The Psychology of Pro-Environmental Communication

The Psychology of Pro-Environmental Communication
Beyond Standard Information Strategies

Christian A. Klöckner
Professor of Social Psychology, Norwegian University of Science and Technology, Norway

© Christian A. Klöckner 2015

All rights reserved. No reproduction, copy or transmission of this publication may be made without written permission.

No portion of this publication may be reproduced, copied or transmitted save with written permission or in accordance with the provisions of the Copyright, Designs and Patents Act 1988, or under the terms of any licence permitting limited copying issued by the Copyright Licensing Agency, Saffron House, 6–10 Kirby Street, London EC1N 8TS.

Any person who does any unauthorized act in relation to this publication may be liable to criminal prosecution and civil claims for damages.

The author has asserted his right to be identified as the author of this work in accordance with the Copyright, Designs and Patents Act 1988.

First published 2015 by
PALGRAVE MACMILLAN

Palgrave Macmillan in the UK is an imprint of Macmillan Publishers Limited, registered in England, company number 785998, of Houndmills, Basingstoke, Hampshire RG21 6XS.

Palgrave Macmillan in the US is a division of St Martin's Press LLC, 175 Fifth Avenue, New York, NY 10010.

Palgrave Macmillan is the global academic imprint of the above companies and has companies and representatives throughout the world.

Palgrave® and Macmillan® are registered trademarks in the United States, the United Kingdom, Europe and other countries.

ISBN 978–1–137–34831–9 hardback
ISBN 978–1–137–34819–7 paperback

This book is printed on paper suitable for recycling and made from fully managed and sustained forest sources. Logging, pulping and manufacturing processes are expected to conform to the environmental regulations of the country of origin.

A catalogue record for this book is available from the British Library.

Library of Congress Cataloging-in-Publication Data
Klöckner, Christian.
   The psychology of pro-environmental communication : beyond standard information strategies / Christian Klockner, Professor in Social Psychology, Norwegian University of Science and Technology, Norway.
     pages cm
   Includes bibliographical references.
   ISBN 978–1–137–34831–9 (hardback) —
   ISBN 978–1–137–34819–7 (paperback)
   1. Communication in the environmental sciences. 2. Environmental psychology. 3. Communication in the environmental sciences—Case studies. I. Title.
   GE25.K56 2015
   304.201′4—dc23
                                               2015003848

Contents

List of Figures, Tables, and Boxes   vii

Preface and Acknowledgements   ix

Part I

1. What Is Environmental Communication and Why Is It Important?   3
2. Potential and Limitations of Environmental Communication   20

Part II

3. Understanding Communication – Insights from Theories of Communication   45
4. Decision Models – What Psychological Theories Teach Us about People's Behaviour   69
5. Communication in Large Social Systems – How Information Spreads through Societies   103
6. Traditional and New Media – About Amplification and Negation   119
7. Target Group Segmentation – Why Knowing Your Audience Is Important   146

Part III

8. An Overview of Communication-Based Intervention Techniques   163
9. Promoting Pro-Environmental Behaviour in Groups and Organisations   179
10. Playing Good? – Environmental Communication through Games and Simulations   197

11 Rock Festivals, Sport Events, Theatre – Some
    Out-of-the-Ordinary Means of Environmental
    Communication   213

References   235

Index   258

Figures, Tables, and Boxes

Figures

1.1	A visualisation of the POET model of environmental sociology	8
1.2	The three elements of social practices	9
1.3	An integrated model of individual behaviour in social contexts	12
2.1	Motivation–opportunity–ability (MOA) model as proposed by Thøgersen (2009)	22
2.2	A model of meat-eating behaviour	35
3.1	A model of human memory	55
3.2	The elaboration likelihood model	59
4.1	The theory of planned behaviour	70
4.2	The norm-activation theory according to Harland et al. (2007)	78
4.3	The value-belief-norm theory according to Stern (2000)	80
4.4	Matching of behaviour models to prevalent goal frame	84
4.5	The comprehensive action determination model	92
4.6	The stage model of self-regulated behavioural change	96
4.7	A comprehensive model framework for environmental behaviour	100
5.1	Diffusion of innovation in a social system through the different types of actors	111
6.1	The protection motivation theory adapted from Floyd et al. (2000)	131
6.2	The social amplification of risk framework	136
7.1	Prototypical structure of Schwartz' basic value orientations	151
9.1	The process of groups shaping group members' behaviour which in turn shapes the group	195
11.1	Positive aspects of a rock festival as identified during the workshop	221

Tables

2.1	A selection of environmentally relevant behaviours in the domain "shelter"	32
2.2	A selection of environmentally relevant behaviours in the domain "food"	34
2.3	A selection of environmentally relevant behaviours in the domain "consumption"	37
2.4	A selection of environmentally relevant behaviours in the domain "mobility"	39
2.5	A selection of environmentally relevant behaviours in the domain "leisure activities"	40
4.1	Overview of communication techniques and their connection to the theory of planned behaviour	75
4.2	Overview of communication techniques and their connection to the norm-activation theory	79
8.1	A structured overview of intervention techniques	177
9.1	Overview of influence strategies spouses use in marital decision-making	182
11.1	Possible contributions of organisers and audience to reduce the negative environmental impact of a big event	215

Boxes

2.1	Environmental design – making the external conditions steer the choice	23
2.2	The potential of household actions to mitigate climate change – an analysis from the United States	26
4.1	Applying the theory of planned behaviour to green consumer behaviour	73
4.2	Habitual behaviour in everyday life	90
7.1	A measurement instrument to detect an individual's stage of change	156

Preface and Acknowledgements

Now that the writing of this book finally comes to an end and I sit here pondering this preface, I ask myself what it was that made me want to embark on such an endeavour. Used to writing scientific papers, I soon found out that writing a book is something very different. What motivated me to go through with it was that I felt that a structured overview of my perspective on environmental communication would help not only me but hopefully also students, practitioners, and other researchers in addressing some of the most pressing challenges we are facing. When the process of writing this book started a couple of years ago, it started as something completely different, just as it usually is when such projects develop over time. A representative of the publisher and I met in my office in late summer 2011, and I proposed an edited book about innovative applications of environmental psychological interventions. The publisher, however, wanted me to write a textbook about environmental psychology. Since there have been a number of high-quality textbooks in environmental psychology published in recent years, I went back to think about new ideas and the result was the seed for the book that you hold in your hands today. I concluded that another general textbook of environmental psychology would not be necessary, but there appeared to be a need for a more focused book on environmental communication with a clear psychological focus. When I proposed this to the publisher, the response was positive and I started conceptualising the book.

This book will have a bias towards psychology, and I did this on purpose because I am an environmental psychologist and quantitative method teacher by training, and not an environmental communicator. I felt that environmental communication, which is traditionally strongly influenced by disciplines other than psychology, would benefit from some psychological theories and methods. At the same time, I think that environmental psychology is too little focused on understanding the processes involved in environmental communication. Even if the main focus will be on psychological theory and methods, from environmental psychology to cognitive and social psychology, I will also consider contributions of other disciplines throughout the chapters of the book.

Another important comment I have to make right at the beginning is that this book became a hybrid between a textbook and proposing new ideas, models, and even data. Each chapter will have the classical review questions in the end; I will provide a list of suggested readings, and the presentation in most sections will hopefully be digestible and helpful for both students on the master level and practitioners who like to get a more comprehensive introduction to psychology-based environmental communication. However, I also felt it useful to use this book to stimulate the development of the discipline by presenting a number of new models, by sketching new lines of research, or by presenting new data.

The book is organised into three parts. In the first part, which consists of the first two chapters, the basic assumptions about environmental communication will be introduced and the key terms will be defined. Furthermore, the chapters will situate environmental communication in the context of other disciplines and traditions within its domain, as well as sketch the potential and limitations evident in environmental communication. In the second part, which consists of Chapters 3–7, the basic theories and empirical findings for understanding how environmental communication works are introduced. This part of the book will give the reader a broad overview about theories and studies that are helpful when designing environmental communication campaigns. In each chapter, conclusions will be drawn, specifically linking the presented models and theories to environmental communication. In the last part of the book, Chapters 8–11, a more case-based approach is chosen. Cases of environmental communication are presented and analysed with respect to the theoretical framework developed in the earlier sections.

I would like to thank a number of people for their input to this book: my colleagues Sunita Prugsamatz, Mehmet Mehmetoglu, Paul Stern, and Ellen Matthies for their stimulating discussions about environmental psychology topics that always help me to get new ideas, identify bad ones, and focus on the good ones. Also thanks to Ida Antonsen, Ingeborg Ljødal, Rut Kristine Tærud Olberg, Lieselotte Roosen, Maria Skogrand, Isabel Richter, and Laura Sommer who critically reviewed earlier versions of the manuscript, my language editor Megan Marks, my editor Eleanor Christie at the publishing office at Palgrave Macmillan for helpful comments and careful guidance, two anonymous reviewers for feedback to the book proposal, and last but not least my wife Silke and my son Phillip who coped with all the hours of weekend and evening writing.

I conclude with a statement that one of my favourite directors made in his first programme when he became director of the theatre in Bochum: Viel Spass! (Have fun!)

Part I

1
What Is Environmental Communication and Why Is It Important?

Chapter summary

This chapter addresses the question of why environmental communication is an indispensable part of environmental strategies. Disciplinary views like environmental economics, environmental sociology, or environmental governance are briefly presented and contrasted to the psychological perspective to gain a comprehensive understanding of the complexity of the topic and the psychological perspective this book is taking. Different forms of communication are outlined (e.g. direct person-to-person; mediated communication via telephone, videophone, print media, TV, radio, or Internet) and their characteristics described. Communication behaviour is contrasted with other forms of human behaviour. The question of how far communication has to include intentionality, or if communication also includes unintended behaviour, is addressed. Furthermore, the difference between verbal and non-verbal communication is outlined. The chapter concludes with a discussion of which understanding of communication is most helpful for the topic at hand, that of describing, understanding, and designing pro-environmental communication strategies. Based on this discussion, a working definition of pro-environmental communication is presented.

1.1 Introduction

As this book addresses the topic of environmental communication, this first chapter has a number of functions. First, it serves to demonstrate that environmental communication is necessary to tackle the environmental problems our societies face and that communication is an essential part of changing societies towards more sustainability. This will be done by placing environmental communication in a context of engineering, economics, sociology, governance, and psychology. Second, communication behaviour needs to be critically analysed along the lines of three dimensions: which forms of communication exist, how is communication different from other types of human behaviour, and what is the difference between verbal and non-verbal communication. Based on these considerations, an attempt will be made to define environmental communication in a way that benefits understanding of this specific type of behaviour for the remainder of this book.

1.2 Why is environmental communication necessary?

Our societies have, through history, been challenged by many different environmental problems such as deforestation, pollution, biodiversity loss, climate change, acidification of the oceans, and depletion of the ozone layer. Two main streams of approaches can be taken to tackle such problems. One is developing new, cleaner, or more efficient technology, thus trying to fix the problem with technological solutions which usually do not imply severe changes in people's behaviour. The other is trying to influence people to reduce damaging behaviours or to shift to alternative, less damaging behaviours. Although the two streams seem to be distinctive at first glance, they have considerable overlap. A binding element in all approaches is that they all depend on environmental communication in one form or another.

1.2.1 The technology-centred approach

When chlorofluorocarbons (CFC) from refrigerators are depleting the ozone layer, engineers must come up with new, less damaging replacements. When carbon dioxide emissions contribute to climate change, new or alternative technologies that improve efficiency and do not rely on fossil fuel need to be developed. When combustion engine cars are a huge environmental problem, then more efficient cars or alternative fuel cars might be a solution. The number of examples in this line of thinking is almost infinite. However, in recent years, a shift from the belief in technology as the prime solution to environmental problems towards behaviour- and lifestyle-centred strategies has occurred (Chapman, 2007). This has several reasons. Some believe that long-term technological progress might be too slow to achieve the necessary reduction in environmental pollution to prevent severe consequences, so short-term behaviour change is necessary (Anable & Shaw, 2007). Another reason is that technological solutions which are not changing people's way of living are often not effective enough to address the environmental problem. Recently, Mitchell (2012) concluded that most scientific and political debates about mitigating climate change are dominated by "technophilic optimism", the belief that technology will save the world, and that this belief is contributing to missing the necessary targets. He argues that more radical societal changes including constraining population growth and reducing consumption are necessary to have an effect large enough to be helpful.

Another aspect is the well-documented rebound effect of efficiency technology. The rebound effect is a concept originating from economic research, with Berkhout, Muskens, and Velthuijsen (2000) defining it as an increase in demand caused by price reductions through efficiency increase. If, for example, cars become more fuel efficient, the demand for fuel to achieve the same product (a driven mile) is reduced. This reduces the fuel price which then in turn increases demand because people can afford to drive more. Usually, such economic rebound effects tend to "eat up" at least parts of the benefits of efficiency improvements (Berkhout et al., 2000). Besides this direct economic rebound, psychological rebound effects have also been shown. Klöckner, Nayum, and Mehmetoglu (2013) have shown that people who bought an electric vehicle not only used it more, but also felt less responsible for the negative environmental effects of car use, which are related not only to direct emissions from the car, but also to the use of space or the production of the car. Furthermore, a study of people exchanging electric resistance heaters with much more energy-efficient air-to-air heat pump technology in Denmark has shown that a large fraction of the technological saving potential was not achieved, because people changed their heating behaviour after installation, such as heating more rooms, having higher room temperatures, or using the heat pump for air conditioning during summers (Gram-Hanssen, Christensen, & Petersen, 2012).

It can be concluded that a technology-centred approach to environmental problems is in most cases not sufficient to eliminate the environmental problem. It needs to be combined with behaviour change to be effective, as new technologies are slow to develop, and this technology-centred approach tends to create rebound effects. Behaviour change requires communication activities, and even in the rare cases where technology actually is the solution to the problem, communication is crucial. Technological change is rarely enforced by law, with the effect that the decision to adopt new technologies is up to the consumer. This implies that some kind of marketing activities or promotion campaigns is necessary to make consumers likely to adopt the clean technology.

1.2.2 Environmental economics

Environmental economics asserts that conservation of natural resources and reduction of environmental pollutants are connected to their price. Unfortunately, the prices of consumer goods often do not adequately reflect the price that society as a whole pays for their use, which in environmental economics is referred to as a market failure (Hanley, Shogren, & White, 2007). Thus, scarce resources are not used in a way where society benefits most. The societal costs of the product use are externalised. Typical solutions for such problems from an economic perspective are either regulating the resource use or the emission and enforcing fines if regulations are not followed, or including the externalised price in the product's price, for example, via emission fees.

Even though environmental economics mostly deals with macroeconomic problems, this way of thinking can also be applied to individual microeconomics. From this perspective, an individual will choose the most beneficial alternative. This can also include non-monetary benefits (Frank, 1997). If the costs do not adequately reflect all societal costs of the behaviour, then this evaluation process is biased towards environmentally damaging behaviours. Personal gains often outweigh the costs, because the costs are partly externalised.

A situation where most of the benefits are personalised but many of the costs are externalised can be described as a "tragedy of the commons" problem (Hardin, 1968; Ostrom, 1990). The commons are collectively owned resources that are used by individuals. A typical example is a common grazing area that all shepherds in a village use to graze their sheep. If it is overgrazed, all shepherds have to pay the price by losing the resource, but the individual benefit of adding just one more sheep to the herd goes to the individual shepherd. There is thus a strong incentive to add additional sheep. One more will not do much harm, but if all shepherds add one more, the price would be high. A typical outcome of such settings is a depletion of the resource. Several strategies can be applied to reduce the negative effects of a common-type situation: most effectively privatisation of the commons, punishment of resource-depleting behaviour, rewards for behaviour protecting the resource, enforcing communication between the actors, or giving feedback about the destructive mechanisms (Bell, Greene, Fisher, & Baum, 2001).

Both macroeconomics and microeconomics assume people are rational actors who select the alternative that gives them the best possible cost–benefit ratio. Research has found, however, numerous examples of deviations from rationality by decision-makers. Most widely known is the work by Kahneman and Tversky (Kahneman & Tversky, 1984; Tversky & Kahneman, 1981, 1986) that shows different presentations of the same choice problem resulted in very different behaviours although the problem in essence was the same. Different forms of presentation are referred to as framing (Tversky & Kahneman, 1986). People react differently if the same event is framed in terms of a loss or in terms of a gain. Tversky and Kahneman (1981) confronted people with two different versions of the same problem: (a) choose between either a sure gain of $240 or a 25% chance to win $1,000 and 75% to win nothing or (b) choose between either a sure loss of $750 or a 75% chance to lose $1,000 and 25% chance to lose nothing. While in situation (a) 84% of the participants preferred the sure gain, in situation (b) 87% of the participants preferred to take their chances to avoid the loss by gambling, though risking an even higher loss.

The example presented in the previous paragraph indicates that people do not behave as rationally as might be assumed, even when they make economic decisions. Furthermore, what is rational for an individual may not be rational from a societal perspective. That makes environmental communication also an important part of an economic perspective on environmental problems. It was shown that how you frame economic choices does matter.

1.2.3 Environmental sociology

Environmental sociology is the branch of sociology that is interested in environment–society interactions. An important part of environmental sociology deals with the question of how environmental problems are caused by social factors and social structures, how environmental problems impact societies, and how they can be solved from a societal perspective (Hannigan, 2006). Because of its focus on communication and discourse, environmental sociology is probably the most dominant theoretical perspective in the field of environmental communication. Environmental sociology focuses strongly on discourses about the environment, the construction of meaning through this discourse, and the reflection of power differences and societal structures in environmental destruction (or conservation). Furthermore, the emergence of technological shifts and their impact on society and the environment are analysed. Typically, environmental sociology describes the complex interdependencies between the human population, its organisational structure, technology, and the environment. In his Population-Organization-Environment-Technology (POET) model, Duncan (1961)

8 *The Psychology of Pro-Environmental Communication*

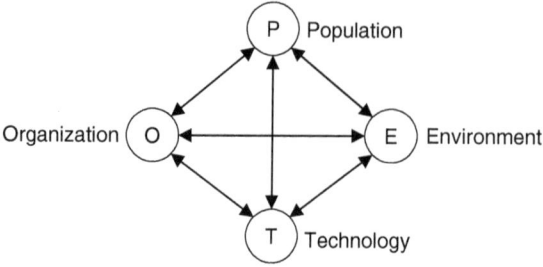

Figure 1.1 A visualisation of the POET model of environmental sociology (Duncan, 1961)

builds on an ecosystem metaphor to describe these four elements (see Figure 1.1). One of the many possible chains of effects within the framework of this model could be that an increasing population leads to a change in organisational structures such as urbanisation. This again leads to the need for changes in technology and together technology, urbanisation, and population growth have a negative impact on the environment.

A second strong tradition in environmental sociology is more closely related to political economy (Hannigan, 2006). An important representative of this tradition, Schnaiberg (1980) coined the phrase of "treadmill of production" by which he describes an economic structure which is dependent on growth and creating consumer demand for new products. This structure then creates societal systems that will extend beyond their physical limits and thus have detrimental effects on the environment.

A sociological theory that has gathered some attention in the environmental domain and explains the way sociology understands environmental behaviour is social practice theory. Researchers sailing under the flag of social practice theory have one common assumption, namely that it is at the scale of human practices that a society is defined and reproduced and that individuals are socialised into a society (Reckwitz, 2002). Social practice theory has a focus on agency and structure and thereby integrates both internal drivers (the agency part) and external drivers (the structure) of behaviour. However, social practice theory does not assume structure and agency to be predictors; they rather interact and together form what is referred to as a practice. Behaviour occurs in a context out of the interconnectedness of agent, structure, and shared knowledge. Strengers (2012) describes the elements of a

What Is Environmental Communication? 9

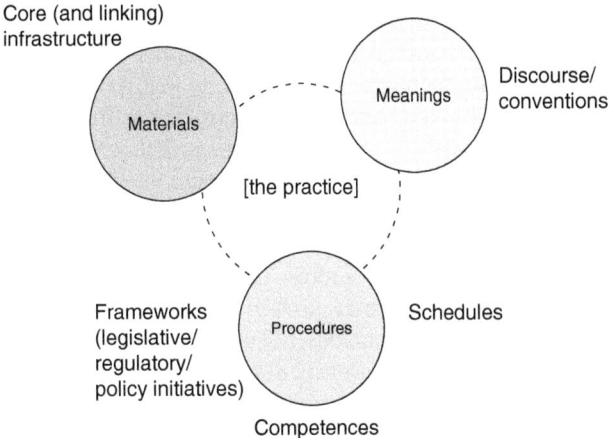

Figure 1.2 The three elements of social practices (Darnton et al., 2011, page 51). Reproduced under the open government licence

practice as practical knowledge, common social understandings, rules, and material infrastructure. Shove et al. define the key elements as materials, meanings, and procedures (Shove & Pantzar, 2005; Shove et al., 2012) (Figure 1.2). Materials are physical objects like technologies; meanings are interpretations, images, symbolism, discourse, and conventions connected to the practice; and procedures are frameworks, regulations, competences, and schedules. This also explains why social practices glue together the re-creation of society and at the same time socialisation of the individuals. Socialisation is the process of an individual being integrated into an existing practice. Knowledge is shared, a context is shared, and technology is shared. At the same time, the individual contributes to re-creating society which is the sum of all practices and reshapes both the individual and the society. Darnton, Verplanken, White, and Whitmarsh (2011) used social practice theory to explain why people use tumble dryers instead of line drying (or vice versa) and found that aspects from all three domains created the practices connected to drying clothes.

The focus of environmental sociology means communication is essential. Communication patterns are the material of which meaning is constructed, which then also impacts people's behaviour. Communication creates the knowledge that is shared in social practices, and the engagement in social practices is understood as communication with other agents.

1.2.4 Environmental governance

Environmental governance is the use of regulatory tools to steer environmentally relevant behaviour of people or institutions. Lemos and Agrawal (2006) define environmental governance as the "set of regulatory processes, mechanisms and organizations through which political actors influence environmental actions and outcomes" (page 298). Governance includes not only government actions, but also other political actors such as communities, businesses, and NGOs (Lemos & Agrawal, 2006). This means that it can address different levels, and when environmental problems are complex, governance across three levels can be necessary. These three levels are described next.

On the *globalised* level, environmental governance focuses on international trade schemes and regulations, as well as international contracts such as climate protocols. However, the globalised perspective is not restricted to regulations between states. Lemos and Agrawal (2006) argue that such regulations have performed notoriously badly. They see an opportunity in a more inclusive global environmental governance paradigm that extends international cooperation between non-governmental social actors, such as corporate interests, social movements, and NGOs. For such types of globalised governance networks, Haas (2004) suggests multilevel, non-hierarchical, information-rich, loose networks of institutions and actors, which have the advantage of being more flexible and adaptive and entice more relevant actors to get involved. Such networks might also be built on cooperation that is not only regulated by legal arrangements. Examples for such emerging networks can be found where large cities across nations cooperate to solve climate change issues.

Parallel to the globalised level, governance also occurs at a *decentralised*, sub-national level. In many countries, the regulation of natural and other resources has been decentralised to regions (Hutchcroft, 2001) where greater efficiency, closer connections between decision-makers and the affected, and better use of precise time- and place-specific knowledge can be achieved (Lemos & Agrawal, 2006).

On the next level, the *market- and agent-focused* environmental governance makes use of economic instruments to steer agents in specific markets to more environmentally friendly choices (Lemos & Agrawal, 2006). As such, they are closely related to the economic perspective described above. Energy taxes or incentives for adoption of new technologies are an example of such instruments.

It is obvious that communication is an essential part of environmental governance not only when agreements are negotiated between different actors, but also when regulations need to be implemented and enforced. Furthermore, communication plays an important role in securing political support for regulatory mechanisms in democratic systems.

1.2.5 Environmental psychology

Environmental psychology is psychology's counterpart to environmental sociology, hence the part of psychology that is interested in people–environment interactions (Bell et al., 2001; Steg, van den Berg, & de Groot, 2012). Conservational psychology, the psychology of pro-environmental behaviour, was not initially part of the core focus of environmental psychology that developed from architectural psychology and research on nature perception and recreational effects of being in nature (Bonnes & Secchiaroli, 1995), but more recently it has become more important (Steg et al., 2012). Since environmental psychology's primary unit of analysis is the acting individual, it is partly related to the economic perspective, but different from the sociological and governance perspectives that mainly analyse at the group level. However, environmental psychology recognises that individual decisions and behaviour are embedded in physical and social structures, which has a strong impact on the individual and is therefore one of the least individualistic sub-disciplines of psychology.

Environmental psychology covers research on many different levels, from mechanisms of attention and decision-making on the level of individual cognitions, to the description and prediction of environmental behaviour in several action models, to models describing behaviour change. All these levels will be presented in detail in Part II. Communication activities are integral to environmental psychology, which will be explained in detail in later chapters.

1.2.6 An integrated perspective

Whereas at first glance the different theoretical perspectives presented in this chapter seem very different from each other, it might be fruitful to look at the potential for integration to achieve a broader and more nuanced picture. Some authors, especially from sociology, strongly oppose such an endeavour and declare, for example, a psychological perspective as non-compatible with social practice theory (Shove, 2010, 2011). Others question this proposition and see benefits

12 The Psychology of Pro-Environmental Communication

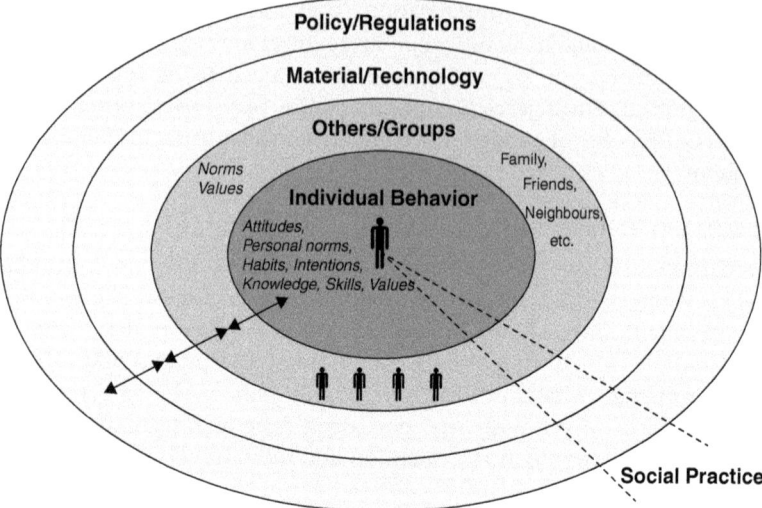

Figure 1.3 An integrated model of individual behaviour in social contexts (Arnesen, 2013, page 27). Used by permission of Arnesen

in combining different theoretical paradigms (Whitmarsh, O'Neill, & Lorenzoni, 2011), even if some basic assumptions differ fundamentally between the research traditions. Arnesen (2013) made an attempt to combine many of the aforementioned assumptions into a theoretical framework model, which is considered helpful for structuring the different perspectives (see Figure 1.3). Arnesen's model assumes that the individual agent is in the centre of several rings, an idea that is congruent with psychological and economical models. This individual actor has attitudes, personal norms, habits, intentions, and other psychological constructs which tell him or her something about the behaviour in question (see Chapter 4 for a detailed discussion). However, this person is embedded in a social context which consists of different sized groups of other people such as family, colleagues, friends, but also larger groups like neighbourhoods or cities, or even members of the same culture. This is compatible with many sociological theories, especially if the material/technological layer that defines behaviour through its context is also taken into account. On the outermost layer, policies and regulations can be found, which links to governance and the economic approach. Social practices in that model can be understood as slices of that system. Each practice is a specific behavioural pattern that consists of agents in a social and physical context interacting with materials/technologies and in a regulative framework.

1.3 Forms of communication

Humans communicate with other humans in many different ways. In this section, three forms of human-to-human communication will be outlined with their specific characteristics: (a) direct communication between two or more people when all of them are present in the same situation; (b) person-to-person communication between two or more people which is mediated by a technological device; and (c) communication via media. All three kinds are used in environmental communication activities. People also communicate with themselves and create meaning in this process, which can also be relevant in an environmental communication context.

Pearson et al. (2011) distinguish between intrapersonal communication, dyadic communication, small-group communication, public communication, and mass communication. In intrapersonal communication, only one person is involved. Dyadic communication between two individuals is rather intimate, offers possibilities for much feedback, is open for many unstructured messages, and there is a high degree of instability as the roles of speaker and listener alternate. When more people are involved, the communication setting is less intimate, the roles are more clearly defined, and there are fewer options for feedback.

1.3.1 Direct person-to-person communication

Humans communicate directly with each other and some of that behaviour is connected to environmentally relevant topics. Family members talk at the dinner table about the new eco-tax that the government is introducing. Colleagues at work debate the importance of recycling. An environmental activist tries to convince people in the pedestrian zone of a city to give their signature or money to a campaign. Such kinds of direct communication are rich. They include (usually oral) language content, but also body language, intonation, mimicry of the communicators, and physical space, for example, physical closeness between the communicating agents. Additionally, there is the physical and temporal context. All aspects convey, sometimes contradictory, meaning. Furthermore, direct communication is interactive and can easily be tailored to the audience. There is the possibility to ask questions, to repeat sections of the communication or to deliver them in another way, and to slow down or fasten delivery. Direct person-to-person communication happens at a specific point in time in a specific context, which makes it unique and non-repeatable.

For environmental communication approaches, direct person-to-person communication has advantages and disadvantages. The richness of direct face-to-face communication aids understanding since more factors than just language content can be used to decipher the meaning (Bordia, 1997). Direct face-to-face communication is also more satisfying to the participants than mediated communication. Attitudes change more in face-to-face persuasion attempts as compared to computer-mediated persuasion, which can be attributed to the fact that more factors are available in direct communication that can be used for peripheral attitude change (see Chapter 3.3.4.2). This means that direct communication can be an effective tool for environmental messages. Not surprisingly, environmental activists who are interested in donations or signatures on petitions usually employ direct communication techniques. The more direct a communication attempt is, the less likely it is that people ignore it and the more likely it is that trust between the parties can develop (Marx, 2000). On the other hand, some people will experience direct communication as more annoying. A problem of face-to-face environmental communication is its high costs in terms of man-power and time. If many people need to be reached, direct communication is hardly practical.

1.3.2 Mediated person-to-person communication

Nowadays, there are many ways of mediating person-to-person communication: phones, e-mail, short phone messages, video calls, or similar services. What unifies all of them is that they are still a communication between two or more parties where all parties can become active in the process and where the flow of the communication can be dynamically adjusted. However, compared to a face-to-face communication, some aspects of the communication process are missing. In telephone conversations, for example, some non-verbal communication is not available and the signs connected to verbal communication (e.g. intonation) are more difficult to detect. In text messages or e-mail, these aspects are missing completely, and a sign language to communicate the emotional tone of the message has developed (emoticons are emotional icons integrated into text messages to transport things like irony). However, Walther and D'Addario (2001) show that emoticons do not transport meaning as efficiently as words in such mediated messages.

Bordia (1997) summarises the literature about differences between face-to-face communication and computer-mediated communication and finds evidence that face-to-face communication produces more distinct thoughts than computer-mediated communication. Furthermore, while face-to-face communication participants are more likely to inhibit socially unacceptable behaviour, in computer-mediated communication people were shown to participate more equally since, for example, the effects of status on participation were reduced. Also social pressure is reduced in computer-mediated communication. Under time pressure, computer-mediated communication was found to be more efficient than face-to-face communication. Lightfoot (2006) noticed that in e-mail communication to university teachers, students were much more reflective than in direct face-to-face communication, demonstrating that mediated person-to-person communication under some conditions gives a chance to reflect more about what is said. This effect was not found in e-mails to other students.

For environmental communication, mediated person-to-person communication can offer a compromise between the advantages of direct communication and the advantages of mass communication. Although people are addressed individually through telephone or e-mail campaigns, the dynamics of the communication can still be tailored to a large degree. The costs connected to such campaigns are lower than seeking face-to-face communication, but higher than for mass media communication, which is described in the next section.

1.3.3 Communication via media

Mass communication can occur through different media such as books, newspapers, TV, radio, Internet, and mobile phones. In a broad sense, artwork, music, and theatre might also be defined as media channels that can be employed to communicate to people. A typical feature of these channels is that many people are addressed at the same time, although the number of people depends on the channel. This communication is not interactive, or only to a very limited degree in modern Internet-based media channels. The message is less targeted and the communication structure is clearly unbalanced: one party is the "sender" of a message; the other has the role of "receiver" who responds to the message. Many of the features of direct person-to-person communication are missing in media communication, although some forms can mimic the non-verbal aspects through, for example, video material. A more thorough discussion of media communication will be given in Chapter 6.

For environmental communication, media communication is most common because it is cost effective, reaching many people at once from a centralised communicator. However, centralised media communication comes at a price. It can miss the specific peculiarities of each receiver, it is less effective in persuading people to change behaviour, and a non-tailored approach has a higher likelihood of adverse reactions from the receiver, thus leading to the opposite of the intended effect. In Section 6.2.4 the use of modern technology to develop hybrid strategies between mass media communication and personalised communication will be discussed.

1.4 Communication behaviour versus other human behaviour

Communication is an important part of human behaviour and much broader than speech. An important question is where communication begins and which part of human behaviour is not communication. The task of defining what communication is has proved to be difficult (Littlejohn & Foss, 2011). Many definitions exist, and they differ enormously in what kinds of behaviours they include and exclude. The difficulties in defining communication have led to Littlejohn and Foss (2011) not suggesting a definition at all.

However, Pearson et al. (2011) define communication as the process of exchanging "meaning through a common system of symbols, signs, and behaviour" (page 23), understanding it as a process that changes over time. If this definition is followed, all activities that lead to the exchange of meaning between people can be defined as communication behaviour. The central part in this definition is the "exchange of meaning". Meaning is understood as a shared "understanding of the message" (page 11) which is constructed by the communicating actors. Behaviour that occurs without the exchange of meaning is not included in communication.

1.5 Verbal versus non-verbal communication

The previous section attempted to define communication behaviour and ended in a rather broad definition that included many activities that contribute to the exchange of meaning. An important distinction that has already been used implicitly in the discussion of different forms of communication above is between verbal and non-verbal communication. Whereas verbal communication is all kinds of communication behaviours that make use of spoken or written language, non-verbal communication includes body language, the non-verbal aspects of language (such as intonation, speed, rhythm, volume), bodily behaviour such as touching, distance to others, eye contact, and the use of time and silence (Littlejohn & Foss, 2009).

Whereas some authors claim that the non-verbal aspect of communication accounts for about two-thirds of all communication (Hogan & Stubbs, 2003), others doubt that the contribution can be quantified and rather assume that verbal and non-verbal communication work together in the creation of meaning and are both important (Power, 1998). It is not debated that the non-verbal aspect is essential for meaning creation and shapes how the verbal part is perceived.

Jurin et al. (2010) analyse the importance of non-verbal communication for the design of environmental communication. They highlight the relevance of considering the effects of matching the body language to the message, the cultural dependence of gestures, the effect of facial expressions, the importance and cultural definition of personal space, the effect of physical appearance and smell, the use of smiles and eye contact, touching, and the physical arrangement of the communication context (such as arrangement of the conference table). They furthermore highlight the effects of non-verbal signs in language, such as articulation, pronunciation, and emphasis.

1.6 Defining environmental communication

In Section 1.4 a definition of human communication was given. Environmental communication is that part of human communication that is related to environmentally relevant human behaviour. However, the question is where exactly the line between environmental communication and other types of human communication can be drawn. Scholars of environmental communication have defined their subject in many different ways.

In his book about environmental communication, Cox (2012) defines environmental communication as the "pragmatic and constitutive vehicle for our understanding of the environment as well as our relationships to the natural world; it is the symbolic medium that we use in constructing environmental problems and in negotiating society's different responses to them" (page 19). Drawing on sociological theories and symbolic interactionism, this definition understands environmental communication both as (a) a pragmatic tool to educate, alert, and persuade people to solve environmental problems and as (b) the medium which constitutes our way of perceiving and interpreting nature and environmental problems. For this book, the former interpretation is more relevant. The second aspect will also be discussed, insofar as it refers to the social construction of environmental problems or non-problems through communication.

Jurin et al. (2010) define environmental communication as "the systematic generation and exchange of humans' messages in, from, for, and about the world around us and our interactions with it" (page 15). This definition is narrow, on the one hand, since it reduces communication to the exchange of messages. In the definition above, communication is the process of exchanging meaning, which is more than just generating and exchanging messages. On the other hand, the definition is very broad since it is applied to messages that are generated and exchanged in, from, for, and about the world around us.

For this book's perspective, a refinement of environmental communication is necessary, since it primarily takes a psychological perspective on communication activities in general and environmental communication in particular. Thus, the following definition explains how environmental communication will be understood, and it is closely related to the definition of communication by Pearson et al. (2011): *environmental communication is a process by which meaning about the environment and environmental problems is exchanged between individuals through a system of common symbols, signs, and behaviour. It includes verbal and non-verbal communication activities.* Although environmental communication can be unintentional, for the focus of this book the area is mostly restricted to intended communication activities. Environmental communication does not imply success, and unsuccessful attempts of environmental communication will also be regarded as environmental communication. Environmental communication is pragmatic in the way that Cox (2012) understands it: it is a vehicle to educate and alert people about environmental problems and influence their mindset and behaviour towards more sustainable lifestyles.

1.7 Conclusions

This first chapter argued for the central place environmental communication should have in addressing the environmental problems our societies are faced with. Irrespective of which paradigm is employed to find a solution for environmental crises, communication is an essential part. Understanding the processes and pitfalls of communication activities is essential to success. Environmental communication is defined first of all as communication, which seems trivial but implies how it is differentiated from other human activities. To narrow the focus, this book will analyse the mechanisms of intended communication about the environment and environmental problems. It explores which communications can make people ultimately change their environmentally damaging behaviour. Furthermore, the book will describe the mechanisms by which environmental communication creates the meaning in environmental actions and defines the problems. By doing that, it includes communication on all levels from dyadic communication to mass communication, direct or mediated communication.

Review questions

- Describe the different theoretical perspectives on environmental behaviour introduced in this chapter. Why is environmental communication important in each of them?
- What characterises different forms of communication?
- Give a definition of environmental communication and explain its elements.

Suggested readings

Arnesen, M. (2013). Saving energy through culture: A multidisciplinary model for analyzing energy culture applied to Norwegian empirical evidence. *(Master), Norwegian University of Science and Technology, Trondheim*. http://www.diva-portal.org/smash/get/diva2:657414/FULLTEXT01.pdf.
Jurin, R. R., Roush, D., & Danter, J. (2010). Communicating without words. In R. R. Jurin, D. Roush, & J. Danter (Eds.), *Environmental Communication*. Second Edition (pp. 221–230). Dordrecht: Springer.
Pearson, J. C., Nelson, P. E., Titsworth, S., & Harter, L. (2006). *Human communication*. New York: McGraw-Hill.
Shove, E., Pantzar, M., & Watson, M. (2012). *The dynamics of social practice: Everyday life and how it changes*. London: Sage.
Tversky, A., & Kahneman, D. (1981). The framing of decisions and the psychology of choice. *Science*, 211(4481), 453–458.

2
Potential and Limitations of Environmental Communication

Chapter summary

The second chapter assesses the potential of the communicative approach of promoting pro-environmental behaviour in relation to other strategies to change environmentally relevant behaviour. This is important to prevent the reader from under- or overestimating the communicative approach to promote pro-environmental behaviour. Based on empirical analyses, it is discussed how strong the impact of behavioural change caused by communication can be, compared to structural or political changes as well as technological developments. Furthermore, potential interactions between structural limitations and opportunities, on the one hand, and communication strategies, on the other, are addressed. The role of communication and discourse for the construction of psychological representations of the material world which then steer behaviour is also discussed. Behaviour domains relevant to people's lives (e.g. shelter, food, other consumption, or mobility) with their subcategories will be individually reviewed, and areas with a particularly high potential as targets for communication strategies will be outlined.

2.1 Introduction

This chapter reflects on how environmental communication can be understood in relation to other types of environmental interventions. Chapter 1 already introduced different approaches to solving environmental problems from the technology-centred to sociological and psychological approaches. This chapter takes the perspective of different types of environmentally relevant behaviour and looks at the potential that environmental communication has in each of them. In the first section, environmental communication will be put into perspective with respect to structural changes, technological developments, and policy changes. In the second section, a brief reflection on the role of environmental communication in the social construction of environmental problems and their solutions will follow, which is extended in the following chapters. In the third section of this chapter, examples of communication-based and other types of interventions will be presented under the themes of the main domains of life: shelter, food, consumption, mobility, and leisure activities. The final section presents a conclusion integrating the previously presented considerations and laying the ground for the remainder of the book.

2.2 Communication in the context of other environmental interventions

As an environmental psychologist, or any other scientist for that matter, it is easy to consider the contribution of one's own discipline to solving environmental problems most central and crucial in the interdisciplinary mix of contributions. Therefore, it is more than an exercise in being humble to take a step back to analyse what contribution environmental psychology in general and a mainly psychology-based approach to environmental communication can make and, more importantly even, what contribution it cannot make.

A relatively simple first approximation of this problem is Stern's ABC model (Stern, 1999). The model assumes that environmental behaviour (B) is fuelled by the external conditions (C) and the attitudes (A) people hold towards the behaviour. In other words, situational conditions become a crucial element in analysing environmental behaviour. If it is made very difficult to perform a behaviour, people are less likely to do it, regardless of how strong the attitudes are; if a behaviour is very easy to perform, it is more likely people will do it again, regardless of attitude strength. This simple model has two implications: (a) situational conditions are important for people to perform environmental behaviours and we should first try to make behaviour as easy to perform as possible by removing the barriers before we start planning a communication campaign; and (b) attitudes, which here can be understood as a stand-in for a richer set of psychological predictors of behaviour, are of most importance for behaviours that have a medium difficulty. In a study on waste recycling, Guagnano et al. (1995) found indications for this curvilinear relationship between attitude and behaviour.

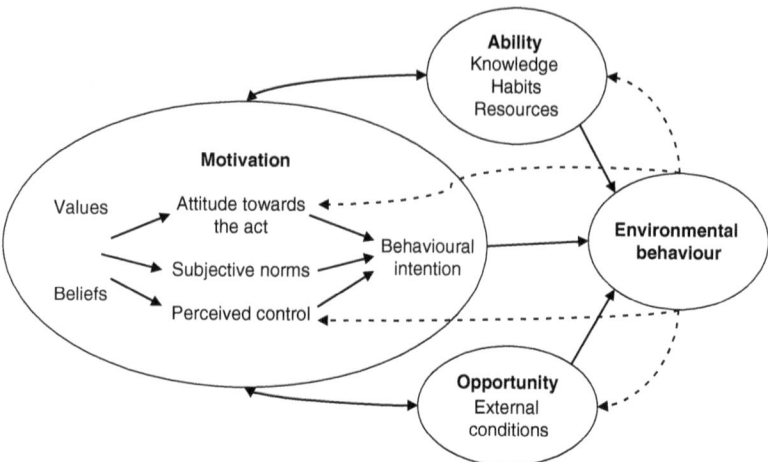

Figure 2.1 Motivation–opportunity–ability (MOA) model as proposed by Thøgersen (2009, page 337). Used by permission of Elsevier

If recycling was made easy by providing curbside pickup, attitudes did not predict behaviour, whereas for the more difficult behavioural option with pickup points, attitudes were a significant predictor of behaviour.

In a more elaborate model, which Thøgersen (2009) refers to as the motivation–opportunity–ability (MOA) model (see Figure 2.1), he differentiates between three main influences on behaviour. Without going into too much detail at this point, since the variables in the model will be explained in Chapter 4, the model assumes that performance of environmental behaviour depends on external conditions (which is an assumption similar to the ABC model) or, in other words, the opportunities to act. The question that needs to be answered here is: do people have a realistic opportunity to perform the target behaviour? Furthermore, people need to be able to perform the behaviour; they need to have the necessary knowledge and resources and not be locked into strong habits to do something else. Only if people have the opportunity and ability to act, motivations can contribute their part.

These considerations lead to implications for the impact that environmental communication can have. If we assume that environmental communication mostly addresses the motivational part of the MOA model, then communication-based interventions will be most effective, if opportunities and abilities are in place. This means barriers to environmental action resulting from lack of opportunity or lack of resources and knowledge need to be addressed *before* any attempt to increase people's motivation to act. Reversing the order might even be counterproductive when people are first motivated and then realise that the action is too difficult for them. Under certain conditions, a change in the opportunities can be enough to make people change their behaviour. If the intended behaviour is so easy to perform that virtually everyone does it, then communication strategies become obsolete. The discipline of environmental design makes use of this assumption by designing products in a way that makes the most environmental-use option the easiest (Elias et al., 2009; Zachrisson & Boks, 2012). Box 2.1 describes an example of a smart product that was designed in a way to minimise energy loss by inefficient user behaviour.

Box 2.1 Environmental design – making the external conditions steer the choice

When using a kettle for boiling water and making tea or coffee, people have problems estimating the correct amount of water that needs to be heated for the purpose. Consequently, most people tend to fill the kettle with much more water than necessary. Aggregated to the country level, the amount of resources wasted on boiling unused water is substantial. It is estimated that the overuse of electricity caused by an average English household per week adds up to enough electricity for lighting a whole house one day.

In 2005, an English manufacturer of small electric appliances constructed a special kettle that, by design, made it very easy to adjust the amount of water in the kettle to be heated to the right amount. This new design was called the eco kettle and has, since its market introduction, sold more than 200,000 products (www.ecokettle.co.uk). Its energy-saving potential is estimated to be around 60% on average. In its newer edition, it also adjusts the temperature of the water to the demand, so that in cases when boiling water is not needed, lower temperatures can be produced automatically.

The eco kettle is a good example of creating opportunities for pro-environmental actions that are very easy to perform and thus override the impact of attitudes. Interestingly, the company producing the eco kettle uses its website for substantial environmental communication, addressing both the purchase stage (why should I buy the eco kettle) and the generalisation of the pro-environmental behaviour shown with purchasing the eco kettle to other behavioural domains.

In the following sections, the potential impact of environmental communication will be explored in regard to three different approaches, namely structural changes, technological developments, and policy change.

2.2.1 Communication versus structural change

From the discussions in the previous section, it can be concluded that structural changes often have an important impact on people's pro-environmental behaviour and should therefore be of high priority in planning a campaign. Steg and Vlek (2009) differentiate in their review paper between informational strategies, referred to as communication-based strategies in this book, and structural strategies. Informational strategies have different aims: some want to increase knowledge; others change perceptions, increase motivation, increase awareness, strengthen perceived norms or values, or provide social models or information about other people's behaviour.

Steg and Vlek (2009) report that environmental research has shown that increasing people's knowledge about environmental problems alone hardly results in behavioural change. Placing prompts, which are small signs with a targeted message (see Section 8.2.2), however, can be effective. Furthermore, if the information provided is carefully tailored to the specific needs and information gaps people have, the effects are stronger (Abrahamse et al., 2007). Section 4.9.2 introduces a stage-based model (Bamberg, 2013a) to tailor information. Communication strategies that strengthen values and norms seem to be more effective than other strategies (Abrahamse et al., 2005). Linking attitudes, intentions, and behaviour closer together by triggering concrete implementation intentions (see Section 4.9.2) seems also to be an efficient strategy when people already have pro-environmental attitudes but do not translate them into behaviour (Bamberg, 2002). Also providing social models and information about behaviour of other people (see Section 8.2.9) can be an effective strategy (Abrahamse et al., 2005). In general, Steg and Vlek (2009) conclude that communication-based strategies are effective when pro-environmental behaviour is convenient and not costly to perform, but become irrelevant in cases where external constraints are strong.

Structural changes, on the other hand, become very important when behaviour is perceived to be costly or inconvenient (note that both aspects refer to *perceived* costs and convenience). Structural changes might include increasing availability of less environmentally damaging alternatives, reducing relative costs by making pro-environmental alternatives less expensive or environmentally damaging alternatives more expensive, or increasing the (relative) benefits of the pro-environmental alternative. Examples of structural changes are increasing the frequency of public transportation, subsidising energy efficiency technology, closing city centres to road traffic, increasing the availability of organic food in the supermarkets, providing recycling bins, introducing a curbside pickup schedule, and offering access to bus lanes for electric vehicles. The consequence of such structural changes is modifications in the reward and punishment structure for different behaviours, thus making the target behaviour more attractive relative to other behaviours. It appears that changes that make the pro-environmental alternative more rewarding tend to be more accepted than strategies increasing the punishment for the damaging alternative (Geller, 2002). Whereas structural changes seem to be powerful tools, their effect also comes at a cost. A downside of implementing structural changes is that they transfer the attribution of the behavioural causes to the external structure: "I have to use the bus, because it is so easy and convenient." This reduces the internal motivation, which ultimately means that behaviour will be terminated when the structural rewards are removed. The most important impact of a focus on structural aspects is certainly the attention to barriers, which make performance of the targeted behaviour very unlikely. If such barriers exist, then communication strategies will be inefficient.

2.2.2 Communication versus technological developments

The previous section introduced us to the notion of the relationship between technological progress and communication (see also Chapter 1). At first glance, it appears to be obvious that technological development can have a huge effect on environmental impacts. More fuel-efficient or alternative fuel cars can reduce the emissions related to travelling considerably, and better housing insulation combined with modern ventilation technology can reduce the energy needed for heating to zero. Compared to such fundamental improvements in the technologies, the contribution of changing consumer behaviour appears marginal. Some authors warn against blaming the consumer and making him or her responsible for negative environmental effects that he or she cannot contribute much to resolve (Evans, 2011; Holm, 2003). These authors see the explanation for negative environmental outcomes rather in the structural, technological, and political context than in individual decision-making. Often, this criticism is articulated in the framework of social practice theory (see Section 1.2.3).

However, an analysis of relatively simple household decisions in the United States argues that even if sometimes low plasticity rates are taken into account (see Section 2.4 and Box 2.2), about 20% of the United States' CO_2 emissions could be reduced by consumer behaviour change alone, based on the technology available today (Dietz et al., 2009). In the famous shortlist of household climate actions (see Box 2.2), both investment decisions into efficient technology and curtailment behaviour, like abandoning the use of "standby" of electric appliances, have been identified. The analysis shows that even if technological developments may contribute significantly to reducing environmental impacts, the consumer sits at a strategically important decision point. The technology has to be implemented and used in the appropriate way, which again makes the need for communication activities obvious.

Box 2.2 The potential of household actions to mitigate climate change – an analysis from the United States

Dietz et al. (2009) tried to identify how big the realistic potential of consumer actions is to reducing CO_2 emissions. Is the impact of household behaviour change really rather insignificant or can decisions on the consumer level make a difference? If they make a difference, which behaviours should be focused on? In a combination of environmental impact assessment and social science, they identified a list of high impact behaviours where a change would lead to significant CO_2 savings, noting behaviours that apply to many people. They then explored the intervention literature to assess how much change in behaviour can be expected realistically. The result was a list of 18 behaviours which realistically can lead to a reduction of 20% of the CO_2 emissions in the United States. If the unrealistic assumption that all people implement the behaviour is made, the theoretical reduction potential would even be 38%. The behaviours in the list were categorised into five areas: weatherisation (W), which means insulation and efficient heating or cooling equipment; energy-efficient technology (E); maintenance (M); equipment adjustments (A); and daily-use behaviours (D). The resulting table of high-priority behaviours is presented below. The potential emission reduction is calculated based on the assumption that all people in the United States would implement the behaviour. It is reported in million tons carbon (MtC), and behavioural plasticity is the percentage of behaviour change that can be realistically expected based on a review of intervention literature. Combining the maximum potential with the plasticity leads to reasonably achievable emissions reduction (RAER). The last column displays how much this realistic reduction of all household-related emissions would be. Even if only behaviours are chosen which do not include any financial investments (only daily and adjustment behaviours), the RAER would be 4%, and with maintenance behaviour included, it would be 5.5%. This illustrates that the impact of household behaviour is significant. However, about 75% of the potential lies in decisions for investing in efficient technology. Currently, several groups are working on localising the list to other contexts.

Behaviour	Category	Potential[a]	Plasticity	RAER[a]	%
Weatherisation	W	25.2	90	21.2	3.39
HVAC equipment[b]	W	12.2	80	10.7	1.72
Low-flow showerheads	E	1.4	80	1.1	0.18
Efficient water heater	E	6.7	80	5.4	0.86
Appliances	E	14.7	80	11.7	1.87
Low rolling resistance tyres	E	7.4	80	6.5	1.05
Fuel-efficient vehicle	E	56.3	50	31.4	5.02
Change HVAC air filters	M	8.7	30	3.7	0.59
Tune up AC	M	3.0	30	1.4	0.22
Routine auto maintenance	M	8.6	30	4.1	0.66
Laundry temperature	A	0.5	35	0.2	0.04
Water heater temperature	A	2.9	35	1.0	0.17
Standby electricity	D	9.2	35	3.2	0.52
Thermostat setbacks	D	10.1	35	4.5	0.71
Line drying	D	6.0	35	2.2	0.35
Driving behaviour	D	24.1	25	7.7	1.23
Carpooling and trip-chaining	D	36.1	15	6.4	1.02
Total		233		123	20

[a] in MtC; [b] HVAC = heating, ventilation, and air conditioning.
Table reproduced with kind permission of PNAS.

2.2.3 Communication versus policy change

Closely related to the question addressed in the previous section is the discussion of the relationship between policy and individual behaviour.

Policy decisions can have a huge environmental impact. Building regulations that increased the energy standard of new buildings have reduced energy use considerably. Regulations in the car sector have forced the industry to include catalytic converters into all new cars. The EU ban on conventional light bulbs had an immediate effect on the composition of light sources in all households in the European Union. Thus, regulations and policy decisions are powerful tools of environmental protection that change people's behaviour by limiting behavioural choice. However, this power comes at a price. Policy decisions need to have public support in a democratic society. Furthermore, regulations tend to be seen as reducing personal freedom which people tend to answer with reactance (Thøgersen, 2005). For that reason, strong policies like bans are not implemented often in the environmental domain unless there is a broad societal consensus or an immediate threat. Weaker policies like subsidy schemes are more common to encourage pro-environmental behaviours. The way the political system works makes it obvious that communication is an essential part of policy making, and that goes both ways. Policymakers need to justify and communicate their decisions towards the public, and the public communicates, often indirectly, with decision-makers about support of policies. Policy making can also be seen as a form of communication in itself. Policies tell us which kind of behaviour is officially accepted in a society and which kind is unaccepted. It also tells us which kinds of problems are addressed and regarded as relevant and which are not. Some reflections on this role of communication will be given in Section 2.3.

2.2.4 Interactions between communication and other strategies

The previous three subsections presented communication-based strategies as something that is opposed to structural, policy-based, or technological interventions. In reality, the picture is more complex, and all four types of interventions usually occur together, depending on each other and their interaction. Structural change often occurs as the result of policy making, which, for example, changes the cost structure of behavioural alternatives. Technological progress often initiates policy making, which then leads to structural changes. Communication accompanies all stages of that process: manufacturers need to market their products – through communication. Support for, and acceptance of, policy making is dependent on successful communication (Steg & Vlek, 2009). When new policies are implemented, they need to be communicated. New technology needs to be used and unwanted rebound effects need to be prevented, usually through communication. New structural conditions need to be made known and accepted. Reactions to perceived infringement of personal freedom need to be addressed (Thøgersen, 2005). When it is impossible to make the structural conditions for a behaviour to be performed automatically, or when strict regulations that ban the unwanted behaviour are impossible, people's attitudinal and motivational factors become central for success. All these aspects underline the crucial importance of environmental communication, even if the effect of communication alone might be marginal. Together with other strategies, environmental communication unfolds its potential.

2.3 The role of communication to construct representations of the world

So far in this chapter, environmental communication activities have been understood as dealing with environmental problems that exist in the physical world because people act in a certain way. However, if we take a social constructivist perspective, then communication has more functions than just to convey information and motivate people to change their behaviour. Social constructivists like Gergen (2011) emphasise the role that language and communication acts have in defining and constructing the world. The way language is structured, which relationships between objects are possible to articulate, and who says what and when and with which level of assigned power define how the physical and social worlds are perceived. Since Gergen (2011) understands relations to other people as the main constructing element of the psychological self, communication becomes the essence of meaning-making in this relational process. This position has received some attention in environmental communication as a discipline, especially in the area that is sociologically dominated. It has severe implications for communication about environmental problems because it questions the existence of scientific objectivity and highlights the structures of power and access to societal resources. Even more fundamentally, it questions the existence of one extra-human nature that needs to be protected and rather assumes that value is attached to certain environmental manifestations and not others in a process of social negotiation (Braun & Castree, 2005). This perspective has contributed significantly to understanding the role of communication in defining problems, while ignoring others, and it will be referred to in more detail in Section 3.4.1.

2.4 The potential impact of environmental communication in different domains of life

In their review of psychological research on encouraging pro-environmental behaviour, Steg and Vlek (2009) address the question of which behaviours should be changed. Environmental psychology has a tradition of focusing on behaviours that are highly visible but have rather limited environmental impact, such as recycling behaviour. However, using resources wisely means to select behaviours which have a balance of environmental impact, plasticity of behaviour, and number of people performing the behaviour (Dietz et al., 2009). Some kinds of behaviours have more environmental impact than others, which can be identified in environmental impact assessment, such as life cycle assessment. Typically, purchasing and investment behaviour has more environmental impact than, for example, recycling or refusing plastic bags in the supermarket (Steg & Vlek, 2009). The second aspect, plasticity of behaviour, refers to the degree to which people are able or willing to change their behaviour. Psychological research has over the last decades contributed much about the degree of behaviour change that can be achieved in different behavioural domains. For example, more people are willing to buy a more fuel-efficient car or change their driving style than sell their car. The final aspect, number of people performing the behaviour, refers to the fraction of the population that performs a targeted behaviour. Using certain kinds of chemicals might have a strong negative environmental impact, and the people doing that might even be willing to change, but if the number in total is low, then the overall impact on a more global level would still be small. In conclusion, environmental communicators should prioritise behaviours that (a) have a large environmental impact, (b) many people are able to change, and (c) many people perform. Steg and Vlek (2009) also suggest to select target groups carefully to use the available resources for a campaign in the best possible way. Chapter 7 will extend this thought about target group segmentation further. Since this book has environmental communication as its focus, a fourth component should also be added: choose behaviours that can be changed by means of communication, or complement a communication campaign with other interventions like structural changes.

In environmental science, the main contributors to people's environmental footprint have been identified. Hertwich and Peters (2009) compared the ecological footprint of nations and found that in industrialised countries, as well as many other countries in the world, the main contributors are shelter and housing (including heating, cooling, and warming water, construction), food, mobility (including transport of people and goods), and other consumption activities (e.g. clothes, electronic devices). Within each domain, a large variety of behaviours appear. The next sections will give some examples and discuss the efficiency of communication-based campaigns. Within each subsection an overview of selected relevant behaviours will be given, with a description of their frequency and monetary investment.

2.4.1 Shelter

Table 2.1 gives an overview of selected examples of behaviours that have an environmental impact associated with shelter. These behaviours differ strongly with respect to the frequency with which they are performed and their monetary costs. Both dimensions are usually strongly correlated. The list of behaviours is not comprehensive but gives an overview about the variety. Some of the decisions people can make with respect to their home have obviously more importance than others and are typically the ones that are more cost intensive and less frequent. Where people choose to locate their residence and what type and size of residence they want to live in defines a large share of their resource use for the years to come, and subsequent decisions have less impact. Travel mode choice is, for example, very dependent on residence location. One could therefore conclude that more focus should be on the decisions that have such long-lasting impacts: choosing a residence to live in, investing in large equipment, deciding building materials and methods, and purchasing appliances and refurbishing. However, the behaviours that are performed frequently on a daily basis and have low costs connected to every act are not negligible if their accumulated effect is analysed. They decide how a person performs with respect to environmental impact within the boundaries set by the large investment decisions. Interestingly, environmental psychology has a tendency to focus more on behaviours that are performed often and have less environmental impact as compared to the big boundary-setting decisions. Maybe this is because some of the big investment decisions exclude the less wealthy groups of society. In the following sections, some key examples will be given to illustrate determining factors of such decisions and ways to address them with communication-based interventions.

Timmermans et al. (1992) modelled the choice of residential location in households with more than one income. They selected a set of 13 attributes of the people in the household and the dwelling, including distance to work, number of working days per week, income, flexibility

Table 2.1 A selection of environmentally relevant behaviours in the domain "shelter"

Behaviour	Frequency	Monetary costs
Choice of a residence type (e.g. house, apartment, size)	Very low	Very high
Choice of residence location (e.g. closeness to infrastructure)	Very low	Very high
Choice of building materials, building standard, and design (e.g. orientation of windows)	Low	High
Choice of providers for building services	Low	High
Purchase of installations for the house (e.g. warm water, heating systems, air condition)	Low	High
Installation of photovoltaic panels, wind turbines, hot water solar panels, or similar technology	Low	High
Decision about refurbishing activities (including energy efficiency upgrades)	Low	Medium to high
Purchase of larger electrical appliances (e.g. freezer, tumble dryer, oven, washing machine)	Low	Medium to high
Maintenance of house-/apartment-related equipment	Medium	Medium to low
Heating/cooling behaviour (e.g. setting of thermostats, switching off heaters/air conditioning in unused rooms or when away)	Medium to high	Medium to low
Everyday water use (e.g. showering, bathing, cleaning, washing, use of water for a pool, watering the garden)	High	Low
Everyday energy use (e.g. standby of electric appliances, warm water use, cooking behaviour, use of tumble dryer, cleaning clothes, use of light)	Very high	Low to very low

of the work schedule, children in the household, type of dwelling, building period, renting or owning, number of bedrooms, size of the town, distance to public transportation, and more. They found that the choice of the residence is a trade-off between the evaluation of the job and the residence environment. The residence environment becomes especially important when the household includes children. People accept longer distances to the workplace if the residence environment and the residence are evaluated more suitable, especially if they have children.

Even if the person and residence characteristics that were used in the analysis are hardly changeable by communication means, the relative importance in the decision-making process might be. Based on that idea, Taniguchi et al. (2014) designed an intervention programme where they included information about the public transportation quality in student residence leaflets and found this had a significant effect on location choice.

In an agent-based model simulation, Sopha et al. (2013) found that the decision for implementing a new, more sustainable heating technology is dependent on the perception of product characteristics, attitudes, perceived efficacy, and norms. All four aspects can be addressed by communication. They used the comprehensive action determination model (see Section 4.9.1) which offers entry points to design interventions (Sopha & Klöckner, 2011).

In a comprehensive review, Abrahamse et al. (2005) presented evidence for the effectiveness of communication-based interventions on energy-saving behaviour, mostly in the everyday behaviour category. A recent meta-analysis (Abrahamse & Steg, 2013) found that especially techniques based on social influence had an impact on resource conservation, in particular the block-leader approach and commitment and social models (see Section 8.2). Another meta-analysis (Delmas, Fischlein, & Asensio, 2013) found that information-based interventions on average reduced energy use by 7.4% and that individualised audits and consulting were most effective. They also found that if energy-related communication was framed with a monetary message such as the potential to save money, the effect was a relative increase in energy use, not a decrease.

These examples show that even if there are strong structural impacts on people's shelter-related decisions, intrapersonal factors also contribute, which can be addressed by environmental communication.

2.4.2 Food

Many decisions are made by individuals and households in the food domain (see Table 2.2). Food decisions, especially how much meat, fish, and dairy products to consume and how much food is wasted, have a huge environmental impact. Within the food domain, however, there are few big investment decisions, which makes it to an area, in theory, where behaviours should be easily changed. Once a person decides to reduce meat consumption, this can be implemented immediately. There are few structural boundaries set by large-scale decisions, although the psychological barriers might still be high.

Table 2.2 A selection of environmentally relevant behaviours in the domain "food"

Behaviour	Frequency	Monetary costs
Decision to home-grow food	Medium	Medium to low
Decision about the diet (e.g. vegetarian, vegan, amount of meat, type of meat, amount of fish, amount of dairy products, amount of exotic fruit and vegetables)	Medium to high	Low
Decision to engage in activism about food-related topics (e.g. signing petitions, demonstrating)	Low to medium	Very low
Disposal of unavoidable food waste (e.g. composting)	Low to high	Medium to low
Decision about the location where the food is produced (local vs. non-local food)	High	Low
Decision about the production methods of the food (e.g. organic vs. non-organic food)	High	Low
Decision to avoid specific food ingredients (e.g. genetically modified food, artificial sweeteners)	High	Low
Decision about seasonal versus out-of-season food	High	Low
Food waste (e.g. amount of food purchased, planning use of leftovers, hygiene standards)	High to very high	Low
Decision about how to prepare food (e.g. how is it cooked, stored)	Very high	Low

A substantial amount of literature can be found about the food domain that demonstrates the effect of information- or communication-based intervention techniques. Again, only selected examples will be presented in the following paragraphs. Most of the published studies address choice of organic versus conventional, local versus non-local, and genetically modified versus non-modified food. Hjelmar (2011) interviewed consumers of organic food and identified two main sources of motivation: convenience and reflexive practices. In the first category, some aspects can be understood as structural improvements (e.g. availability, price difference, visibility), whereas the second category embraces aspects such as political, ethical, health, and quality considerations. Whereas communication can to a certain degree also address the first category, the second category is clearly more targeted by communication campaigns. Janssen and Hamm (2012) systematically studied how the willingness to pay for organic food depends on the consumer perception of different types of eco-labels. They found strong variance in willingness to pay, and that the consumers' perception of eco-labels was more dependent on subjective evaluations than knowledge about the labels. Stolzenbach et al. (2013) could even show that information about local food, in their case apple juice, impacts the perception of taste positively.

Few studies have been conducted on the choice of diet. Recently, Zur and Klöckner (2014) proposed a model of determinants of reduced meat consumption and found that ethical, social, and health considerations were important (see Figure 2.2 and Chapter 4 for more information about the variables). Many variables in the described model are good entry points for communication interventions. The model shows that meat consumption was mostly determined by habits, but reduction intentions had a significant impact. Intentions were dependent on attitudes, health-related beliefs connected to consumption of meat, and moral beliefs about meat consumption. For the moral beliefs, descriptive norms (what others do) and perceived behavioural control (PBC) were most relevant.

Rothgerber (2013) found in a study of strategies that students used to justify their meat consumption that males were direct in their

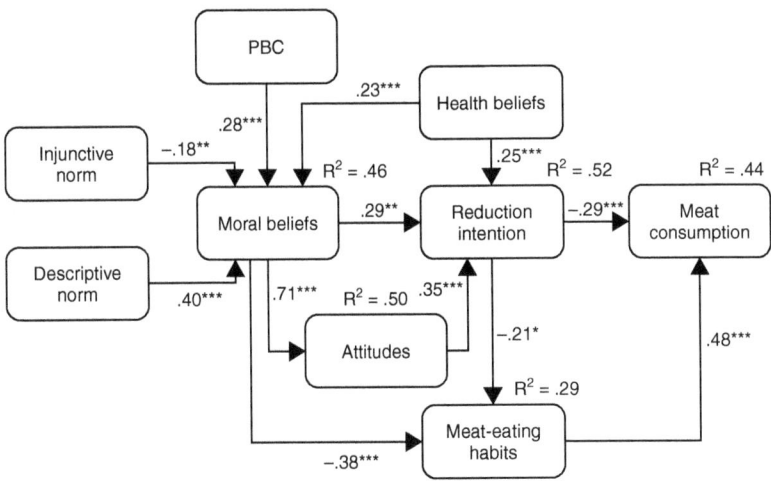

Figure 2.2 A model of meat-eating behaviour (Zur & Klöckner, 2014, page 635). Used by permission of Emerald group publishing

strategies. They endorsed pro-meat attitudes or denied animal suffering and provided health or religious reasons for eating meat. Females were more indirect and dissociated meat from animals and avoided thinking of animals suffering. Meat consumption was also closely linked to masculinity. Studies on meat consumption show clearly that it is a behaviour which should be receptive to communication-based interventions, even if the consumption of meat is deeply rooted in cultural conventions and practices (Schösler et al., 2012).

Recently, the focus on food waste has increased. In a Romanian study, Stefan et al. (2013) looked at shopping routines. They found that minimising purchases of too many or too big food items and planning routines for preparing food during the week were the two main drivers of reducing food waste. Intentions to reduce food waste had no significant impact if these two were controlled for. The main predictors of implementing good routines were moral attitudes and perceived control. The strong relationship between intentions to reduce food waste and moral attitudes was not translated into behaviour. Nomura et al. (2011) studied whether feedback on the performance of one's neighbourhood in a food waste reduction programme had an impact on participation and found that getting feedback increased participation rates. Again, the two examples show the potential for communication-based intervention types.

2.4.3 Consumption of other goods

In the domain of other consumption-related activities, the situation is comparable to the shelter domain. Many decisions are investments, although medium-sized in this domain, which set boundaries for the use-stage afterwards. For example, which kinds of consumer electronics are purchased has a huge impact on the energy consumption in the use-stage. However, there are also other decisions that are less bound by single investments: cosmetic brands can easily be replaced by others; purchase decisions on clothes are made regularly and the impact of the use-stage is minor, although the decision for quality clothing has a considerable impact on the replacement time (Table 2.3).

Jiménez-Parra et al. (2014) studied predictors of consumer intentions to buy remanufactured, professionally checked, and updated second-hand laptops. They found that besides attitudes and social norms, a focus on financial and environmental benefits and less focus on latest technology had an impact. Furthermore, availability through distribution channels like normal retail stores or Internet shops positively influenced the intention, whereas a focus on the design of the laptop and the brand image influenced negatively. Tailored marketing

Table 2.3 A selection of environmentally relevant behaviours in the domain "consumption"

Behaviour	Frequency	Monetary costs
Purchase of consumer electronics (e.g. PCs, tablet, smartphones)	Medium	Medium
Purchase of clothes and shoes	Medium to high	Medium to low
Purchase of cosmetics or similar	Medium to high	Low
Purchase of services (e.g. hairdresser, massages)	Medium to low	Medium to low
Purchase of printed communication means (e.g. books, magazines, newspapers)	Medium to high	Low
Use of virtual communication means (e.g. Internet, telephone)	Medium to high	Low
Decision to engage in collective ownership (e.g. sharing appliances, loaning books)	Low to high	Low
Decision to buy second-hand or remanufactured products	Low to high	High to low
Handling of non-food waste	High	Low

could thus be an efficient strategy to increase the market share of remanufactured consumer products.

With respect to smartphone technology, the topic of environmentally driven consumer choice seems to be almost absent from research, which might reflect that consumers and producers do not yet consider the topic relevant. However, this might change, since in 2013 a small company in the Netherlands introduced a smartphone to the market which claims to be produced with less environmental impact and under fairer conditions for the workers (www.fairphone.com). Inspired by this event, a study was conducted to find out how much more the average consumer was willing to pay for a smartphone with an eco-label or a fair-trade label (Gavelin & Sjöström, 2014). The consumers in the study's small sample reported on average a willingness to pay about 1300 Swedish crowns (about 140 Euro or about US$195) extra for a smartphone with an eco-label and about 600 Swedish crowns (about 65 Euro or about US$90) more for a fair-trade-labelled smartphone. This shows that communication via an accepted labelling system has the potential to impact consumer choice.

Kim et al. (2012) analysed the impact of social norms (see Section 4.4.1) and environmental concern on the intention to buy eco-friendly clothes. Both social norms and environmental concern were significant predictors. In addition to that, the type of environmental claim communicated by the company had an impact on the strength of the relations. If the company claimed that the product itself was produced in an environmentally friendly way (intrinsic claim), the relationship between environmental concern and buying intentions is stronger, and the impact of injunctive social norms is weaker than if the company communicated that a donation to an environmental cause will be given after the purchase. This underlines the complexity of communication around environmental aspects.

2.4.4 Mobility

The mobility domain is characterised by big decisions. Location of residence defines the distance to be travelled and the available transport infrastructure. Also investments in a car, or to a much smaller degree in a bicycle or a bus pass, will set boundaries for the following use-stage. Residence location and the type of car will have an impact on mobility-related resource use for a long time – even if the car is sold after a few years it will be used by other people and impact their resource use. However, the consumer has room to make an impact with smaller use-related decisions within the boundaries set by these big decisions: maintaining the car properly, not transporting unnecessary weight, reducing the number of trips, carpooling or trip chaining as well as cycling, walking, or using public transport for as many trips as possible will reduce the impact of mobility (Table 2.4).

The literature on mobility-related behavioural choices is extensive. Again, only very few selected examples can be given but they represent a whole spectrum of different behaviours. Recently, research on determinants of car purchase has intensified as a result of the introduction of alternative fuel cars (Nayum & Klöckner, 2014; Nayum et al., 2013; Peters et al., 2011). This line of research paints a very complex picture of the car purchase decision and shows that psychological variables like intentions to buy fuel-efficient cars, and also brand loyalty, contribute significantly to car choice behaviour. Even though structural variables had an impact, their importance was less strong when psychological variables were controlled for, which opens new opportunities for communication-based approaches. In another study, Klöckner (2014) modelled the dynamic decision-making process before buying an electric vehicle and found support for a stage-based approach (see Section 4.9.2).

Table 2.4 A selection of environmentally relevant behaviours in the domain "mobility"

Behaviour	Frequency	Monetary costs
Decision about location of the residence (see also shelter)	Very low	Very high
Purchase of a car and which type (e.g. size, brand, fuel efficiency, engine type)	Low	High
Purchase of a bicycle or similar	Low to medium	High to medium
Purchase of a period ticket for public transportation (maybe subscription)	Medium	Medium
Membership in a car-sharing organisation	Low	Medium
Maintenance of the vehicles (e.g. tyre pressure, engine)	Medium	Medium
Removal of unnecessary weight or wind-resistant objects (e.g. the ski box from the car)	Medium	Low
Decision for home office work	Medium to high	Low
Decision for virtual meetings instead of business trips	Medium	Low
Travel mode choice for individual trips	Very high	Low
Trip chaining	Very high	Low
Choosing a fuel-saving driving style	Very high	Low

The decision of whether to use the car, public transportation, bicycle, or to walk has been modelled in literally hundreds of studies with different combinations of structural and psychological predictors. In a meta-analysis, Gardner and Abraham (2008) analysed the importance of psychological predictors of car use and found that car use habits and intentions had the strongest relation. The strongest reasons for choosing to drive the car were found to be perceived control about the choice, importance of the environment, and attitude to non-car use. Friman et al. (2013) found that Swedish soft policy programs that aimed to reduce car use had positive effects, even if the structural conditions in Sweden are more in favour of car than in many other countries. Bamberg (2014) reflects on psychological interventions and concludes that the potential for such interventions is good, if they are delivered in conjunction with structural improvements and go beyond the "one-size-fits-all" approach and tailor the intervention to the specific needs.

Dogan et al. (2014) analysed the impact of feedback on the adoption of an eco-driving style. One group received feedback about the monetary savings they achieved by eco-driving, a second group received feedback about the environmental savings, and the third group did not get any feedback. The results showed that even though both types of feedback were increasing eco-driving, the environmental benefits were valued higher.

2.4.5 Leisure activities

In this final domain, it is important to keep in mind that leisure activities have become more important in western societies. Short weekend trips to far away cities have become affordable and thus popular, and holiday destinations spread across the globe are far more accessible. Many people exercise regularly in fitness clubs and interestingly travel there by car. Even if everyday decisions and big decisions about the residence, food, and mobility might have bigger impact, the leisure sector is of growing importance for the environment (Table 2.5).

In the last domain, two studies will be discussed as examples for choice of travel mode to a holiday destination and choice of holiday activities. Hergesell and Dickinger (2013) analysed a large number of travel mode decisions to holiday destinations by students in different European countries. They found that the price was the main driver for the decision, followed by travel time. Convenience was less important. The choice was, however, also impacted by the students' general environmental behaviour, indicating that their (non-)environmental lifestyle had an impact. An interesting hypothesis is proposed by Nawijn and Peeters (2014) that a potential explanation for unsustainable travel patterns to holiday destinations might be the aim to reproduce experiences of happiness connected to memories from trips already

Table 2.5 A selection of environmentally relevant behaviours in the domain "leisure activities"

Behaviour	Frequency	Monetary costs
Decision about holiday destination	Medium	Medium
Decision about holiday activities	Medium	Medium
Decision about travel mode to holiday destination	Medium	Medium
Decision about sports and exercise (e.g. jogging vs. fitness club) and how to get there	Medium	Medium
Decision about going out (e.g. restaurant, cinema)	Medium to high	Medium to low
Decision about other hobbies	Medium to high	Low to high

made. Kaklamanou, Jones, Webb, and Walker (2015) found that many holiday travels tend to trade off bad environmental behaviour (taking a flight to a far-away destination) by doing good things while being at the destination (using public transport).

Chiu et al. (2014) studied how experiences during a holiday within the ecotourism sector impact the environmental behaviour of the tourists, assuming that eco-tourists are not per se more environmentally friendly but may be more so in their holiday environment. They found that the perceived value of the holiday via engagement in activities and satisfaction with the experience impacts pro-environmental behaviour.

2.5 Conclusions

The purpose of this chapter was to situate environmental communication within a context of other environmental interventions and within the context of different domains of human life. The chapter explored the role environmental communication has in constructing and defining the very core of its target: environmental problems and who believes which ones need to be addressed. Understanding environmental communication is important in not getting trapped in what Gergen (2011) refers to as the "games of language" (the definition of realities by language) without knowing the rules.

As a tool to change people's environmentally relevant behaviour, it is important to see the potential and limitations that environmental communication has. Often, people's behaviour is restricted by structural boundaries, whether they be cultural, physical, economic, or a lack of skills and abilities. Without addressing such barriers first, all attempts of environmental communication can be of little effect. On the other hand, once the structural conditions give people some "room to move", environmental communication can make the difference.

If we take a look at the different domains of human life, it appears that shelter and mobility are largely characterised by big investment decisions that have the largest impact because they define the use-stage for a long time. The food domain, the leisure activity domain, and, to some extent, the consumption domain are characterised by more flexibility within the repeated decision-making. Whereas in the first two domains, environmental communication needs to focus on affecting the big decisions before they happen, the window of opportunity is larger for environmental communication addressing the other domains.

However, one of the biggest decisions of all, deciding to have children, has not been addressed in this chapter, despite its huge impact.

Review questions

- What is the potential and what are the limitations of environmental communication in the context of other possible environmental interventions?
- What role does the consumer have in the environmental domain?
- Give examples of typical behaviours in the different domains and explain what the characteristics of these behaviours are.
- Argue for the potential impact of environmental communication in the different behavioural domains.

Suggested readings

Abrahamse, W., Steg, L., Vlek, C., & Rothengatter, T. (2005). A review of intervention studies aimed at household energy conservation. *Journal of Environmental Psychology*, 25(3), 273–291.

Delmas, M. A., Fischlein, M., & Asensio, O. I. (2013). Information strategies and energy conservation behavior: A meta-analysis of experimental studies from 1975 to 2012. *Energy Policy*, 61, 729–739.

Nayum, A., & Klöckner, C. A. (2014). A comprehensive socio-psychological approach to car type choice. *Journal of Environmental Psychology*, 40, 401–411.

Steg, L., & Vlek, C. (2009). Encouraging pro-environmental behaviour: An integrative review and research agenda. *Journal of Environmental Psychology*, 29(3), 309–317.

Thøgersen, J. (2009). Promoting public transport as a subscription service: Effects of a free month travel card. *Transport Policy*, 16(6), 335–343.

Part II

3
Understanding Communication – Insights from Theories of Communication

Chapter summary

This chapter first presents an overview of the most important theory families within communication research, namely the rhetorical, the semiotic, the phenomenological, the critical, the cybernetic, the sociopsychological, and the sociocultural traditions. For each tradition, central assumptions and their importance for environmental communication are presented. Central concepts in two theory families which are important for the scope of this book are introduced and discussed in more detail: the sociopsychological and the sociocultural traditions. Sociopsychological concepts of attention, human memory, attribution, persuasion, and automaticity in communication are explained and their relevance for environmental communication is explored. Sociocultural concepts of social constructivism, social construction of meaning, and the concepts of the self and identity are introduced and their importance for environmental communication is explored.

3.1 Introduction

This first theory chapter gives a brief overview of the most relevant theory families used by researchers on human communication. Communication research is a large field and cannot be explored extensively in the limited space of one chapter. Following the general overview, two theoretical families will be explored in more detail as they are relevant to the psychological scope of this book: the sociopsychological and the sociocultural theory families. The basic approach of the cybernetic communication theories will be discussed next. For readers interested in the basics of communication and its manifestations on all levels of communication (communicator, message, conversation, relationship, group, organisation, media, culture, and society), the author recommends reading the comprehensive presentation of theories in *Theories of Human Communication* by Littlejohn and Foss (2011).

3.2 Overview of communication theories

In the following section, the main families of communication theories will be introduced and their relevance to environmental communication analysed. In introducing the families, the same categorisation as suggested by Littlejohn and Foss (2011) based on an overview paper by Craig (1999) will be used, even if the categories are overlapping and placement of theories within the families is not always distinct.

3.2.1 Rhetorical communication theories

Probably, the oldest tradition in communication theories can be traced back to ancient Greek philosophy. Rhetoric is the human use of symbols and the art of constructing arguments and speech making (Littlejohn & Foss, 2011). Its original use was persuasion, but, in modern communication research, the rhetoric tradition addresses all human use of symbols to affect other people and to construct the worlds in which we live (Littlejohn & Foss, 2011). A central characteristic of rhetoric is to present arguments for all positions in a structured manner and weigh them against each other.

Based on the ancient art of rhetoric, the modern rhetoric tradition analyses communication along the following five aspects of a speech: invention, arrangement, style, delivery, and memory. *Invention* is the process of assigning meaning to symbols (e.g. words) through interpretation, which emphasises the subjectivity of communication. *Arrangement* is the process of organising the symbols: what is going to be said when and in which context and order. *Style* refers to the presentation of the symbols: which system of symbols is chosen, which meanings are given to them, and also other aspects, such as clothing, gestures, and furniture that support the presentation. *Delivery* is the process of presenting the symbols in a physical form, which could be speech, written presentation, or non-verbal communication. *Memory* finally covers not only the cognitive processes connected to memorisation and retrieval of information, but also the cultural memory that affects our interpretation of symbols.

The contribution of rhetoric to environmental communication provides a structured framework that can improve an environmental communication strategy. First of all, rhetoric stresses the importance of presenting arguments for both sides. The effect this has on reception of a persuasive attempt will be analysed more closely in Section 3.3.4. Rhetoric also recommends paying attention to the form of presentation and the order or arrangement of the message, as well as the context of delivery.

3.2.2 Semiotic communication theories

Semiotics also has its roots in ancient philosophy and is related to rhetoric but was, according to Craig (1999), catalysed by John Locke's work in the 17th century. The semiotic approach to analysing human communication focuses on studying the function of signs in representing objects, ideas, states, feelings, situations, or conditions. Semiotics thus analyses how signs (e.g. words) are connected to objects and how their meaning affects the communication process. "Signs" are a central concept in the semiotic tradition. Language is a very important system of signs, but there are also other systems such as gestures. Signs always represent something in reality. Signs are not understood as tools that are used by communicators but rather like entities that affect the communicators, or as Craig (1999) puts it: "We do not use signs; rather they use us" (page 134). Signs become an inter-subjective mediator between perspectives of individuals.

As one of the first modern representatives of semiotics, Peirce (1974) defines the process of communication through signs, the semiosis, as the relationship between an object, a sign, and a meaning. The sign becomes a representation of the object in the mind of the interpreter. The sign is then not the object itself, but the thoughts, associations, or interpretations connected to the object (Littlejohn & Foss, 2011). According to semiotics, misunderstandings in communication originate from using different systems of signs, different "languages". If one person attaches a different sign to an object than another or if a sign has a different meaning for one person than for another, their communication is distorted. The discourse about climate change is a good example of how semiotics can contribute to environmental communication. When Hurricane Katrina hit New Orleans in 2005 (the object), many people in the United States saw this as a sign of climate change manifesting in a concrete event, even if single local events like a hurricane are difficult to relate to a global phenomenon like climate change. Consequently, they associated the event with the increased likelihood of similar events in the future and felt motivated to take action. Others interpreted the same hurricane as an extreme but natural event (they attached a different sign to it) and thus did not feel any impulse to act against climate change. More generally speaking, an important contribution of semiotics to environmental communication is the conclusion that whatever signs I use in my communication, whatever words or pictures I use, will have different meanings for different people and will trigger different associations. Being aware of this is very helpful.

3.2.3 Phenomenological communication theories

In the phenomenological approach, the basic assumption is that people understand and make sense of the world by direct experience with phenomena (Littlejohn & Foss, 2011). Deetz (1973) formulates three principles of phenomenology: (1) knowledge is created by direct experience with the world in a conscious experience; (2) the meaning of things is connected to its potential for a person's life. Things that potentially have a stronger impact on your life will be assigned a more important meaning. Thus, meaning is directly related to function; and (3) language transports meaning. The experiences that lead to knowledge are made through the channel of language. Through a process of interpretation, the world is constructed for the individual. This interpretation is an active process of the mind, characterised by oscillating back and forth between a state of experience and a state of assigning meaning to the experience (Littlejohn & Foss, 2011). This process is also referred to as the hermeneutic circle: first we experience something, then we interpret that experience and assign it a meaning, then we test this interpretation again in the next experience, reinterpret, and so on.

An important lesson from phenomenology for environmental communication is the importance of personal experience. One problem of communication about the seriousness of climate change is, for example, that climate change is an abstract phenomenon that is difficult to connect to personal experiences (Weber, 2006). People will be more affected by environmental messages if they have personal experiences of the issue rather than if it is a problem mediated by reports from other people or media. Phenomenology also emphasises the importance of personal relevance. People will more likely relate to environmental problems that have negative effects on something that is personally relevant for them or their loved ones than on some distant people or distant ecosystems. Creating arenas for personal experience, for personal contact to the phenomenon and making it relevant, is thus the main message to be taken from phenomenological theory traditions.

3.2.4 Critical communication theories

The focus of the critical tradition of communication theories is the analysis of how communication contributes to creating power distribution in societies, for example, who defines meaning of communication, who structures and sets the agenda. Feminist communication theories as well as post-colonialist and postmodern theories can be found under this label. All critical theories try to understand and question the taken-for-granted systems, power structures, beliefs, and ideologies of society (Littlejohn & Foss, 2011). Critical theorists identify who is allowed and given room to speak and who is not. They ask who defines meanings and who defines what is to be talked about. Finally, they identify who profits from the arrangements as they are and who is disadvantaged. Critical theorists then try to uncover the systems of oppression and offer alternatives that can liberate and emancipate the oppressed. They typically merge theory and action closely, with a moral need for action originating from this type of research. Structures of discourse that stabilise the oppressive structures are of utmost interest. How power differences are transported and manifested through language and other means of communication is high on the research agenda and critical discourse analysis is a common tool.

This tradition has implications for environmental communication. Environmental messages cannot be separated from the societal context and power structures. Identifying who is setting the agenda choosing the environmental problems to be addressed and which are ignored, for example, is an important focus of environmental communication. Who is defining which solution is advocated? Who benefits from advocating this and not another solution? Who assigns me the right and power to influence other people into an environmentally friendlier way of living? These are important questions that critical environmental communicators should ask themselves. It seems also like power and environmental concern or attitudes are often negatively correlated.

3.2.5 Cybernetic communication theories

The cybernetic tradition of communication research has its origin in its analogy to complex (mostly technological) systems and focuses on information processing (Craig, 1999). Computer analogies are not uncommon in the cybernetic tradition. It treats communication as the outcome of the complex interaction of many different small elements that influence and control each other (Littlejohn & Foss, 2011). In the complex system, states of equilibrium and states of change can occur between the different parts. The complexity makes the outcome of the system different from the outcome of its single parts. Each part of the system is dependent on other parts and is constrained by them; often feedback loops and self-regulation loops are parts of such a system and the relationships are non-linear. The system also interacts with its environment by taking input, processing it, and outputting something else to the environment. Simpler systems can also be embedded in more complex systems, which again can be contained within even more complex systems.

Many of the theories which are presented in Chapter 4 can be understood as belonging to the cybernetic tradition; at least they borrow the idea that different components of a decision-making process can be identified and that the outcome of the decision-making process is determined by the complex interplay of its parts. Thus, the impact of the cybernetic tradition on environmental communication will be discussed in more detail in the next chapter.

3.2.6 Sociopsychological communication theories

In the sociopsychological tradition, the communicating individual and intrapersonal processes are the focus of the analysis. Even if the individual is understood as part of a physical and social environment which has an impact on their decisions, the main unit of analysis is one individual (Littlejohn & Foss, 2011). Aspects such as personality, attitudes, emotional states, perception, and social cognition are assigned to individuals which then impact the way this individual communicates (Craig, 1999; Littlejohn & Foss, 2011). Social psychology, which is the origin of this family of communication theories, is characterised by strong reliance on empirical, often experimental, research and thereby questions other research traditions which lack empirical proof, as social psychologists would say (Craig, 1999). The sociopsychological tradition has become one of the most influential theoretical traditions in communication research and many different psychological and cognitive mechanisms have been studied under its name. Some examples that the author considers most relevant for environmental communication will be introduced and discussed in more detail in Section 3.3.

3.2.7 Sociocultural communication theories

The sociocultural research tradition takes a focus that is very different from the sociopsychological tradition. The group, the interactive creation of meaning, identity, and knowledge are the focus of the sociocultural approach (Littlejohn & Foss, 2011). This approach has its origins in sociology, which is the study of the behaviour of collectives. As such, the sociocultural tradition is interested in how groups collectively construct meaning, norms, roles, social rules, and identities of both the group and its members. It asserts that reality is not an objective entity but the product of social negotiations, which also implies that realities vary even for one individual depending on the group the individual belongs to or attaches himself or herself to at a given point in time. This means that reality also changes when the group changes. This approach also offers specific methods of research. As sociocultural theorists assume that reality is constructed and that language has a crucial part in that construction process (Littlejohn & Foss, 2011), research itself will have an impact on the object of research and is a result of processes of construction of meaning.

A central concept in the sociocultural tradition is identity which is the intersection of the individual with social, community, and cultural rules. Identity is negotiated and context-dependent which makes the contextualisation of communication a central research question in this approach. What happens on the micro-level is always influenced and can only be understood by knowing the macro-level context. As Craig (1999) puts it: "Communication in these traditions is typically theorized as a symbolic process that produces and reproduces shared sociocultural patterns" (page 144). Also this tradition has tremendous implications for environmental communication as it emphasises the importance of the context. Selected aspects of this theory will be discussed in Section 3.4.

3.3 Selected aspects of sociopsychological communication theories

After the brief overview about the basic assumptions of sociopsychological communication theories, this section will present selected aspects that have been analysed. The overview starts with two aspects of information processing, namely attention and information storage and retrieval. Afterwards an introduction to attribution theory, how we assign explanations for behaviours, will be given and the theory of persuasion presented. The section ends with an overview about automatic processes that affect communication, an aspect that will also reoccur in the next chapter. For each aspect, its relevance to environmental communication is explored.

3.3.1 Attention

If we move through our environment and organise our daily lives, we need to make sense of the extremely rich information content. Our cognitive capacity to process information is limited, which means we need to select the information that might be relevant for us and ignore the rest. The process that makes this selection is referred to as attention.

In 1958, Broadbent published a book that outlined an influential psychological theory of attention, which he referred to as the selective filter theory of attention (Broadbent, 1958). The main assumption is that the human brain has a memory system that stores all available information from the environment for initial processing. This system, which is also referred to as sensory memory, stores enormous amounts of information, but only for a couple of milliseconds up to a number of seconds (Sams et al., 1993). The sensory memory is permanently overwritten with new information as we move around. There is separate sensory memory for each sensual modality (e.g. vision, hearing). The information stored in the sensory memory is preliminarily scanned for physical features that make it potentially relevant for the individual (e.g. visual features that indicate an approaching, potentially threatening object). According to Broadbent (1958), only information that is identified as relevant in this first step is passed on to higher cognitive processing into the working memory where it is semantically analysed and where meaning is attached to the information. What is regarded as relevant or irrelevant depends both on top-down influences (e.g. which goals does a person have at a point in time – see also goal-framing theory in Section 4.6) and on bottom-up influences (e.g. stimulus intensity) (Lachter et al., 2004).

Broadbent asserts that information processing for unattended stimuli, those stimuli that go unnoticed, is halted by an early attention filter. This has been challenged by a series of influential experiments (Treisman, 1960). Participants in the experiment were asked to wear earphones that presented two different audio-streams of spoken words into each ear. They were then asked to repeat the message that they heard in one ear and ignore the message in the other. During the experiment, the messages unexpectedly changed from one ear to the other and after a very short period of confusion, the participants continued repeating the message they reported before the switch. This means that they were aware that the message continued in the ear that went unnoticed, which implies some level of semantic processing of this information. This led Treisman (1960) to conclude that Broadbent's filter mechanism seems not to work as an on/off filter where information is either passed on or totally blocked. It seems rather like a threshold filter, where all information that reaches a certain conscious processing threshold is processed.

Deutsch and Deutsch (1963) propose a selection mechanism that occurs rather late in information processing. For example, imagine the cocktail party effect: you are at a cocktail party talking to someone.

Around you are many other conversations going on that you are not paying attention to, but as soon as someone in those conversations mentions your name, you are likely to shift attention. According to Deutsch and Deutsch, all input is processed semantically, with a selection made of which information reaches consciousness and which is filtered out.

Another important line of research on attention focuses on divided attention. We often do several things at once, for example, driving and having a conversation with our co-driver, or reading a book while listening to music. It has already been said that separate sensory memories are assumed to exist for different modalities. On that level, interference between competing information on the same modality is to be expected, but no interference will occur between information on different modalities. While there is some evidence that the interference is stronger within the same modality, research shows that multitasking also impairs the quality of performance across modalities (Salvucci & Taatgen, 2008). Salvucci and Taatgen's "threaded cognition" theory also predicts that interference between tasks becomes smaller when the tasks are well trained, which makes their performance more and more automatic (see also Section 3.3.5).

For designing environmental communication, knowing about limited cognitive processing capacity and the role attention plays as a filter is crucial. An environmental message needs to make it to conscious processing to have a chance to be perceived. In the vast stream of information that people are confronted with, environmental messages can easily be filtered out as irrelevant by the attention system. This is especially the case for people that do not already have a pro-environmental goal, which makes it especially complicated. However, research on the effects of priming suggests that it can be possible to prime a certain goal set on the subliminal level (see also Section 4.6). This confirms that it is better to present environmental communication in situations where people are relatively free from information overload. However, late-selection models of attention suggest that environmental communication might even achieve an effect if people do not attend to it directly, an assumption that is also related to what is referred to as the periphery route of persuasion (see Section 3.3.4.1).

3.3.2 Information storage and retrieval

In the psychological tradition, memory processes can be separated into three distinct processes: (1) encoding, (2) storage, and (3) retrieval. Encoding is the processing and adapting of incoming information so that it can be transferred to memory. Storage is the process of keeping the information in memory for some time. Retrieval refers to pulling information back from the memory so that it can be used again. In their famous multi-store model, Atkinson and Shiffrin (1968) propose a three storage model. The first part of memory is the sensory memory, sometimes also referred to as the sensory buffer or sensory register (see previous section). Some of that information enters short-term memory, filtered through processes of attention. Short-term memory is where information is actively processed and manipulated. It has a limited capacity and memory traces fade quickly if information is not actively rehearsed, usually within 20–30 seconds (Peterson & Peterson, 1959). The capacity of the short-term memory is considered as being seven plus/minus two distinct items (Miller, 1956). From short-term memory, some information is transferred into long-term memory, which is virtually unlimited and can store information for a very long time. If information from long-term memory is needed to solve some task, it needs to be retrieved back to short-term memory.

The multi-store model (Atkinson & Shiffrin, 1968) has been criticised as an oversimplification. It makes sense to assume that the sensory memory is mode-specific, meaning it has at least three separate components: iconic memory that stores visual information, echoic memory that stores auditory information, and haptic memory that stores information from our haptic sensors or touch (Baddeley, 1997). Baddeley and Hitch (1975) proposed a model of working memory which differentiates the short-term memory into three components: (1) the phonological loop that processes words, (2) the visuo-spatial sketchpad, which processes visual and special information, and (3) the central executive that integrates and steers the two other processes and also acts as the attention-steering entity. Baddeley (2000) added an episodic buffer, which processes temporal information as a fourth process. Long-term memory is not a uniform memory structure and is broken up into declarative memory ("the know what") and procedural memory ("the know how"), which stores learned skills (Tulving, 1972; Ullman, 2004; Wood et al., 2012). The declarative memory has two sub-dimensions: semantic memory (factual knowledge) and episodic memory (memory of events in a temporal chronology). Figure 3.1 displays an integrated model of human memory.

Retrieval of information from long-term memory can come in two forms: recognition (e.g. knowing familiar objects when encountering them again) and recall (freely reproducing previously learned items of information). Ratcliff (1978) describes the retrieval process as sending

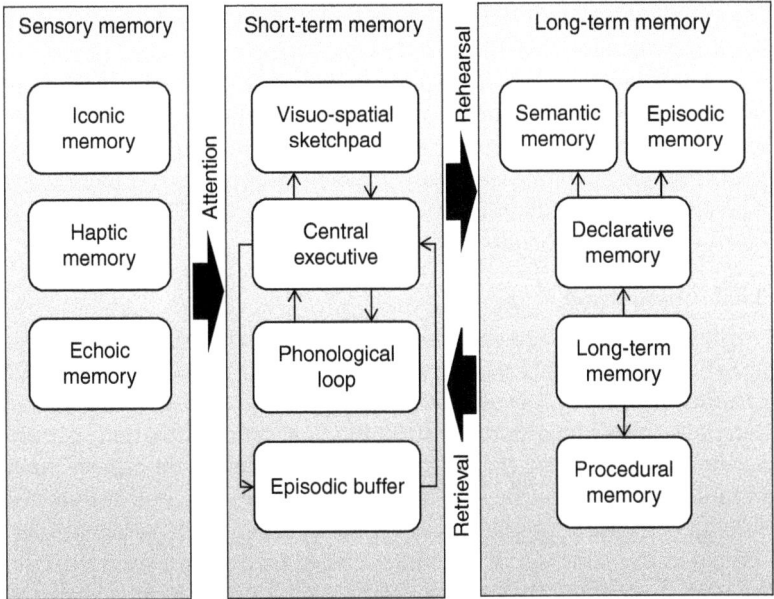

Figure 3.1 A model of human memory

a probe or a cue through the memory networks. The more the probe resonates with a memory structure, the stronger the retrieval of this memory into short-term memory. Tulving and Thomson (1973) formulate the encoding specificity principle which states that memory retrieval is easier when the retrieving stimulus or probe matches the context of the learning situation. In other words, things are easier to remember if a person is in a similar situation or state. A number of aspects have been shown to impact ease of retrieval, including the notion that retrieval is easier and faster if attention is focused on the retrieval process rather than taken up with something else (Baddeley et al., 1984). Also strong motivation seems to enhance the accuracy of memory retrieval (Roebers et al., 2001).

This brief overview of memory processes has some implications for environmental communication design. For example, if we want to educate people in pro-environmental actions, it is beneficial to provide them with knowledge about the reasons for why an environmentally damaging behaviour should be substituted with a less damaging one. We may also want to provide them with procedural knowledge and hence the skills to perform the behaviour. Communication needs to attract people's attention (see also Section 3.3.1) to make it into short-term memory. We then need to make people motivated enough to memorise the information we provide them with, to make them store it in their long-term memory. We also need to make sure that people retrieve the relevant information when they are making their decisions. Following the encoding specificity principle, this retrieval is more likely when the decision situation matches the learning situation or when cues occur that make recognition possible.

3.3.3 Attribution

Attribution theory deals with the question of how people deduce causes of behaviour or events. This applies for our own behaviour, behaviour of other people, and explanations of occurring events. Kelley (1973) describes three dimensions to attributing cause in a situation: person, entities, and time. For example, if a student failed a test and we want to find out where the cause of that failure lies, we can look at how this student performed in other tests over time and how other students performed in the same test. If the student failed many of the exams before, we tend to attribute the cause to the student – he or she is a weak performer. If the student passed most of the exams, but also many other students failed this specific test, we tend to attribute the cause to the test – it was too difficult. If the student usually passes exams and most other students also passed this specific test, the attribution will most likely go to something in the particular circumstances of the event, may be a mismatch of the test and the way the student prepared this time, or "bad luck".

Weiner (1972, 2001) extended the theory of attribution by introducing three new dimensions (locus of control, stability, and controllability) and linking the attribution to both emotional reactions to it and willingness to help a person. Locus of control refers to where the cause of a behaviour or event is located. If it is inside a person (e.g. personality, skills, knowledge, or effort), then Weiner speaks of an internal locus of control; if it is outside (e.g. difficulty of the task or circumstances), the locus of control is external. Stability refers to the temporal variability of the cause. Whereas personality as the cause would be assumed to be stable, effort might vary over time. Controllability analyses if the cause is under the control of the individual or not. Whereas the effort a person puts into something can be controlled, factors such as aptitude would be regarded as uncontrollable. Whereas the difficulty of a task can be controlled by someone, luck in guessing the correct answer, for example, cannot. If the cause for a negative event seems controllable, either shame and guilt (in case of attribution of one's own behaviour) or blame and anger (in case of others) is felt. The impulse to help others, who we feel would have had control to achieve a better result, is low. Stable causes that lead to success lead to feelings of hopefulness when approaching the next task ("I know I can do that"), whereas stable causes for failure cause hopelessness and consequently a lack of effort. Stable causes for failure might motivate others to help, whereas unstable causes are regarded as "passing quickly".

In an important paper, Ross (1977) describes a general tendency to overestimate the influence of internal causes on people's behaviour, an effect referred to as fundamental attribution error. We tend to attribute behaviour to the individual's characteristics rather than circumstances. However, this applies mostly to other people's behaviour as for our own behaviour we are much more willing to attribute the cause externally, especially for failures.

Attribution theory has important implications for environmental communication. We need to know how people attribute the causes of environmental behaviour to target our communication attempts. If persons perceive the causes of their behaviour as uncontrollable, they will not react positively to attempts to change it. If the causes are attributed externally, there will also be little willingness to invest effort in change, at least not before the external causes, barriers in this case, have been removed. We should also be aware that the fundamental attribution error might affect both us as designers of a communication campaign and the targets. Whereas we will tend to attribute the causes of environmentally damaging behaviour internally ("people are lazy, greedy, unaware"), people themselves will most likely attribute externally ("I cannot do anything, it is so difficult to be environmentally friendly"). The role of ascription of responsibility is introduced in Section 4.4.1 as a related topic.

3.3.4 Persuasion

Environmental communication is essentially persuasion; we communicate to make people change their attitudes, intentions, and consequently their behaviour. Much psychological research has focused on how and when persuasion is effective. Some of the theoretical background will be presented in the following sections, before the last section presents the weapons of influence that Cialdini (2006) outlines in his best-selling book on persuasion.

3.3.4.1 Cognitive dissonance theory
Cognitive dissonance theory, proposed by Festinger (1962), assumes that people strive for harmony between their cognitions (thoughts). If two or

more cognitions do not match, a feeling of unease is caused that individuals will try to reduce. They have four options to reduce the tension between the cognitions: (1) changing one of the cognitions, (2) reducing the importance of one of the cognitions, (3) increasing the overlap between the two conditions, and (4) re-evaluating the cost/benefit ratio. For example, let us assume a person is a dedicated car driver and enjoys driving the car, but at the same time he is of the opinion that car traffic is an important cause of environmental damage. The two cognitions together cause cognitive dissonance. Now he can either change one of the cognitions (e.g. by changing his positive association with car driving or by denying the environmental damage). Or he can reduce the importance of the joy of driving or the environmental problem in his reasoning, and he can argue that his way of driving causes minimal damage as compared to the alternatives (and thus make the overlap stronger). Another possibility would be to conclude that the benefit of driving is so great that it outweighs the environmental costs (or vice versa).

One way to change people's minds is to create cognitive dissonance by planting ideas in people's minds that contradict their cognitions related to an environmentally relevant behaviour. However, the problem is that cognitive dissonance theory predicts that there will be many ways to reduce cognitive dissonance and only a few of them include changing attitudes or even behaviour. Consequently, Kollmuss and Agyeman (2002) use cognitive dissonance theory more as an explanation for why people *avoid* information about environmental problems than as a tool for attitude change. Thøgersen (2004) uses cognitive dissonance to explain why people might generalise environmental behaviour across domains. Dissonance explains why people who behave environmentally friendly in one behavioural domain have a higher likelihood of doing so also in other domains.

3.3.4.2 The elaboration likelihood model

Petty and Cacioppo (1986) proposed the elaboration likelihood model to explain how the mechanisms of attitude change differ depending on how much elaboration we put into the process. Figure 3.2 shows that the model assumes two routes of persuasion: the central route and the peripheral. The central route is an active process demanding our attention and using cognitive resources. We only take that route, meaning we think about presented arguments, if we are both motivated and capable of doing that.

So, what happens to communication aimed at persuasion according to the model? The first question is if we are motivated to process it.

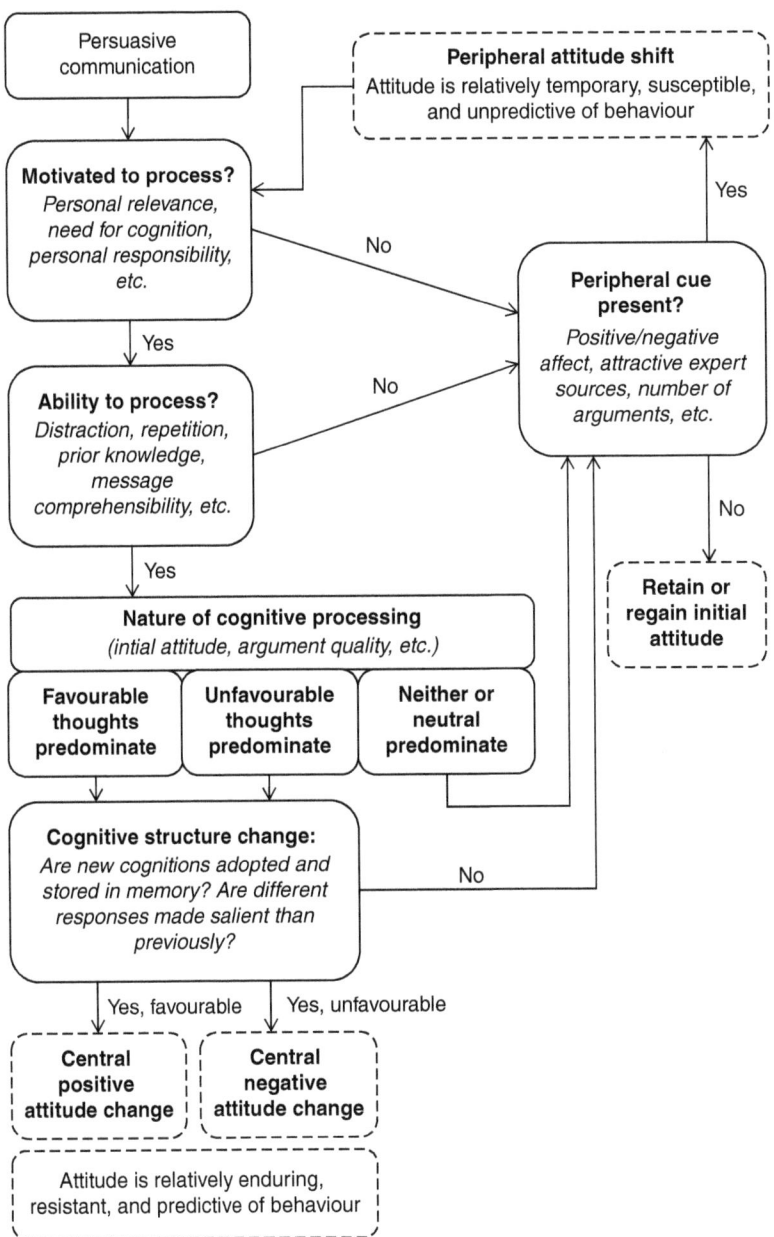

Figure 3.2 The elaboration likelihood model (Petty & Cacioppo, 1986, page 126). Used by permission of Elsevier

This depends on, for example, personal relevance of the topic, personal responsibility, or the need for cognition implied in the communication. The next question is if we are capable of processing the communication. We may be distracted, have little prior knowledge, or the message may be incomprehensible, so we might answer "no". The next step is cognitive processing and in the end positive or negative thoughts might dominate. The next question is if the communication succeeds in changing our cognitive structure. If there is a change in the cognitive structure, it can be in a more favourable or unfavourable direction. If that happens, we have achieved an attitude change through the direct route of persuasion. Attitudes that have been formed or changed in the direct way tend to be enduring, resistant against change to a certain degree, and determine behaviour.

The peripheral route is activated if we are not motivated or able to process the persuasive communication. It also happens if no clear dominance of favourable or unfavourable thoughts is achieved or if no change in cognitive structures occurs. Here, not the arguments themselves, but other cues are processed in a rather superficial way. Do I get a positive or negative affective reaction when I listen to the communication? Is the communicator attractive or appears to be an expert? How many arguments are presented? A peripheral attitude shift occurs if there is a positive affective reaction, an attractive or expert communicator, or if many arguments are presented. This shift, however, is often temporary and the attitudes created in this way do not predict behaviour as well as attitudes formed or changed via the direct route.

This model can also be used in environmental communication. If we want to achieve an enduring change in behaviour, we need to make sure that people process our communication attempts via the central route. This means we need to address people in situations when they are motivated to use some cognitive effort to process the arguments we confront them with. The topic should be relevant to them and they should be likely to accept responsibility. Furthermore, they should not be distracted and the message should be presented in a way that they can relate to and that is understandable. We need to be aware of people's opinions regarding their prior knowledge and attitudes. However, we should also not underestimate the power of the peripheral route. Even if the attitude change created this way might be less enduring and less predictive for behaviour, an environmental communicator should pay attention to the attractiveness and compatibility of the communicator for the target group, the emotional reaction induced by the communication, and features like number of arguments.

3.3.4.3 Theory of inoculation

The theory of inoculation was developed by McGuire (1964) and draws on a medical analogy: just like in a vaccination where a reaction to a small amount of the virus immunises against a serious infection with the same virus later, the idea of inoculation is to immunise people against persuasion by confronting them with some mild arguments for the opposing negative side and make them argue against them. If they are later confronted with more serious counter-arguments, they will be much more able to withstand them and not change their attitudes. An interesting application in environmental communication could, for example, be to confront people who believe in human-made climate change with a number of weak arguments presented by climate sceptics that they can easily argue against. If they are later confronted with more serious or massive counter-arguments, they will be more resistant against them, according to inoculation theory. Though inoculation theory is widely used in marketing (Bither et al., 1971) and health interventions (Duryea, 1983), Kemp et al. (2012) find only limited support for an inoculation technique in the environmental domain (such as in a study focusing on recycled water).

3.3.4.4 The weapons of influence

In his book, Cialdini (2006) presents six principles of successful persuasion which he refers to as the "weapons of influence". The principles are (1) reciprocity, (2) commitment and consistency, (3) social proof, (4) liking, (5) authority, and (6) scarcity.

The *reciprocity* principle builds on the fact that humans like to repay their debts. If someone does me a favour, I feel obliged to repay that person by also doing them a favour. This principle is widely used in marketing when small gifts, trial periods, or other gains are provided by a company. An application in the environmental domain could be in the marketing of pro-environmental products, but a more subtle variation could be to give people something they want, for example, an energy audit, and then afterwards approach them about changing their behaviour.

Commitment and consistency utilise the fact that people want to appear consistent in their behaviour (see also Section 3.3.4.1). If we can get people to commit to performing a behaviour, they will feel obliged to actually perform it to keep consistency intact. In Section 8.2.8, commitment as an environmental intervention strategy will be introduced in more detail.

Social proof plays on the human tendency to analyse and copy other people's behaviour. We tend to do what most other people in the same situation do, an effect that is analysed in Section 8.2.9 under the themes of social models, descriptive norms, and social norms.

Liking is a factor that builds on the tendency to be persuaded more easily by people we like. Liking is basically caused by two factors: attractiveness and similarity. Environmental communication should thus not underestimate the importance of attractive communicators that match the target group on dimensions such as gender, age, and social status (see Section 8.2.9).

Authority means that people are more easily persuaded by people they perceive as experts in the field, sometimes not even in the field but on a more general level. Advertising makes heavy use of this principle by hiring scientists to promote products. In environmental communication, the role of expertise is also important.

Scarcity, finally, is a principle that is also exploited in marketing. Declaring a product as scarce makes people more willing to buy it, fearing that they will miss out on the opportunity to buy it later. In environmental communication, scarcity could be induced by creating time-limited opportunities to act, such as if you act now your action will have an extra large impact. However, this strategy also needs to have a believable background.

3.3.5 Automatic processes in communication

With the elaboration likelihood model presented in Section 3.3.4.2, we already discussed the impact that automaticity can achieve in communication. Several other mechanisms also affect the way humans communicate on a subconscious level: routines, habits, heuristics, and mental models to name just an important few. Heuristics and mental models will be discussed in the next two sections, routines and habits later in Section 4.8.

3.3.5.1 Heuristics

Simon (1972) coined the term "bounded rationality" by which he wanted to express the idea that even if people strive to make rational decisions, this rationality is not necessarily the same rationality as an outsider would have utilising the full array of available information. He also introduced the concept of "satisficing", meaning that most people will stop searching for the best solution when they have found a solution that is "good enough". Tversky and Kahneman (1974) were interested in how people make decisions in situations in which not all information is available, such as outcomes. They identified a number of simplifying rules of thumb, referred to as heuristics, that people use to make decisions in such contexts. Usually, such heuristic decisions free cognitive resources for other tasks because they reduce the amount of information that needs to be processed. Three of the most famous heuristics presented below are the representativeness heuristic, the availability heuristic, and the anchoring heuristic (Tversky & Kahneman, 1973, 1974).

The *representativeness heuristic* is applied when the probability of an event is inferred from how representative a described case is for a prototype. Information about base rates is ignored in that process. For example, a person is described with features that are perceived as prototypical for an environmentalist, and then others are asked how likely it is that this person is a banker or a leader of a national environmental movement. People tend to overestimate the likelihood of this person being an environmental leader and underestimate the likelihood of that person being a banker, because it is ignored that there are far more bankers than environmental leaders.

The *availability heuristic* describes that the estimated probability of an event is positively correlated with the ease with which people can make this event come to life in their minds. Things that are continuously communicated and illustrated in the media, like violent crime, are thus overrated in the perceived likelihood, whereas the probability of events that are more difficult to imagine is underrated. This can be important for environmental communication. Environmental problems that are easy to envision will be perceived as more pressing than abstract problems that are not connected to vivid mental representations. Furthermore, the likelihood of negative environmental effects will be underestimated if they get little media coverage as compared to other societal problems.

The *anchoring heuristic* emphasises the importance of the first piece of information over information given later. What is given to people first serves as an anchor for all information presented later, which means the later information will be interpreted in relation to the anchor information and will be biased towards it. If, for example, a high number of environmental incidents per year is presented, people will adjust their own perception of the likelihood of such instances upwards.

Cornelissen et al. (2008) use the availability heuristic and the representativeness heuristic to explain the self-perception of pro-environmental behaviour. If it is easy for a person to recall instances of pro-environmental behaviour, this person should be more likely to judge himself or herself an environmentalist. If previous pro-environmental behaviour is in a domain that is prototypical for this person, the same occurs.

3.3.5.2 Mental models

Mental models are simplified cognitive representations of complex processes in the outside world (Johnson-Laird, 1980). They consist of assumptions about the important key elements and their relationships to each other. Imagine driving a car. Only few of us really know how the engine works, how all the technical elements interact with each other, how many components there are, and what their functions are. What we have, however, are assumptions of what happens when we press the accelerator or brakes. And most of us also have a simplified representation of how a car engine generates power and how that is transferred to the wheels. Mental models help us to form expectations about the world around us, but they also influence which kind of information we attend to and which we ignore.

Mental models are very relevant for environmental communication since many environmental problems are part of complex systems. How people construct their knowledge about climate change is important for communicating with them. People often have misconceptions in their mental models; many people confuse, for example, climate and weather; falsely assume that the ozone layer depletion is related to climate change; or have false assumptions about which actions are related to climate change (Bostrom et al., 1994). Exploring the mental models of people is thus an essential part of designing an environmental communication strategy because it needs to be targeted to people's assumptions about the world.

3.4 Selected aspects of sociocultural communication theories

The sociocultural perspective of communication has a different focus to the sociopsychological that has been described in the previous section, namely how social processes and especially communication create collective realities, define meaning, and provide identities for the participants in the communication process. In the remainder of the chapter, social constructivism as an underlying epistemology will be introduced, and the role of language in defining reality will be discussed.

The creation of identities for individuals and also groups will end this theoretical chapter.

3.4.1 Social constructivism and the social construction of meaning

The development of social constructivism is closely related to the work of Lev Vygotsky who further developed Jean Piaget's cognitive constructivism (DeVries, 2000). Both were interested in how learning occurs, how children develop an understanding of the world, and how they create a reality to live in. According to social constructivism, learning occurs through social interaction with other people, such as parents, teachers, and other children.

Stetsenko and Arievitch (1997) describe the essence of social constructivism in the following three principles: (1) human development is a process, not static; (2) it is an activity and does not just happen to an individual, that is the individual is actively engaged in making the development happen; and (3) it is an ongoing, contextualised interaction which is mediated by language in a cultural and historical context. Stetsenko and Arievitch (1997) state that social constructivism "conceives of human development as not a 'natural' process but as a social 'artifact' (i.e. created by human individuals), as a social co-creation of new reality of psychological processes by people acting together in a sociocultural milieu" (page 161). As such, social constructivism has had an enormous impact on the pedagogical discourse about learning.

Understanding learning in this way also has implications for the understanding of communication. If communication is a process of construction of knowledge and reality, then communication becomes the essence of being human. Meaning of concepts is no longer attached to the things themselves but is generated by communicating about them. Each group, each local culture, develops its own way of communicating and thus also creates an idiosyncratic version of reality. Consequently, not one but many realities exist, and meaning cannot be verified objectively, only locally within a given discourse.

If reality and meaning of physical as well as social entities are constructed and negotiated, the communication process becomes a co-constructive process, rather than just asserting more knowledge or a new idea. Environmental communication must understand contextualised discourses and redefine people's understanding of concepts and meaning in lieu of them. Social constructivist ideas have mostly found their way into environmental education through local and experiential learning activities (Pruneau et al., 2003).

3.4.2 The role of communication to create identity

Another important concept in the sociocultural branch of communication theories is *identity*. According to sociocultural theories, identity is the collected history of social interactions that provide us with unified but flexible tools to adjust ourselves to the discourse contexts we are located in (Littlejohn & Foss, 2011). Identity is thus not something that is only connected to the individual and consistent across contexts, like personality in the sociopsychological tradition, but dynamic, and yet coherent.

In symbolic interactionism (M. H. Kuhn, 1964), a central idea is that the *self* of a person is the product of social interaction with other people. Who you are as a person is defined by the symbolic interactions, the creation of meaning about yourself together with other people, and sometimes with yourself. We define ourselves in interactions with others that are important to us, the so-called *orientational others*. The self is a social object which develops over time in communications with others, and the self-concept is our plan for ourselves, our identities, our interests, goals, self-evaluations, and most importantly attitudes (Littlejohn & Foss, 2011).

Goffman (1959) uses the metaphor of a theatre to describe the role of the self. According to him, people are like actors on the different stages of everyday settings and play their roles to impress their audiences. Their different selves are the roles they perform in the given contexts. The self thus has an instrumental function; it is displayed to achieve a reaction in the audience. Interestingly, individuals are both actors and an audience for others. All participants in a situation present their self, and the different presentations together create a usually unified and coherent identity for the group. This group identity then again steers which self-presentations are adequate and which will be sanctioned.

The role of identity expression in pro-environmental behaviour has been analysed by a number of researchers. Dono et al. (2010), for example, found that the social identity people have of themselves has an impact on environmental activism, but this impact was indirectly mediated by environmental citizenship, which can also be understood as a measure of identity via belongingness to certain societal groups. Whitmarsh and O'Neill (2010) analysed the role of a "green" self-identity for spillover effects of one behavioural domain to another and found some hints to support this idea. It appears that identity can be a vehicle for behaviour change towards more environmentally friendly behaviour, and this impact is at least partly independent of other determinants of pro-environmental behaviour. This again is relevant for environmental communication. If being environmentally friendly can become part of an identity, we need to set the stage so that a green identity is accepted.

3.5 Conclusions

This chapter started with a brief introduction to different theoretical traditions within communication research and explored two of them in more detail: the sociopsychological and the sociocultural tradition. For environmental communication, this chapter presents many bricks that when built together can be helpful in designing a communication strategy. The bricks do not necessarily fit together in one theoretical building, but they are relevant nonetheless. The take-home message of this chapter is that communication is an incredibly complex phenomenon and many perspectives can be taken to understand parts of the picture. Together, the concepts give us a rich understanding of what we might encounter in the communication process. What has been presented in this chapter is only a very brief overview, a rigorous selection made by the author; other authors might select completely different aspects and would still have been able to write a chapter of the same length, probably several times.

Review questions

- What are the central assumptions of the seven families of communication theories and what do they contribute to understanding and designing effective environmental communication?
- What are different theoretical positions regarding attention and how is attention relevant for environmental communication?
- How is human memory organised and what are the relevant implications for environmental communication?
- What does attribution theory assume and how might attribution processes affect environmental communication?
- What are models and tools of persuasion that can be useful in environmental communication?
- What is the role of heuristics and mental models in communication? How does that affect environmental communication?
- What is social constructivism? What role does language have and how is that relevant for environmental communication?
- How is identity relevant for environmental communication?

Suggested readings

Atkinson, R. C., & Shiffrin, R. M. (1968). Human memory: A proposed system and its control processes. In K. W. Spence & J. T. Spence (Eds.), *The Psychology of Learning and Motivation* (Vol. 2, pp. 89–195). New York: Academic Press.

Cialdini, R. B. (2006). *Influence – the psychology of persuasion*. New York: Harper Business.

Goffman, E. (1959). *The presentation of self in everyday life*. Garden City, NY: Doubleday.

Lachter, J., Forster, K. I., & Ruthruff, E. (2004). Forty-five years after Broadbent (1958): Still no identification without attention. *Psychological Review*, 111(4), 880.

Littlejohn, S. W., & Foss, K. A. (2011). *Theories of human communication*. Long Grove, IL: Waveland Press.

Tversky, A., & Kahneman, D. (1974). Judgment under uncertainty: Heuristics and biases. *Science*, 185(4157), 1124–1131.

Weiner, B. (2001). Intrapersonal and interpersonal theories of motivation from an attribution perspective. In F. Salili, C.-y. Chiu & Y.-y. Hong (Eds.), *Student Motivation* (pp. 17–30). New York: Springer.

4
Decision Models – What Psychological Theories Teach Us about People's Behaviour

Chapter summary

This chapter introduces the most common environmental psychological decision models and analyses their relevance for the design of environmental communication strategies. The theories introduced in the first half of the chapter are the theory of planned behaviour, the norm-activation theory, the value-belief-norm theory, and goal-framing theory. In the remainder of the chapter, the role of the decisional context is analysed by discussing the ipsative theory of behaviour. The role of routines and habits is introduced, and the comprehensive action determination model as an integration of the aforementioned theories is presented. Decision models are contrasted with behaviour change models, such as the trans-theoretical model and the stage model of self-regulated behaviour change. The concluding section of the chapter drafts a framework that integrates the chapter's conclusions into a complex model that can guide design of communication strategies.

4.1 Introduction

The previous chapter introduced the basic psychological principles relevant for describing and designing environmental communication, while this chapter moves a step closer to environmental behaviour. It presents the most important decision models that psychological research and intervention design is based on. Shortcomings of the models are identified, and some less commonly used but nevertheless helpful theoretical approaches are presented. In each subsection, the relevance of each theoretical approach for designing environmental communication is explored. A distinction between action models and change models will be made.

4.2 The theory of planned behaviour

The theory of planned behaviour (Ajzen, 1991, 2012) is the most often used theoretical framework in environmental psychological decision-making research. It draws its popularity from its structural simplicity and general applicability across many different behavioural domains, especially within environmental behaviour. The theory is an extension of its predecessor, the theory of reasoned action (Fishbein & Ajzen, 1975). The theory builds on attitude research and describes how and under which conditions attitudes predict people's behaviour. Generally, the theory is understood as belonging to the reasoned action approach, which means that it is best applied to behaviours that are deliberately performed.

4.2.1 The variables and structure of the theory

The theory of planned behaviour assumes that the choice of one behavioural alternative over another can be understood by exploring people's intentions to do so. The main assumption in the model is that people mostly do what they intend to do. Intentions are in turn formed based on a rational choice process which weighs three different components against each other: attitudes towards each behavioural alternative, subjective norms, and perceived behavioural control (PBC). Figure 4.1 displays the structure of the variables in the theory of planned behaviour.

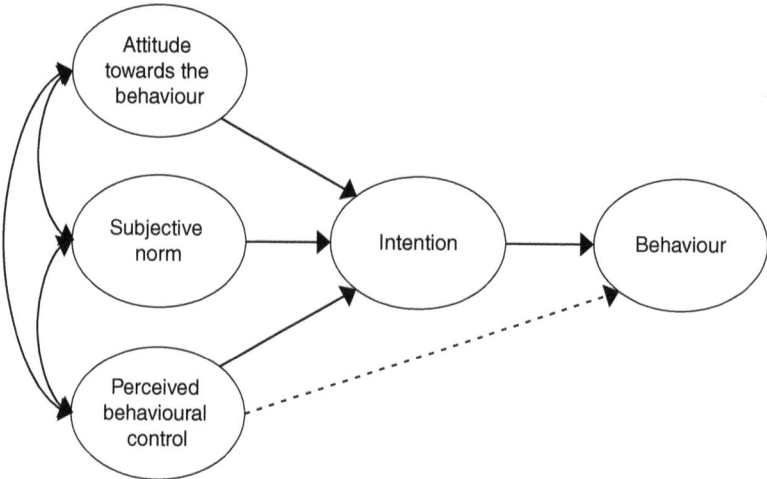

Figure 4.1 The theory of planned behaviour (Ajzen, 1991, page 182). Used by permission of Elsevier

Attitudes towards the behaviour are understood as a general evaluation of favourable or unfavourable behavioural alternatives. The attitude is the sum of all beliefs about a behaviour. Beliefs are the product of contemplating the probability of a certain behavioural outcome and the degree to which this outcome would be regarded as positive or negative. If the behaviour would be the purchase of organic vegetables instead of conventionally grown vegetables in a supermarket, the person might hold the following beliefs: (1) organic vegetables have a high probability of being healthier than conventional vegetables and that would be very positive; (2) organic vegetables have a high probability of being more expensive than conventional vegetables and that would be negative; (3) organic vegetables have a small probability of being less fresh because fewer people buy them, which would be regarded as negative; and (4) organic vegetables have a medium probability to taste better, which would be very positive. The beliefs are then integrated into a general evaluation of favourability of the organic vegetable purchase. Furthermore, it needs to be recognised that people usually do not activate all beliefs they hold about a behavioural alternative in every decision-making situation. Attitudes can therefore vary even if the person has not changed any belief.

Behaviours are performed in a social context, even if no other people are present. Subjective norms, which are the social pressure towards a certain behavioural alternative, might support or counteract attitudes in their impact on intentions. Subjective norms also have beliefs as their building bricks – this time social beliefs. Social beliefs are an evaluation of what a person perceives other people expect from them, combined with the willingness to comply with these expectations. Returning to the organic food example it might be that the person perceives his or her partner has strong expectations that they should buy organic food, whereas his or her friends have expressed several times that they consider buying organic food a waste of money. Based on a meta-analysis, Rivis and Sheeran (2003) argue that subjective norms should be complemented with descriptive norms, which are a subjective representation of other people's *behaviour*. This might be different from what they *tell* other people to do. Often, descriptive norms have a stronger impact than subjective norms, especially in younger samples (Rivis & Sheeran, 2003).

The third variable that impacts on intentions is PBC. This aspect represents perceived limits of resources, abilities, or opportunities to perform the behaviour. PBC is also constructed of beliefs, which are referred to as control beliefs. How far a person feels a behaviour is easy or difficult to perform also decides if he or she intends to perform it. In the organic purchases example, PBC describes how difficult a person perceives the purchase of organic food, for example, with respect to price differences or availability in the store. Unlike attitudes and subjective norms, PBC can also have a direct impact on behaviour (see Figure 4.1). This direct link is caused by two effects (Ajzen, 1991): (1) strong PBC makes people more persistent in trying to implement behaviour. This means that a person who perceives to have more control should try harder to perform a behaviour than a person with the same intention but lower perceived control; and (2) PBC is often a proxy for objective behavioural control. Objective control is a factor that sets boundaries to people's options (see also Section 4.5). More recently, Ajzen (2012) has reconceptualised this direct impact, which now assumes a moderation effect rather than a parallel direct impact of perceived control on behaviour. This means that the link between intentions and behaviour becomes weaker when perceived control is low.

4.2.2 Applications of the theory in environmental domains

Since its publication, the theory of planned behaviour has become one of the most successful social psychological theories and has been applied in numerous behavioural domains. Several meta-analyses of the theoretical structure have been conducted with positive results. Armitage and Conner (2001) found that the structure of the theory is supported and that all variables significantly explain intentions or behaviour as predicted. Subjective norms usually have the weakest impact.

In the field of environmental psychology, Heath and Gifford (2006) used the theory of planned behaviour to explain bus use and found that subjective norms were the strongest predictor of bus use intentions. They also found that intentions, perceived control, and the interaction between the two explained actual bus use. Wauters et al. (2010) applied the theory to explain the implementation of soil erosion protection by farmers and found attitudes to be the most important factor. Tonglet et al. (2004) used the theory to explain participation in recycling programs and also found attitudes to be the most relevant single aspect. Many more examples can be found. An interesting conclusion is that the structure of the theory seems consistent between cultures, behavioural domains, and target groups, but that the relative impact of the variables varies, indicating the variability of environmental behaviours. Another example of an application of the theory of planned behaviour is described in Box 4.1.

> **Box 4.1 Applying the theory of planned behaviour to green consumer behaviour**
>
> Vermeir and Verbeke (2008) analysed the intention of young Belgian adults to buy a (hypothetical) sustainable dairy product. They started with the variables of the theory of planned behaviour, but separated PBC into two constructs: (a) perceived availability; and (b) perceived consumer effectiveness, the latter being a measure of the perceived difference sustainable consumption can make for the environment. This variable is theoretically related to locus of control. Furthermore, they assumed that the relation between the four variables and intentions depends on both confidence that the product does what it promises to do and general value orientations.
>
> For the total sample, half of the variance in purchase intentions could be explained by the four explanatory variables. Attitudes were by far the strongest predictor, the two components of perceived control (availability and consumer effectiveness) came second, and social norms last. Separate analyses of the effects for participants with high and low levels of confidence in the product show that social norms lose their influence in the low confidence group. Using criterion from Schwartz's value orientations (Schwartz, 1994), differences between participants with different value orientations could be found.
>
> The results of the study show two interesting things: first, the theory of planned behaviour is a suitable framework for predicting intentions to act environmentally friendly and, second, the pattern of how important the different variables are depends on other factors such as confidence in the product or value orientations in this case.

4.2.3 Strengths and weaknesses of the theory

The strengths of the theory of planned behaviour are clearly its simplicity and applicability across different behavioural domains. The variables are relatively easy to measure, and the standardisation makes studies applying the theory easily comparable. The theory has proven able to identify relevant determinants of environmental behaviour, especially if the variables are measured on the same level of specificity as behaviour and in close temporal proximity to behaviour.

The strengths of the theory are, on the other hand, also related to its weaknesses. The theory of planned behaviour is proposed as a general model of deliberate behaviour. This means that specific variables that might be relevant for certain types of behaviour may not be included. Consequently, many studies extending the theory of planned behaviour by other constructs have been published. Conner and Armitage (1998) identified in a review study the following variables as the most promising candidates for extending the theory of planned behaviour: habit strength, moral norms, belief salience, self-identity, and affective beliefs. These extensions deal with weaknesses the theory shows in specific domains of behaviour:

- By including habits the theory's applicability extends to domains where behaviour is repeated (see Section 4.7).
- Including moral norms deals with a weakness of the theory with predicting behaviour in morally laden situations, which often applies to environmental behaviour (see Section 4.3).
- Belief salience asserts that beliefs of all three types as described in Section 4.2.1 need to be activated to become relevant.
- Self-identity is the attempt to include a wider social context into the theory of planned behaviour. It represents a conceptualisation of a behaviour being critical to defining who a person is: "doing this or that is who I am". In some studies, self-identity measures had an additional influence on intentions for green consumerism in parallel with attitudes, subjective norms, and perceived control (Sparks & Shepherd, 1992).
- Finally, including affective beliefs tries to address the problem that the emotional reaction to behavioural alternatives is not well captured in the standard attitude measures. The anticipated emotions with performing a behaviour are not necessarily in accordance with the non-emotional evaluations of the same behaviour.

4.2.4 Implications for environmental communication

In its standard form, the theory of planned behaviour offers three levers to change people's intentions to behave environmentally friendly (Hardeman et al., 2002): (1) change the attitudes of people so that attitudes towards the pro-environmental alternative become more positive or the attitudes towards the environmentally damaging alternative become more negative, (2) shift subjective norms towards the pro-environmental alternative away from the damaging alternative, and

(3) increase PBC for the pro-environmental behaviour or decrease control for the damaging alternative. Furthermore, environmental communication can try to make the links between pro-environmental attitudes, intentions, and behaviour stronger by removing barriers. Table 4.1 shows an overview of the techniques discussed in Chapter 8 and how they relate to the variables in the theory of planned behaviour.

Table 4.1 Overview of communication techniques and their connection to the theory of planned behaviour

Attitudes	Subjective norms	Perceived behavioural control	Attitude–intention–behaviour link
Increase the number of *positive* beliefs about the pro-environmental behaviour	Social models	Increase control beliefs for the pro-environmental behaviour	Strengthen perceived behavioural control
Decrease the number of *positive* beliefs about the environmentally damaging behaviour	Increase the salience of descriptive norms for pro-environmental behaviour	Provide knowledge and skills to act environmentally friendly	Remove barriers, constraints to behaviour
Decrease the number of *negative* beliefs about the pro-environmental behaviour	Decrease the salience of descriptive norms for environmentally damaging behaviour	Feedback about effects	Provide procedural knowledge
Increase the number of *negative* beliefs about the environmentally damaging behaviour	Communicate injunctive norms (what is expected)	Anticipatory addressing of potential barriers (everyday problem solving)	
Prompting	Legal regulations, fees, subsidies, or penalties		

4.3 The norm-activation theory

Another popular theory in environmental psychology is the norm-activation theory (Schwartz & Howard, 1981), which originally aimed to explain altruistic behaviour like helping people in an emergency. Unlike the theory of planned behaviour, it was not intended to apply to all types of behaviour but to situations in which moral considerations are relevant. However, the theory became popular in environmental domains because it is able to describe the moral background of environmental actions much better than the theory of planned behaviour.

4.3.1 The variables and structure of the theory

The central assumption of the norm-activation theory is that peoples' behaviour in moral situations is determined by a feeling of moral obligation to help. The theory refers to that feeling as a *personal norm*. The theory further assumes that personal norms are not always determining behaviour, but need to be activated (Schwartz & Howard, 1981). First, a person needs to be aware that someone (or something) is in need of help, a variable that is referred to in the theory as *awareness of need*. Transferred to the environmental domain, this would mean that the first step to activate peoples' personal ecological norms would be to draw their attention to environmental problems. Taking the example of food waste, the first step to reduction of food waste according to the norm-activation theory would be to raise awareness of food waste as an environmental problem. Second, even if a person is aware that there is a need to act, they need to be made aware that their behaviour contributes to the problem or can contribute to its solution. The theory refers to this aspect as *awareness of consequences*. Many people accept that wasting edible food is an environmental (and ethical) problem, but do not see the link to their personal behaviour ("I never waste any food"). A related variable that often is used instead of awareness of consequences is *ascription of responsibility*. It captures to which degree a person ascribes himself or herself responsibility for the negative effects. In the domain of food waste, a typical barrier in the norm-activation process could be that people do not see responsibility at their personal level. They see it at the level of producers, retailers, and restaurants. Third, even if a person sees a need to act and feels responsible, activation of personal norms is still not given. If the person feels unable to act, the personal norm might still not be activated. This process is comparable to what the theory of planned behaviour describes as perceived behaviour control, and many applications of the norm-activation theory actually use PBC.

Personal norms are assumed to be representations of personal values in a given situation, but are also described as being generated in an internalisation process. Thøgersen (2006) proposed a taxonomy of norms from the most externalised norms to the most internalised. He considers descriptive norms to be the most external version of social norms, where the mere observation of other peoples' behaviour gives an indication of what is acceptable behaviour in a situation. The next step is subjective social norms, which are the perceptions of what other people expect in a given situation. A person who complies with social norms would not act against social expectations in situations where other people are present. The next step of internalisation are introjected norms for which the driving force is an anticipated feeling of shame towards relevant other people. This feeling is created when someone acts against other people's expectations, even if they are not present. The most internalised version of norms is the integrated personal norm, where the driving force is a feeling of guilt for not acting in accordance with your own values, irrespective of other people. This complex link has been implemented in a simplified version in the norm-activation theory as the assumption that personal norms mediate the influence of social norms on behaviour. The term social norm is used here interchangeably with subjective norms in the theory of planned behaviour.

4.3.2 Applications of the theory in environmental domains

The norm-activation theory has been applied to many different environmental domains. However, a problem with the theory is that Schwartz and Howard (1981) did not formalise the theory so that many alternative versions, partly with different subsets of variables, are used in parallel. Harland, Staats, and Wilke (2007) proposed the version that is depicted in Figure 4.2 and applied it to two very different behaviours: car use and turning off the tap. They use the norm-activating variables that have been described above, but differentiate ascription of responsibility into two parts: situational responsibility and denial of responsibility. The two aspects appear to be closely related and hard to distinguish empirically. Furthermore, they separate two sub-dimensions of perceived control: perceived ability to perform a behaviour and perceived efficacy of this behaviour to help the need. They found empirical support for their version of the theory from their data. A structurally very similar version of the theory has been proposed by Hunecke, Blöbaum, Matthies, and Höger (2001) and applied to travel mode choice.

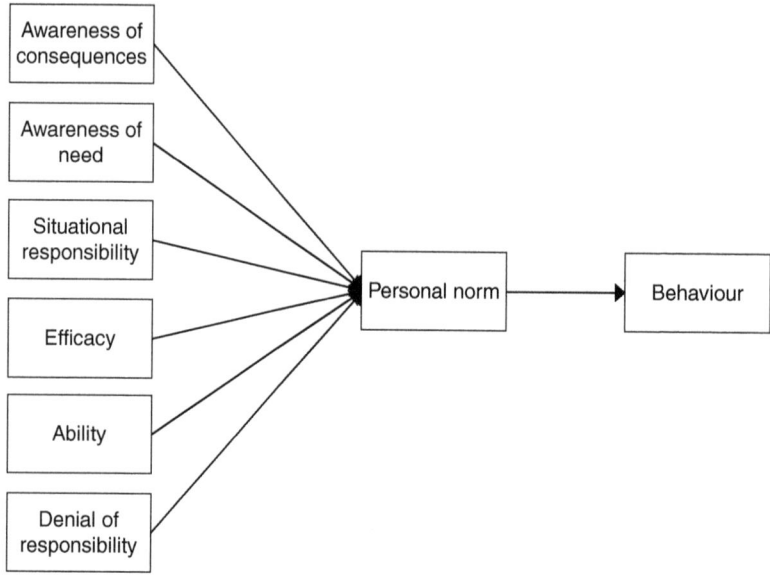

Figure 4.2 The norm-activation theory according to Harland et al. (2007, page 324). Used by permission of Taylor & Francis

4.3.3 Strengths and weaknesses of the theory

The norm-activation theory has become popular because of its documented strength to capture the normative dimension much better than the theory of planned behaviour. However, an obvious weakness is that the theory has not received the same degree of formalisation that the theory of planned behaviour has. Furthermore, the theory is more complex in its assumptions. Both aspects have led to a considerable variability in how the theory has been applied and tested, and to less conclusive results.

When variables of the norm-activation theory have been added to the theory of planned behaviour, especially personal norms, a typical result is that personal norms significantly predict intentions, adding to the other variables in the theory of planned behaviour. However, the influence on behaviour is usually mediated by intentions (Bamberg & Möser, 2007; Bamberg et al., 2007; Klöckner, 2013a). This underlines not only that the norm-activation theory is able to describe a process important for environmental behaviour that is not well captured in the

Table 4.2 Overview of communication techniques and their connection to the norm-activation theory

Awareness of need	Awareness of consequences	Ascription of responsibility	Personal norm
Provide information about environmental problems and the need for action	Personalised information about environmental effects of own behaviour (e.g. carbon footprint calculators)	Create localised experiences of negative environmental impacts on emotionally relevant entities (e.g. national parks)	Strengthen antecedents of personal norms
Use social media to document and share environmental problems	Individual feedback	Hypocrisy paradigm, induce cognitive dissonance	Commitment
Environmental education	Write a diary/photo diary		Block-leader approach
Nature experiences	Environmental education		Foot-in-the-door technique

theory of planned behaviour, but also that the norm-activation theory alone is not well suited to explain environmental behaviour.

4.3.4 Implications for environmental communication

As well as the theory of planned behaviour, the norm-activation theory also identifies a number of levers for behaviour change through communication events in a broader sense. Some variables are to a large degree identical with the theory of planned behaviour and will not be addressed again. Table 4.2 presents a summary of how the remaining variables can be connected to communication-based interventions (see Chapter 8).

4.4 The value-belief-norm theory

The value-belief-norm theory as proposed by Stern (2000) is an extension of the norm-activation theory as it formalises the relationship between the central variables and extends the norm-activation chain further back in the direction of basic value orientations.

4.4.1 The variables and structure of the theory

Figure 4.3 displays the relationships between the core variables in the value-belief-norm theory. The main assumption of the theory is that several types of pro-environmental behaviour are motivated by a feeling of moral obligation to act, an assumption that is taken from the norm-activation theory described above. The value-belief-norm theory assumes that these feelings of obligation need to be activated. First, an understanding needs to be in place that something valuable is in danger, such as a nature reserve or clean air. This is referred to as awareness of consequences (AC). If a need to act is perceived, the second prerequisite for norm activation is a perceived ability to reduce the threat (AR), a variable comparable to perceived self-efficacy or PBC. The new assumptions in the value-belief-norm theory are that the likelihood that a need is perceived depends on the degree to which a person embraces an ecological worldview. The ecological worldview is often captured by a standard measure referred to as the new ecological paradigm (NEP) (Dunlap, Van Liere, Mertig, & Jones, 2000). This measure includes people's reactions to statements about basic beliefs about nature and humans' place in it, such as "humans have the right to modify the natural environment to suit their needs", "the earth has plenty of natural resources if we just learn how to develop them", or "the balance of nature is very delicate and easily upset" (Dunlap et al., 2000, page 433). Different basic value orientations about the environment can be found behind an ecological worldview. Egoistic values mean that a person values personal gains, power, and pleasure. Altruistic values on the contrary mean caring for other people, justice, and the environment. Biospheric values

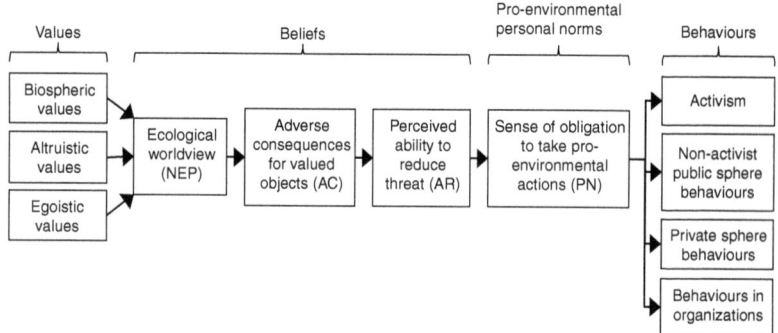

Figure 4.3 The value-belief-norm theory according to Stern (2000, page 412). Used by permission of John Wiley and Sons

mean caring for other species and habitats. People that embrace altruistic or biospheric values are more likely to have an ecological worldview and people that embrace egoistic values are more likely to have a non-ecological worldview.

4.4.2 Applications of the theory in environmental domains

Oreg and Katz-Gerro (2006) used an adapted value-belief-norm theory to predict several environmental behaviours in a 27-country sample and found strong support for the suggested causal chain from values to behaviour as proposed in the theory. Also Kaiser, Hübner, and Bogner (2005) found relevant results for the value-belief-norm theory explaining a general environmental behaviour index, but the structural equation model also revealed a potential mismatch between the strict causal chain proposed in the model and empirical results. Furthermore, the authors found that the theory of planned behaviour explained general environmental behaviour better than the value-belief-norm theory. Nordlund and Garvill (2002) not only present results that support the causal chain as the main structure carrying the impact from values to action, but also show that some of the impacts of variables earlier in the chain on those later in the chain are not completely mediated by the other variables in the chain. This result was also found by Steg, Dreijerink, and Abrahamse (2005) and Jansson, Marell, and Nordlund (2010). Especially biospheric values seem to have a direct effect on all variables in the causal chain.

4.4.3 Strengths and weaknesses of the theory

A strength of the value-belief-norm theory is that it formalises the relationships between variables proposed in the norm-activation theory in a more stringent and testable way. It actually makes very strict assumptions about the causal order of variables and extends the causal chain by including more basic psychological variables such as worldviews and value orientations. It also receives empirical support for its structure and is usually able to explain a significant portion of variation in environmental behaviour, especially if applied to policy support or generalised environmental behaviour. Its stringent, structural form is, however, also its weakness. Many studies find that the proposed structure seems to be the main transferral of effects from values to behaviour, but that some of the variables break out of this line and have additional direct impacts on variables later in the chain.

An important strength of the theory, however, is often overlooked in the studies. The value-belief-norm theory predicts that activated personal norms can express themselves in many different behavioural domains. If a person feels obligated to act pro-environmentally, they can express that obligation either in policy support or activism, changes in private sphere behaviour such as home energy use, or organisational behaviour (e.g. support and participation in the company's meatless Monday campaign). It is hard to predict in which domain feelings of obligation are expressed. This is most likely the reason why the value-belief-norm theory performs so well when applied to more generalised pro-environmental behaviour. The theory thereby also provides an explanation of why specific pro-environmental behaviour is harder to explain.

4.4.4 Implications for environmental communication

Since many variables used in the value-belief-norm theory have already been discussed in Section 4.3.4, only new perspectives that can be derived from the theory shall be discussed in the following paragraphs.

One implication of the theory is that activating personal norms will not necessarily lead to the intended change of behaviour; it might be that people react to the feeling of moral obligation by choosing to show environmental action in another behavioural domain. This means that one should pay attention to the wider context if the effect of environmental communication is to be evaluated.

Another implication of the model is that value orientations and worldviews have an impact on environmental behaviour, even if this impact is rather indirect. That raises the question of which processes steer value change. Generally, values and also worldviews are regarded as some of the most consistent psychological constructs; people do not change their value orientations based on simple communication measures. According to Inglehart and Welzel (2005), who analysed change of value orientations on a societal level, only big societal restructuration like during the industrial revolution or more recently post-industrialism leads to changes in value orientations. However, whereas Inglehart and Welzel (2005) analyse prevailing cultural values in a society, value orientations on the personal level might also change due to other experiences. Schwartz (2006) describes characteristics of values that also make them interesting on a person level: (1) values are beliefs that are related to affect, (2) values refer to desirable goals (see also Section 4.5 for a discussion about goals), (3) values are linked to behaviour in specific situations, (4) values serve as moral standards, (5) values are ordered by importance, and (6) the relative importance of values guides actions. Especially, assumptions (5) and (6) are relevant from an intervention perspective. It can be assumed that people embrace all value orientations to a certain degree, but vary in the relative importance they ascribe to each value orientation. Very few people would, for example, disagree that we should protect nature, but more would disagree with the statement that nature protection is more important than economic prosperity. Thus, communication measures targeted at value orientations may focus on not only changing value orientations per se, but also the relative importance values have, which might be less stable.

4.5 Goal-framing theory

Goal-framing theory is related to what has been discussed in the previous section, that is, different things can be regarded as important at different times and in different situations. What is important for a person at a given point in space and time is referred to as a *goal*. Elliot and Fryer (2008) define a goal as "a cognitive representation of a future of an object that the organism is committed to approach or avoid" (page 244). They define "object" very broadly, including any kind of entity, event, or experience. In other words, a goal is a thing or a state that a person strives to achieve in the near future. Goals determine how a person interprets a situation.

4.5.1 The variables and structure of the theory

Goals are the central variable in goal-framing theory. Goals are assumed to govern what people attend to (see also Section 3.3.1), which knowledge and attitude structures become most accessible, and which behavioural alternatives will be considered (Lindenberg & Steg, 2007). Furthermore, goal-framing theory assumes that people will have many goals at the same time and that they are hierarchically ordered. The ones that are most important at a given time guide information processing and decision-making, whereas goals that have been downgraded in importance have no such impact. Furthermore, goals may not be compatible with each other. If the goal not to be away from your family for a long time collides with the goal to travel environmentally friendly to a conference, a conflict occurs: whereas the latter goal would exclude taking the plane from the list of alternatives, the first goal would exclude taking the train.

Which goal becomes activated or prioritised in a given situation depends on many other variables, such as what cues does the situation give, are there other people present, what do they do? No matter which goal ends up highest on the list of priorities, a person always tries to behave within the boundaries of what is interpreted as appropriate behaviour within that goal frame. However, what is regarded as appropriate behaviour depends on the cognitive representations that become activated by the respective goal frame. Lindenberg and Steg (2007) identify three overarching goal frames: (1) the hedonic goal frame, (2) the gain goal frame, and (3) the normative goal frame. Within the hedonic goal frame, aspects such as avoiding effort, gaining pleasure, and avoiding uncertainty or negative thoughts are activated. Within the gain goal frame, gain of resources (or prevention of resource loss) is the central aspect. The normative goal frame activates goals like doing the "right thing". In other words, the way of thinking in a hedonic goal frame is "what would make me feel best at the moment", within a gain goal frame is "what is in it for me", and within a normative goal frame is "what would be the right thing to do here in my social situation".

It is furthermore assumed in the theory that each goal frame has an a priori value, which means that one person may have a higher likelihood of activating a hedonic goal frame than another person irrespective of the situation the person is in. He or she would therefore need less of a push to activate it than the other person.

Interestingly, Lindenberg and Steg (2007) propose goal-framing theory also as a meta-theory that decides within which of the model traditions introduced in the previous sections behaviour determination can be described. Figure 4.4 displays this relationship. If a person acts within an activated gain goal frame, rational choice theories like the theory of planned behaviour describe behaviour best. Within a normative goal frame, normative theories like the norm-activation theory or the

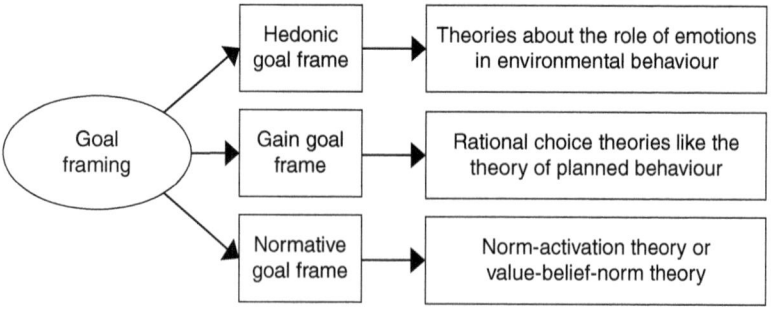

Figure 4.4 Matching of behaviour models to prevalent goal frame

value-belief-norm theory are more suitable in describing the decision-making process. With respect to the hedonic goal frame, research is less developed. This may be due to the notion that environmentally friendly behaviour is mostly seen as not serving hedonistic objectives. However, this might be achieved if pro-environmental behaviour is framed as an act which can increase personal well-being, as recently proposed by Venhoeven, Bolderdijk, and Steg (2013).

4.5.2 Applications of the theory in environmental domains

The interesting aspect of goal-framing theory is that all three goal frames can be utilised to promote environmental behaviour. Within a hedonic goal frame it would be expected that people show pro-environmental behaviour if it makes them *feel good*. If a person considers buying an electric car, then choosing a stylish electric car may have an emotional reward. Within a gain goal frame, pro-environmental behaviour can be motivated through personal resource gains (e.g. financial incentives) or loss avoidance (e.g. penalties for environmentally damaging behaviour). For a person with a gain goal frame, the decision to buy an electric car would then be primarily motivated by incentives such as reduced tax or access to parking space. Finally, a person with a normative goal frame might consider buying an electric car if it feels right for this person to do it as an environmental action; here, the perceived environmental benefit of the electric car compared to a combustion engine car might be the motivating aspect.

There are very few studies that empirically test goal-framing theory directly in the environmental domain. Most studies interpret results they find within the goal-framing framework. Handgraaf, Van Lidth de Jeude, and Appelt (2013) used goal-framing theory to find that public social rewards were the most effective incentive for saving energy in an office setting, as compared to public and private monetary incentives and private social rewards. They argue that public social rewards activate the normative goal frame. Miao and Wei (2013) present interesting data on the dependence on context of goal frames. They found that in a household setting the normative goal frame is most relevant for people engaging in pro-environmental behaviour, whereas a hedonic goal frame was the strongest (negative) predictor for pro-environmental behaviour of the same people in a hotel context.

4.5.3 Strengths and weaknesses of the theory

The greatest strength of the goal-framing theory is that it accounts for behavioural variability within an individual. It can explain why the same person sometimes acts very pro-environmentally and sometimes not. This is something that the other theories presented above do not explain. However, this aspect also makes the theory partly circular, since the prevalent goal frame determines behaviour, but is also inferred from behaviour. The theory also provides relatively vague predictions, which means it is used as a general interpretive framework rather than a behavioural model.

4.5.4 Implications for environmental communication

Goal-framing theory predicts that a person's mindset decides what kind of information he or she attends to and how he or she processes and interprets this information. Thus, a goal-framing approach to communication would focus on finding ways to change the goal frame people are in, for example, from a hedonic or gain frame to a normative goal frame. Norms are communicated via context. Littered areas or areas with a high degree of visible vandalism will lead people to assume that the norm is that littering or vandalism is accepted (Keizer, Lindenberg, & Steg, 2013). This effect is even more distinct if the norm communicated by the context is disagreeing with norms communicated, for example, by prohibition signs (Keizer, Lindenberg, & Steg, 2011).

Goal priming is another approach to inducing a goal frame in people. Priming is a procedure where perceiving one stimulus (e.g. a word, a text, or a picture) influences the response to an unrelated later stimulus (e.g. a selection of products in a supermarket) by unconsciously activating a related mental representation, which could also be a goal (Tulving & Schacter, 1990). A typical priming procedure is asking people to identify a word in a scrambled sentence that does not belong there (Bargh & Chartrand, 1999). For example, the scrambled sentence could be "very chains recycling important is". The sentence is actually "recycling is very important" and the misplaced word is "chains". Either the sentence or the target word can be related to the goal to be primed, such as belonging to a normative goal frame. After solving a number of sentences with the same theme it is assumed that the goal to be environmentally friendly is primed (salient in memory), which then affects how people perform later tasks such as shopping for food. Other less artificial types of priming stimuli such as pictures or colours have also been used (Carr, McCauley, Sperber, & Parmelee, 1982; Folk & Remington, 2008). In the environmental domain, very few studies have analysed the effectiveness of priming on conservation behaviour. McCalley, Kaiser, Midden, Keser, and Teunissen (2006) primed participants in a study with either a neutral goal, a meta-level goal ("I should save energy"), or an action-level goal ("I should wash at a low temperature"). They found that the action-level primed participants saved more energy using their washing machines. Clarke, Bell, and Peterson (1999), on the other hand, found that pro-environmental priming had no influence on the value ascribed to public environmental goods.

4.6 The role of the context

In the models described so far in this chapter, the decision-making context as an information source that can trigger people to follow a specific goal frame was only explicitly mentioned in goal-framing theory. In the following sections, some characteristics of situational impact on decision-making will be analysed.

4.6.1 The underrated impact of the decisional context

Whereas outside psychology the context in which decisions are made is often treated as the strongest or even the only determinant of people's behaviour, psychological models have a tendency to ignore this. For example, people and even traffic planners often assume that less expensive bus tickets or more bus services make people more likely to use the bus. Each decision is made in a situation that is defined by physical opportunities and barriers; some behaviours are possible while others are physically restricted. Furthermore, legal and economic regulations also define behaviour, but are less restrictive than physical boundaries; if an action is prohibited it is still possible to perform it, but most people would not.

Whereas many environmental psychologists do not primarily focus on the role of context, Stern (2000) in his ABC theory explicitly conceptualised attitudes *and* context as determinants of environmental behaviour. He furthermore assumed that they interact non-linearly. Environmental attitudes only have an impact on behaviour if the context is not too restrictive or too enabling; in other words, when a behaviour is too difficult or too easy to perform, levels of environmental attitudes do not differentiate between people. This way of thinking of an interaction between behaviour difficulty and strength of the attitude–behaviour link has also been referred to as the low-cost hypothesis, where high behavioural costs (e.g. monetary costs or effort) would reduce the impact of attitudes (Diekmann & Preisendörfer, 2003).

4.6.2 Objective versus subjective constraints

While context has an important influence on people's behaviour, it should also be noted that its impact on behaviour is usually mediated by a subjective representation of it, hence a psychological variable. Very few aspects of context can directly impact behaviour without psychological processing. For example, it is not the price of different products that directly impacts people's behaviour but a representation of the price in relation to other products or the same product at a previous point in time, for example, cheap versus expensive, appropriate versus inappropriate.

4.6.3 What do we choose between? Generation of choice sets

A question that has been mostly ignored in environmental psychology so far is how people generate behavioural alternatives. Most studies are based on choice between behavioural alternatives defined by the researcher rather than the participant, with this perhaps biasing results of such studies. Imagine a travel mode choice study where the alternatives in the questionnaire are car, bus, and bicycle. What if a participant usually does not decide between these three but between the car and walking? How realistic would the results from the questionnaire be for that person?

The methodological problems connected to an alternative approach where the participants define the choice categories may explain why it has not been used often. Hoogendoorn-Lanser and Van Nes (2004) are an interesting exception. They were interested in people's choices when making multi-modal trips where the train is the main mode of transportation. Participants decided which modes of transport they used to get to and from the train. Hoogendoorn-Lanser and Van Nes (2004) were able to show that people usually made a choice between a very limited set of alternatives which is much smaller than the theoretically possible set.

4.6.4 The ipsative theory of behaviour

Most environmental psychology theories try to explain why people behave in a certain way, hence finding determinants for environmental behaviour. The ipsative theory of behaviour (Tanner, 1999) takes another perspective, aiming to explain why people do *not* act. It assumes that environmental behaviour is prevented by a number of different constraints, and people are more likely to act environmentally friendly if the constraints are removed. The interesting contribution of the theory is that it differentiates constraints into three different sets:

ipsative constraints, subjective constraints, and objective constraints. Ipsative constraints prevent the activation of a behavioural alternative, as an alternative is not even evaluated because it never enters the choice set (see also Section 4.6.3). Subjective constraints prevent that an alternative is preferred, for example, it appears too expensive or too difficult. Objective constraints finally prevent a chosen alternative from being performed. So in other words, the theory predicts that pro-environmental behaviour will only be shown if it is (a) objectively possible, (b) considered in decision-making, and (c) preferred over other alternatives. In her study, Tanner (1999) found evidence that both subjective and objective constraints prevented car drivers from switching to other travel modes.

4.6.5 Implications for environmental communication

Context has an important influence on choosing between behavioural alternatives. This means that context should be included in the design of communication strategies. Any communication attempt aimed at making people behave more environmentally friendly will fail if the context does not enable people to be environmentally friendly. Hence an analysis of the context is a crucial first step. Important barriers to behaviour need to be removed *before* communication even begins to make people consider changing behaviour.

However, it also needs to be recognised that subjective representations of context are often more important determinants than objective constraints. It is more important how a person perceives his or her opportunities for action rather than how they objectively are. Usually, the subjective opportunities are perceived smaller than the objective, but in certain cases it can be the opposite. Thus, addressing a mismatch between perceived opportunities and objective opportunities can be the focus of an effective communication strategy. Free trial periods are used in marketing to overcome exactly this barrier; people can experience a product and learn how easy it is to use without committing themselves. Free public transport trial tickets for new customers are becoming common. Gronau and Kagermeier (2004) show in a qualitative study that trial tickets were a key component in convincing participants that public transportation is a viable alternative to the car.

Finally, it is important to make sure that the behavioural alternative promoted through a communication strategy actually is in the set of alternatives a person chooses. Here prompting can be a helpful technique, making alternatives salient that might not be considered otherwise. Increasing decisional involvement by linking a decision to the values a person has (see also goal framing in Section 4.5) or reducing time pressure in the decisional situation can help.

4.7 Routines and habits

So far we have analysed environmental behaviour without differentiating between behaviour that is performed often (e.g. showering) and behaviour that is performed less often (e.g. buying a new car). Is it realistic to assume that the decision-making processes are identical? Most likely they are not. This section analyses behaviours that, although differing from our big decisions, are still very relevant for their environmental impact: everyday behaviours.

4.7.1 Specifics of everyday behaviour

In a study Wood, Quinn, and Kashy (2002) found that many of our daily activities can be categorised as habitual behaviour (see Box 4.2). We perform behavioural routines or habits, investing neither much thought nor emotion in them. The study showed the potential advantages of routine decision-making, such as the need for little cognitive capacity to perform habits, freeing resources to think about more important things.

Box 4.2 Habitual behaviour in everyday life

Wood et al. (2002) conducted two diary studies where participants reported once every hour what they were doing, thinking, and feeling over one or two days. They also reported the frequency of the respective behaviour in the past month and if it was usually performed in varying or the same locations. The authors found between 35% and 53% of all reported behaviours were habits. A habit according to their definition was a behaviour that is performed frequently (almost every day) and at the same location every time, indicating a high consistency of the situational circumstances.

The authors also analysed how emotionally engaged the participants were in the reported behaviour and if they were thinking about the behaviour or let their thoughts wander. Whereas non-habitual behaviours emotionally engaged people and kept their thoughts focused on the behaviour, habitual behaviours were characterised by low levels of emotional engagement and wandering thoughts.

4.7.2 Routines and habits

The previous section showed routines or habits make it easier for us to structure and process the enormous amount of information we deal with in our daily life. They develop over time by successfully repeating behaviours in stable situational contexts. Simply put, a habit or routine stores information about a decisional context and which previous behaviour led to a satisfactory outcome (Klöckner & Verplanken, 2012). Over time, situational cues and behavioural patterns become associated with each other (Neal, Wood, & Quinn, 2006), with similar situations triggering performance of the behaviour, bypassing deliberate decision-making processes.

Ouellette and Wood (1998) found in a meta-analysis that the link between intentions and behaviours was weaker for frequent behaviours than infrequent behaviours, meaning deliberately formed intentions have less impact on habitual behaviours. The same effect has been shown for the relationship between personal norms and behaviour (Klöckner & Matthies, 2004; Klöckner, Matthies, & Hunecke, 2006), demonstrating that the two most important models used in environmental psychology (the theory of planned behaviour and the norm-activation theory) have reduced predictability for frequent behaviour.

Research has furthermore shown that people with strong habits pay less attention to information regarding alternative behaviours. They are more selective in the amount of information they choose and base their decisions on a few restricted pieces of information (Aarts, Verplanken, & Van Knippenberg, 1997; Verplanken, Aarts, & Van Knippenberg, 1997). This means that people who have strong habits will most likely not perceive or process information that would be related to behavioural alternatives to their habits.

4.7.3 Implications for environmental communication

Strong habitualisation of behaviour has important implications for attempts to change behaviour. It has been argued that habits reduce information uptake and processing, meaning it is very likely that a communication attempt to persuade for alternative behaviours will fail if people have strong habits. Intervention strategies need to be designed differently for strongly habitualised behaviours (see Section 8.3.1).

4.8 Integrated approaches

In recent years, several attempts have been made to integrate several of the aforementioned models and variables into more comprehensive models to overcome their limitations. One of those models which has been proposed by the author of this book will be presented in this section.

4.8.1 The comprehensive action determination model

Klöckner and Blöbaum (2010) argue that the theory of planned behaviour and the norm-activation theory have weaknesses that can be addressed if the two theories are combined and extended by including context and habits in the model. The model has since been applied in several environmental domains and developed further in a number of papers (Klöckner, 2013c; Klöckner & Oppedal, 2011; Sopha & Klöckner, 2011). Most recently, the structure of the model has been confirmed in a meta-analysis (Klöckner, 2013a).

Figure 4.5 depicts the most elaborate version of the model which has been published in Klöckner (2013c). Environmental behaviour is assumed to be directly determined by intentions and PBC. Objective constraints are included in the model as well as PBC, which is the subjective representation of the context. Most of the objective constraints' impact should be mediated by PBC, but some of their impact might affect behaviour directly by physically constraining certain alternatives.

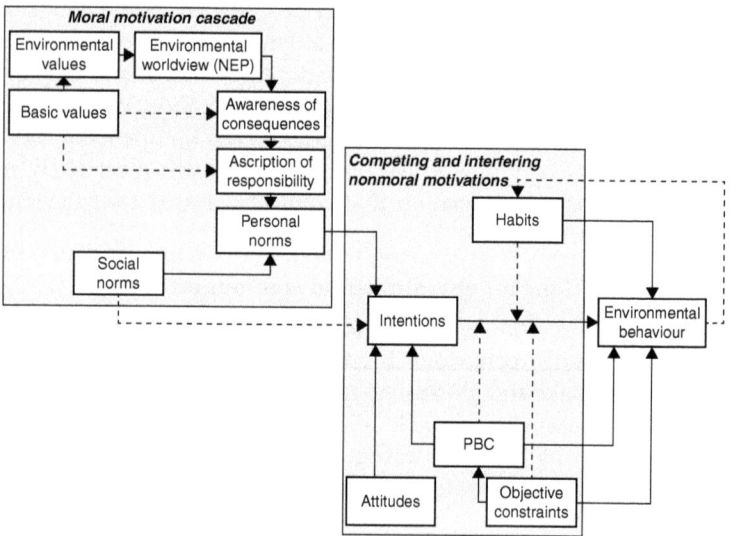

Figure 4.5 The comprehensive action determination model (Klöckner, 2013c, page 462). Used by permission of Springer

Habits are included as a third predictor, assuming the direct association between situation and behaviour determines performance when habits are strong. PBC, objective constraints, and habits are assumed to moderate the relationship between intention and behaviour. This means that a strong link between intentions and behaviour can only be expected if habits are weak and perceived and objective control are high enough.

Intentions are a variable integrating the influence of attitudes, PBC, and social norms. However, the comprehensive action determination model assumes social norms do not have a strong direct influence on intentions. This impact is mediated by personal norms. It is assumed that personal norms are generated from internalised social norms. They are triggered in a chain that goes from the most basic value orientations over environmental values, beliefs, awareness of consequences, and ascription of responsibility. Since studies of the value-belief-norm theory show that some effects from values in the latter parts of the chain are both direct and indirect, the comprehensive model also assumes some short cuts although the main effect should follow the proposed chain.

The final assumption is that habits develop over time by repeatedly performing a behaviour successfully, linking habits to behaviours at earlier points in time (Klöckner & Matthies, 2012).

4.8.2 Implications for environmental communication

All implications for environmental communication that have been outlined previously in this chapter also apply here, since the model uses the same building blocks. However, the model has some additional implications. First, it is obvious that communication attempts targeting the moral cascade might have a more indirect effect than assumed earlier. Even if people manage to develop and activate their norms, the link to behaviour might still be affected by other factors such as other motivations, habits, or constraints. This makes moral interventions vulnerable as long as they are not combined with strategies to unfreeze habits and remove barriers. One should also address potentially counterproductive attitudes in parallel because they may counteract the impact of personal norms.

Second, the interplay between habits and intentions makes the model suitable for several types of behaviour, ranging from repetitive actions to single big decisions. However, that means that the level of habits needs to be known and taken into account. Even for repetitive behaviour, not all individuals have the same degree of habitualisation. If habits are strong, deactivation strategies need to be part of the communication package.

4.9 Decision models versus change models

The models described in this chapter so far can all be called decision models; they aim to describe how people make decisions if and how to engage in pro-environmental behaviour. What they have in common is that they all have a focus on describing a decision at one point in time. They do not describe how people *change* their behaviour. Recently, behaviour change models have become more popular. They mostly refer to stage models from health psychology, most prominently the trans-theoretical model (Prochaska & DiClemente, 1994). This section will first introduce the basic idea of a change or stage model using the trans-theoretical model as an example and then discuss the most comprehensive stage model that environmental psychology has to offer at the moment, the self-regulation model of behavioural change (Bamberg, 2007, 2013a, 2013b).

4.9.1 The trans-theoretical model

The trans-theoretical model was proposed by Prochaska and DiClemente (1994) to explain how people change their health-related behaviour, for example, starting to exercise. The most important assumption is that behaviour change is not a single-, but a multiple-step process. Before people start considering a change in their behaviour, they are referred to as being in the pre-contemplation stage; in other words, they do not see any problem. At some point in time, they start considering a change in their behaviour, for example, because they notice some negative health effects (e.g. they realise that their blood pressure is too high). They enter stage two, contemplation stage, where they decide between different behavioural alternatives (e.g. changing their diet, exercising at the gym, walking to their job), often including non-action. If they finally make a decision, they enter stage three, preparation stage, where the implementation of the chosen behaviour is planned (e.g. a training schedule for the next three weeks is made). During stage four, action, the behaviour is implemented for the first time, which marks the transition into the last stage, the maintenance stage. Here the main issue is to prevent relapse into old behaviours and resist temptations. However, the trans-theoretical model does not assume that the transition is linear through all stages. It is assumed that people often oscillate between stages, for example, between periods of pre-contemplation and contemplation, or go in circles, where a progression from stage one to five is followed by a relapse and a period of pre-contemplation. It might even be that after some cycles the progression is terminated and no more cycles of contemplating, preparation, action, and maintenance are added.

A stage model like the trans-theoretical model has important implications for communicating with people. According to the model people are in different stages of change; therefore, the same communication does not affect all people in the same way. Whereas some people are in the pre-contemplation stage and have not even considered a certain behaviour a problem, others have long passed that stage and are planning how to implement the change they decided to make. It is obvious that people in different stages of change need different pushes to reach the next stage. From pre-contemplation to contemplation, the important step is to realise a problem. This can be achieved by problem information and communication that strengthens the personal feeling of responsibility (see Section 4.3.4). For transition from contemplation to preparation, communication is relevant that helps decision-making between behavioural alternatives. Basically, anything that affects attitudes towards different alternatives, self-efficacy, and perceived control should be effective here (see Section 4.2.4). In the preparation stage, concrete action knowledge is relevant to enable people to make good and realistic plans. In the action stage, it is important that people have positive experiences with the behaviour to enter maintenance stage where the most relevant communication is to help people resist temptation and to deal with relapse.

4.9.2 The stage model of self-regulated behavioural change

Bamberg's stage model of self-regulated behavioural change (2007, 2013a, 2013b) is a substantial extension of the trans-theoretical model. It is specifically adapted to environmental behaviour. Its first assumption is that people are able to change deliberate and habitualised behaviour through a process of self-regulation. Like the trans-theoretical model, it assumes that this requires a multi-stage process of consecutive steps and that circles and oscillation between stages are likely. However, the self-regulation model formulates expectations about which variables trigger and mark the transition into the next stage and how these variables are predicted by other variables. The model offers testable predictions and also more detailed expectations about which kind of communication will affect which part of the model. Figure 4.6 depicts the model.

The first stage in the model is the predecisional stage, corresponding to the pre-contemplation stage in the trans-theoretical model. The second stage is the preactional stage, which has the same function as the

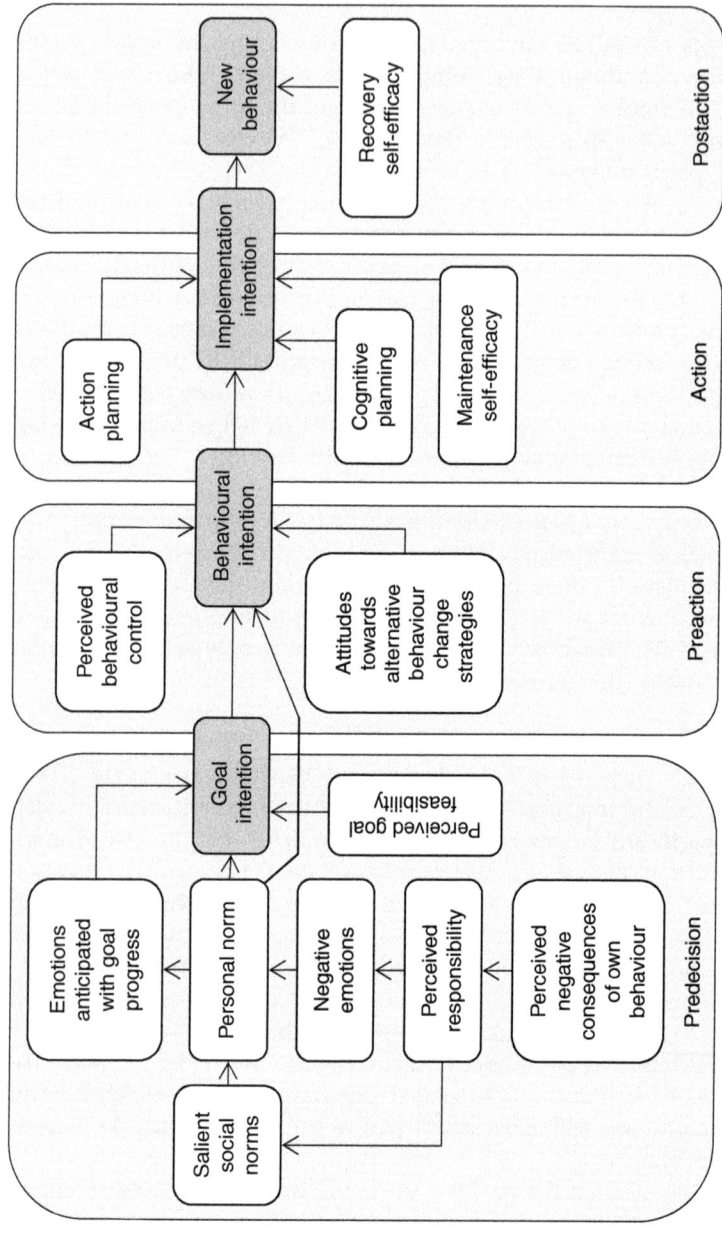

Figure 4.6 The stage model of self-regulated behavioural change (Bamberg, 2013b, page 153). Used by permission of Elsevier

contemplation stage in the trans-theoretical model. In Bamberg's model the preparation stage and the action stage from the trans-theoretical model are merged into a single action stage, because the action itself is usually of such a short duration that it cannot be captured in an empirical study. The final stage is the postactional stage, which corresponds to maintenance in the trans-theoretical model, if the behaviour is repeated.

According to Bamberg's model, transition between the stages is marked by forming a specific type of intention. The transition from pre-decision to preaction is marked by forming a goal intention (I intend to do *something* with/against x). The transition from preaction to action is marked by forming a behavioural intention (I intend to perform the behaviour y in the near future). The final transition from action to postaction is marked by forming an implementation intention (Next time I am in situation z I will do y). Applied to the example of reducing meat consumption, the three important steps to action would be (1) forming the intention to reduce meat consumption, (2) forming the intention to do that by substituting meat with fish, and not, for example, becoming vegetarian or reducing portion size, and (3) forming the intention to buy fish instead of meat when shopping the next time.

The model also describes which variables contribute in each stage to forming the respective intention. The predecisional stage is about becoming aware of a problem, realising one's own contribution, and feeling able to do something about it. The variables are to a large extent taken from the norm-activation model (see Section 4.3). The stage model assumes that perceived negative consequences of a behaviour, which is the same as awareness of consequences in the norm-activation model, lead to perceived responsibility, which would be referred to as ascription of responsibility in the norm-activation model. Perceived responsibility for negative consequences of a behaviour makes social norms about this topic more salient and leads to negative emotions, a step which is implicit in the norm-activation model. Both the social norms and negative emotions then activate personal norms, which together with perceived goal feasibility determine if a goal intention is formed or not. Goal feasibility is a very general version of perceived control, not specific to certain behaviours but connected to a goal (Would it be possible for me to reach this goal?). If reaching the goal is anticipated to lead to positive emotions, it is more likely that a goal intention is formed.

In the preactional stage, different behavioural alternatives are evaluated against each other. Here, the attitudes towards each alternative and the specific PBC for each alternative become relevant. These are two familiar variables from the theory of planned behaviour (see Section 4.2). However, personal norms might still have some impact also in this stage as the moral dimension might be used to disqualify some alternatives.

In the next stage, planning abilities and cognitive capacity come into play, as well as maintenance self-efficacy (How able am I to maintain this behaviour?). These variables cannot be found in the models presented above. The assumption is that people who have the ability to plan well, anticipate and cope with challenges, and organise their day efficiently are more able to succeed to the next stage. However, these abilities can also be taught, for example, by providing concrete action knowledge. In the final stage, recovery self-efficacy refers to a person's perceived ability to recover from relapse. How easily does a person perceive returning to the intended behaviour after they did not succeed previously?

4.9.3 Implications for environmental communication

The most important implication of the stage models, and especially the stage model of self-regulated behavioural change, for environmental communication is that communication needs to be tailored to the stage a person is at. Communication attempts based on the norm-activation theory (see Section 4.3.4) should be most effective to get people from the predecisional stage to the decisional. In addition, using techniques to make people aware of discrepancies between what they do and who they want to be, which is referred to as self-discrepancy (Higgins, 1987), might also be effective in this first stage transition. Communication designed from the theory of planned behaviour (see Section 4.2.4) will most likely be best for people in the decisional stage and may get them into the action stage. Providing people with information on how to implement behaviour changes will be relevant to the action stage, but it is crucial to provide an information package that is as tailored to the individual needs and the concrete action as possible. What is it a person needs to know to be able to successfully plan an implementation? Which cognitive strategies can be used to increase planning abilities and skills? A communication strategy for people in this stage should also try to anticipate common barriers and challenges and provide possible solutions on how to work around them. The everyday problem-solving procedure described in Section 8.2.15 is also an appropriate intervention at this stage. Successes in implementing the behaviour can show that it is possible to make the change, and in the last stage also to sustain it. Social support, linking people in the same situation so they can communicate how they solve problems, overcome temptations, and relapse, is a suitable approach for people in the last stages, as is feedback about the good effects behaviour changes had for the environment.

4.10 Conclusions

This chapter presented many different perspectives on describing, predicting, and changing environmentally relevant behaviour by reviewing the most prominent and interesting models and theoretical assumptions. Each section has described how the perspectives of each model are relevant for designing environmental communication. This last section aims to present an integrated model framework (see Figure 4.7) that is based on the reviewed models and ideas. The model is not supposed to be an empirically testable model, which would be difficult in its complexity, but rather a framework whose processes may be relevant when planning an environmental communication strategy.

The first important conclusion of this chapter is that behaviour is always embedded in a situational context, which has both enabling and limiting characteristics. The first step of each communication strategy thus needs to analyse the context and identify barriers that need to be removed before it can communicate. The behaviour needs to be sufficiently easy to make communication attempts effective.

Another function of the context is to trigger three different mechanisms: (1) goal framing, (2) choice set generation, and (3) automatic processes, most importantly habits. If people hold strong habits, the whole decision-making process might be cut short and behavioural patterns might be directly cued by the context. However, the self-regulation model tells us that people might also be able to overcome habitual constraints if the behaviour change is important enough for their self-perception. The context also triggers a goal-framing process, which frames a choice context as either hedonic, gain-related, or normative. If the goal frame is normative, the processes in the predecisional stage of the stage model can begin. It links value orientations via many variables to developing a goal intention. If the goal frame is gain-related or hedonic, behaviour may still change, but then this change will be due to hedonic or other benefits (gain). Which alternatives are considered in the preactional stage depends on the generation of choice sets. This process might be thorough or heuristic. Heuristics may also cut the evaluation process short.

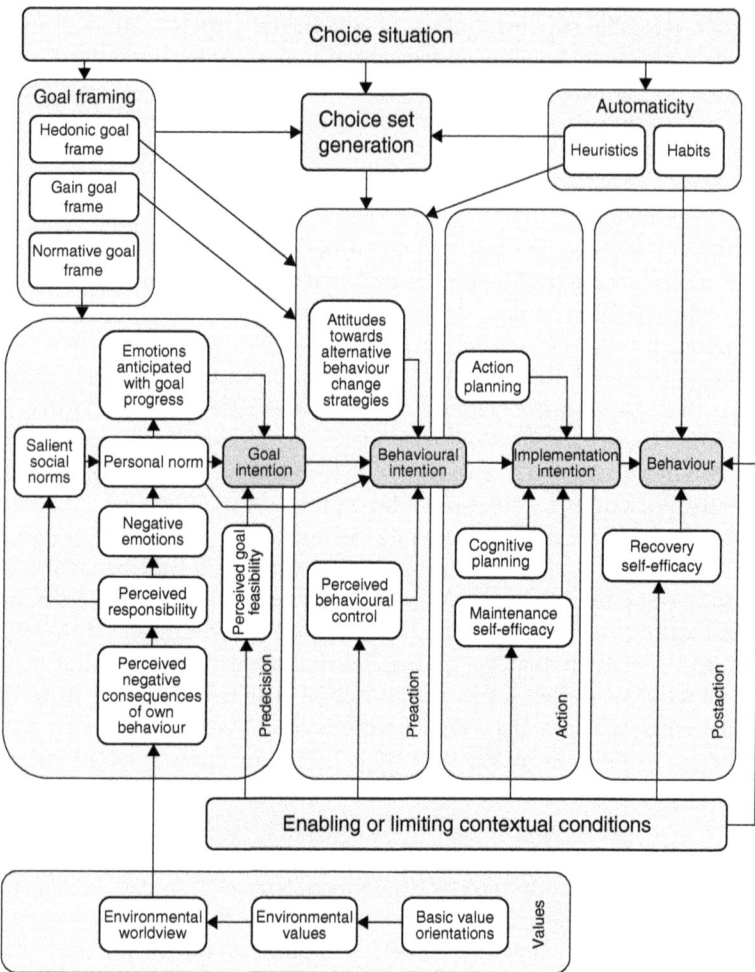

Figure 4.7 A comprehensive model framework for environmental behaviour

The contextual conditions are not only represented as an initial trigger of decision-making, but also reflected via subjective representations almost along the entire chain of decision-making.

If we assume that people can be in different stages of change in the centre of the model, then the variables are of different importance for each person. Goal-framing processes can frame the same situations differently for a person even if he or she is in the same stage of change. For example, a dedicated environmentalist planning to change behaviour does not frame a situation as normative and thus does not relate it to environmental protection.

Different communicative strategies have been discussed in the previous sections, and so they will not be repeated here. The final message of this chapter is that both behaviour and behaviour change have many determinants and the picture is complex. However, there are some mechanisms and rules that can be identified, and keeping the bigger picture in mind when designing a communication strategy is certainly helpful.

Review questions

- Describe the main components of the theory of planned behaviour and how they relate to each other. How can the theory be used to derive communication strategies?
- Which communication-based techniques can be connected to the theory of planned behaviour and how are they expected to work?
- What are the main assumptions of the norm-activation theory and the related value-belief-norm theory?
- How can the norm-activation theory and the value-belief-norm theory be used to improve environmental communication?
- Describe the assumptions of goal-framing theory and how people can be persuaded into a different goal frame?
- What is the effect of habits, routines, and heuristics on behaviour and what does that mean for environmental communication?
- What is the difference between the stage model of self-regulated behavioural change and decision models, and what implications does the self-regulation model have for environmental communication?

Suggested readings

Ajzen, I. (2012). *Values, attitudes, and behavior: Methods, theories, and empirical applications in the social sciences*, 33–38.

Bamberg, S. (2013b). Changing environmentally harmful behaviors: A stage model of self-regulated behavioral change. *Journal of Environmental Psychology*, 34, 151–159.

Hardeman, W., Johnston, M., Johnston, D., Bonetti, D., Wareham, N., & Kinmonth, A. L. (2002). Application of the theory of planned behaviour in behaviour change interventions: A systematic review. *Psychology and Health*, 17(2), 123–158.

Klöckner, C. A. (2013a). A comprehensive model of the psychology of environmental behaviour – A meta-analysis. *Global Environmental Change*, 23(5), 1028–1038.

Klöckner, C. A., & Verplanken, B. (2012). Yesterday's habits preventing change for tomorrow? About the influence of automaticity on environmental behaviour. In L. Steg, A. E. van den Berg & J. I. M. De Groot (Eds.), *Environmental Psychology: An Introduction* (pp. 197–209): Wiley-Blackwell.

Lindenberg, S., & Steg, L. (2007). Normative, gain and hedonic goal frames guiding environmental behavior. *Journal of Social Issues*, 63(1), 117–137.

Schwartz, S. H., & Howard, J. A. (1981). A normative decision-making model of altruism. In J. P. Rushton, Sorrentino, R. M. (Ed.), *Altruism and Helping Behavior* (pp. 189–211). Hillsdale: Lawrence Erlbaum.

Stern, P. C. (2000). New environmental theories: toward a coherent theory of environmentally significant behavior. *Journal of Social Issues*, 56(3), 407–424.

Verplanken, B., & Wood, W. (2006). Interventions to break and create consumer habits. *Journal of Public Policy & Marketing*, 90–103.

5
Communication in Large Social Systems – How Information Spreads through Societies

Chapter summary

This chapter introduces the diffusion of innovation theory which describes how new technologies and practices are adopted in a population. The chapter analyses the characteristics of innovations, innovation adopters, and diffusion networks that make the diffusion process more effective. It also outlines the innovation adoption decision process. These aspects are discussed from an environmental communication perspective. Lastly, agent-based modelling (ABM) as a tool for analysis of complex diffusion processes is introduced and analysed with respect to its implications for environmental communication research.

5.1 Introduction

In the previous chapters, the dominating unit of analysis has been the individual decision-maker, which is a typical approach for psychology. This chapter will take a different perspective by combining the individualistic and the social perspectives. In the first part of the chapter, one of the most influential theories about how technological and social innovation spreads in social systems will be introduced, the *diffusion of innovation theory* (E. M. Rogers, 2003). In the second part, an increasingly popular methodological approach in psychological research will be presented, namely *agent-based modelling*. ABM in itself is not a theory but a tool, but it can be used to study the dynamic processes that occur in large groups of people communicating about environmental innovations. What both approaches have in common is that they explicitly investigate time as a relevant factor in communication analysis. Whereas the theories presented in the previous sections analyse snapshots of populations and try to identify differences between people and their environmental behaviours, both diffusion of innovation theory and ABM focus on changes over time.

5.2 The diffusion of innovation theory

When Rogers, in the 1960s, began to study how agricultural innovations spread in a rural community, he soon realised that the pattern of diffusion of such innovations appeared to be more universal than he initially assumed. He started collecting examples of diffusion of innovations all over the world and found that not only new hybrids of corn and harvesting technology, but also birth control practices, HIV protection, and new environmental behaviours usually follow the same prototypical diffusion curve. This began decades of intensive research on what aspects impact the speed of diffusion of an innovation, who adopts innovation first, and who is reluctant to adopt the change. In his influential book *Diffusion of Innovations* (E. M. Rogers, 2003), Rogers summarises the entire research field and also critically discusses its flaws and pitfalls. The next paragraphs will present a brief summary of his theoretical framework. The adoption of electric cars in Norway will be used as an example throughout the chapter to illustrate the different aspects.

Diffusion of innovation is defined in Rogers' theory (2003) as "the process by which (1) an *innovation* (2) is *communicated* through certain *channels* (3) over *time* (4) among members of a *social system*" (italics and numbers in the original, page 11). Throughout his book, Rogers formulates a number of generalisations which usually can be found in diffusion of innovation processes. Not all of them are always applicable, but, as a general summary, they are helpful.

5.2.1 The S-shaped diffusion curve

When Rogers analysed how innovations spread, he recognised a common pattern that emerged (E. M. Rogers, 2003). Initially, only very few individuals in a population adopt the innovation, while the overwhelming majority sticks to the traditional technology or behaviour. After some time, news about the innovation spreads from the very early adopters to other people and the rate of adoption starts to increase. When a critical mass is reached, the adoption rate grows exponentially for some time, before the amount of individuals in the population who have not yet adopted becomes so small that the adoption rate decreases again and asymptotically approaches zero. If the cumulative percentage of individuals in a population who have adopted an innovation is plotted against time, this pattern of first increasing, then levelling out, then decreasing adoption rate leads to the famous S-shaped diffusion curve.

The diffusion of innovation curve can then be used to analyse many different aspects of the diffusion process. (1) Different innovations can be compared within the same population, where some spread faster than others indicated by a steeper slope of the S-curve. The resulting research then tries to identify characteristics of the innovation itself that make it prone to a faster adoption process. Furthermore, which types of innovation reach near full marked penetration, which means their cumulative adoption curves approximate 100%, and which innovations already approach their maximum adoption for lower percentages of the population can be analysed. Finally, it can be asked which adoption processes fail, resulting in non-S-shaped diffusion curves, because the initial diffusion process is reversed after some time. Section 5.2.3 discusses this. (2) For a single innovation, which characteristics earlier adopters have and which characteristics later adopters have can be analysed. Section 5.2.4 discusses this. Finally, (3) the diffusion of the same innovation can be compared across different social systems to identify characteristics of culture that promote innovation uptake. Section 5.2.5 will discuss this aspect.

5.2.2 The innovation-decision process

At the core of E. M. Rogers (2003) theory is a model of how an individual makes a decision about adopting an innovation. The model assumes that innovation adoption is a five-stage process, not unlike the stage models described in Section 4.9 (Bamberg, 2013b; Prochaska & DiClemente, 1994). The first step to innovation adoption is to gain *knowledge* about the existence of an innovation. Characteristics of the decision-maker, such as socio-economic characteristics, personality, or communication behaviour, determine both at which point of innovation diffusion they receive knowledge and also how fast they proceed through the process (see below). Rogers distinguishes three types of knowledge which are necessary for innovation adoption: (1) *awareness knowledge*, which is knowledge that the innovation exists; to adopt an electric car, people need to be aware that electric cars exist; (2) *how-to knowledge*, which is the necessary information on how to use the innovation properly, such as information about the electric car range and how to recharge its batteries; and (3) *principles knowledge*, which is information about how the innovation functions. Even if in the example of the electric vehicle it is not necessary to fully understand how such a car works, it will help in the adoption process to have some understanding of batteries and electric engines to see the advantages.

The second step in innovation-decision is persuasion. Perception of innovation characteristics, such as relative advantage over old practices, compatibility with the system used, complexity, trialability, and observability, becomes relevant in choosing to use an innovation (see Section 5.2.3 for a deeper analysis). In the next step, *decision*, an innovation is either adopted or rejected. If a decision for adoption is made, this decision may be revised at a later point in time, leading to discontinuance. Rejection can be revised and turned later into adoption. If it is decided to adopt an innovation, the *implementation* stage is entered and concrete plans of implementation need to be made. At this stage, it is not unlikely that the innovation is reinvented, meaning it is implemented in a different way than suggested by the promoters. In the early years of innovation diffusion research, reinvention was either ignored or regarded as a problem, but has recently become the focus of interest. Now, reinvention, or the adaptation of an innovation to the local context, is regarded as a positive quality which ensures a higher speed of innovation diffusion and more likely sustainability of the implementation. In the final *confirmation* stage, the implementation of the innovation is evaluated and a decision to discontinue the adoption or reinvent the innovation can be made. Communication activities impact the deciding individual in all five stages.

Prior conditions play an important role in the innovation-decision process. For example, if the previous practice is similar to the new practice or the new practice can be easily blended into existing routines, then the innovation-decision process will proceed faster. If the person sees a need for change or experiences a problem with the old practice, the likelihood for innovation adoption will also be higher. People who, in general, are more innovative, more interested to test new developments, will be faster to take up all kinds of innovations. If the social norms in a system are criticising the new practice, then uptake will be slowed and, in the worst case, restricted to people who are already social outsiders.

Different types of communication channels are relevant at different stages. Whereas for knowledge, especially awareness knowledge, mass media channels are most effective, person-to-person communication channels on a local level are more effective in the persuasion stage, especially for later adopters.

5.2.3 Innovation characteristics supporting diffusion

Under similar conditions, different types of innovations spread with different speed in a population. Much of the research on innovation diffusion has focused on identifying the characteristics of an innovation that encourages early adoption. The most important are relative advantage, compatibility, complexity, trialability, and observability.

Relative advantage refers to the benefit an individual gets from adopting an innovation compared to the technique/practice already implemented. If a high relative benefit is perceived with high certainty, then the innovation has a high relative advantage and is likely to be adopted. Electric cars in Norway are promoted by the government with powerful incentives that increase their relative advantage. Buyers of electric vehicles do not have to pay purchase tax; have reduced annual car tax; are exempted from parking fees, road tolls, and ferry tolls; and are allowed to drive in bus lanes. All of that makes an electric vehicle highly beneficial, especially for people living in or close to urban areas.

Compatibility refers to the degree of implementation of the innovation that requires breaking with established values, beliefs, previous ideas, or needs. If an innovation is compatible with the established norms and practices, it will be much more likely adopted than if not. Again, the electric car is a good example of a highly compatible innovation. Buying an electric instead of an ordinary car does not require much adaptation from the innovator, especially if the electric car is purchased as a second car. How an innovation is named is also part of the compatibility, because the name partly defines the expectations of the innovation.

Complexity refers to the degree of difficulty in comprehending or implementing an innovation. If an innovation is extremely complex to implement, the rate of adoption will be slower. Electric cars, in general, require little learning for people that already drive a car, so they can be regarded as innovations of little complexity, even if an electric car is a complex system. However, since most people are not able to understand and repair their cars anyway, the difference between an electric and combustion engine car is not significant. The electric car engine is actually less complex than a combustion engine.

Trialability of an innovation refers to the ability to try an innovation first. Trialability reduces the risk an innovator takes by offering an exit, should the innovation not satisfy. By offering this, a barrier for innovation adoption is removed, especially if the necessary investment is high. Many promoters of new products offer free trial periods to address this aspect. Trialability of electric cars is relatively low, except for test drives.

In the beginning, some producers of electric cars actually offered the potential early customers longer trial periods.

Observability refers to the visibility by other people of the implementation of the innovation. Observable innovations spread faster than unobservable innovations. For example, it is interesting how electric cars diffuse in neighbourhoods. It is easy to observe if your neighbour has bought a fancy new electric car, which may persuade you to purchase an electric car. Since interpersonal communication about an innovation is especially important in the persuasion stage, it is not surprising that observability, which is also an expression of descriptive norms (see Section 4.3.1), is an important feature of effective diffusion processes.

5.2.4 Innovator characteristics supporting diffusion

E. M. Rogers (2003) used the normal distribution of adoption rates over time to also group adopters into different groups. He applied the simple statistical measures of mean and standard deviation to define five segments of adopters in the adoption curve. First, he divided the area under the curve into two parts at the mean. Then all people who adopted earlier than the mean were categorised into one out of three groups based on how much earlier than the mean they adopted. People who adopt innovation very early (defined as the mean minus two standard deviations) are referred to as "innovators". People who adopt innovation after them but earlier than most others (between mean minus two and mean minus one standard deviation) are referred to as "early adopters", and people that adopt innovation slightly earlier than the mean (mean minus one standard deviation to mean) are referred to as "early majority". People who adopt innovation slightly later than the mean (mean to mean plus one standard deviation) are referred to as "late majority", while the remaining very late adopters are referred to as "laggards". The use of standard deviation and mean to define the groups also results in the percentage each group constitutes of the total population.

Afterwards, E. M. Rogers (2003) characterised a prototypical member of each category based on research results about innovation adopters. The typical innovator is venturesome, risk taking, and cosmopolite. Usually, the innovators are not well integrated parts of the local community; they are too far ahead in terms of trying new things. They are usually also friends with other innovators, often across long geographical distances. Innovators are usually financially powerful and well educated. Their role in the diffusion of innovation is to be a gatekeeper who actively imports innovations into the local system.

Early adopters are much better integrated into the local community and well respected. Often, they are important opinion leaders who are the nodes of local communication networks. Contrary to innovators, early adopters are localites. Because they are less advanced than innovators, they are more suitable role models for later adopters and often help in triggering the critical mass. Some researchers even detect a threshold that an innovation process needs to overcome to really be taken up. This threshold, which is also referred to as "the chasm", is usually crossed when the early adopters implement the innovation and the early majority also begin to adopt the innovation.

The early majority are usually not opinion leaders, but above-average active in communication networks. The innovation-decision process of members of the early majority is longer than for early adopters. They like to see proof within their social system that an innovation works.

The late majority is more sceptical than the early majority. They adopt innovation basically because of peer pressure (note that more than half of a population already adopted the innovation when they start) and economic necessity, not because of enthusiasm. Usually, members of the late majority have less resources available than the groups that adopt earlier. The late majority first starts adopting when insecurity about the benefit of an innovation is removed.

The last group are the laggards. They are traditionalists with no opinion leadership and are the most localite category. Laggards tend to make decisions which favour past behaviour. Laggards are not communicating frequently with members of the other earlier adopter groups and are suspicious of innovation.

Even though Rogers sorted the innovation adopters into categories, he is very explicit that innovativeness on the personal level is a continuum. This variable has been related to a large number of socio-demographic variables, including social status, personality, and communication behaviour.

5.2.5 Diffusion network characteristics supporting diffusion

Diffusion of innovation is a process of communication through social networks. The more people talk about an innovation, praise its potential and benefits, and share their experiences, the more quickly it will be adopted. A paradox in diffusion of innovation lies in the tendency of social systems to be resistant to change. Members of a social system, in general, tend to be more influenced by people equal to them on a number of psychological and socio-economic dimensions (homophily), than by people different from them (heterophily). The problem is that innovations are usually promoted by a person outside the social system (a change agent), for example, a scientist or a government agency. Most members of a social system are not very likely to be convinced by such a person.

This is where the roles of innovators, early adopters, and opinion leaders come into play. The innovator is usually too different from the ordinary member of a social network to have a relevant direct influence. An anecdote from a focus group study conducted on energy behaviour in Norway (Klöckner et al., 2013) illustrates this problem. One participant in one focus group discussion reported his substantial investment in energy upgrades to his house. After some time, other members of the focus group started wondering if this person could be real or was rather a plant by the researcher who was supposed to trigger reactions by the other participants, which he was not. He was obviously too innovative to connect to the rest of the participants. Innovators are rather the gate keepers that take an innovation into the social system and convince the opinion leader. Opinion leaders are the advocates of innovation in the system, given that the social norms in the system do not sanction change in general. They have the credibility and degree of similarity to the ordinary members of the system that is needed to spread the innovation further. However, the role of weak communication links to distant people, mostly belonging to other systems, should not be underestimated for innovations spreading over larger distances. Otherwise, the boundaries of the local society would become the boundaries of innovation diffusion. Once the opinion leaders are adopting the innovation, the adoption process speeds up and members of the early majority who are communicating with the opinion leaders start adopting. Members of the late majority start adopting when more and more peers (not only opinion leaders) have adopted and start communicating with them. The laggards will either adopt very late or not adopt at all, since their communication network is only loosely connected to members of the earlier adopter groups. They usually communicate with other laggards. Figure 5.1 shows a typical communication pattern in a diffusion network.

5.2.6 Applications of the diffusion of innovation theory in the environmental domain

The diffusion of innovation theory has frequently been applied to pro-environmental innovations. Ozaki (2011) employs the theory to analyse why some consumers sign up to green electricity while others do not. He identified weak social norms, uncertainty, and inconvenience as main

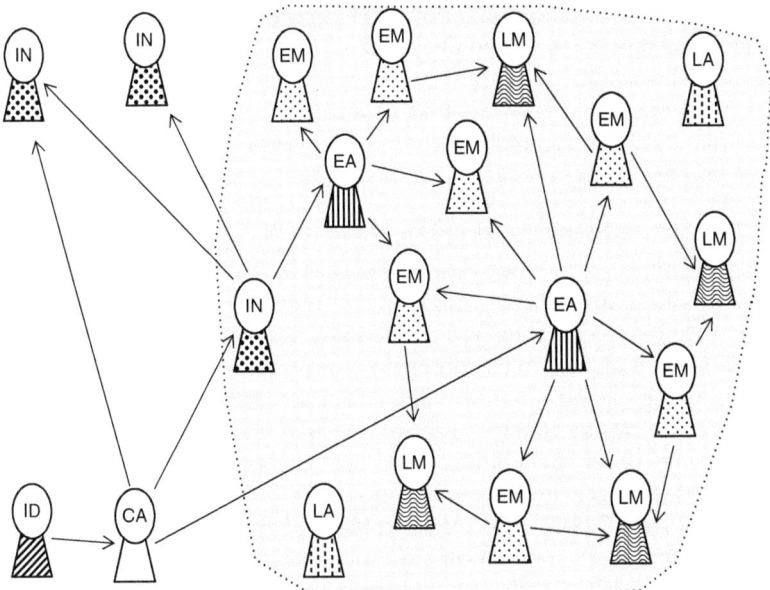

Figure 5.1 Diffusion of innovation in a social system through the different types of actors
ID = innovation agency (developing the innovation), CA = change agent (promoting the innovation), IN = innovators, EA = early adopters (often opinion leaders), EM = early majority, LM = late majority, LA = laggards.

barriers to adoption. Jansson, Marell, and Nordlund (2011) combined the diffusion of innovation framework with factors identified in the theory of planned behaviour (Ajzen, 1991) in a study on purchase of alternative fuel vehicles. With respect to diffusion of innovation-related aspects, they found that adopters of such cars are more novelty-seeking and rank the attributes of cars differently (e.g. the car's CO_2 emissions). In line with Rogers' theory, adopters see a higher relative advantage of an alternative fuel car, perceive it as more compatible with their lifestyle and less complex, and see the purchase as less risky and the innovation as more observable. In a second study based on the same data, Jansson et al., 2009 cluster-analysed their participants based on their beliefs and involvement in eco-innovation adoption. They found clear evidence for a group of ecological innovators, which they referred to as *ecovators*. Crabtree and Hes (2009) analysed the diffusion of sustainable housing in Australia and found that unfamiliarity with new sustainable technologies and unclear communication channels were among the two main barriers for adoption, two aspects that Rogers' theory would predict to be crucial. In a theoretical paper on hybrid car purchase, Ozaki and Dodgson (2010) argue that the diffusion of innovation theory's assumptions about the adoption of an innovation should be supplemented by assumptions about the consumption of innovations, namely the *meaning* of an innovation for the adopter/consumer.

5.2.7 Strengths and weaknesses of the theory

Rogers' diffusion of innovation theory has had a huge impact on research in many different domains. Its main strength is its universality; it applies in the same way to diffusion of a technology in Northern America as it applies to the diffusion of pregnancy protection practices in Asia. The same mechanisms and effects are postulated. However, the theory also has weaknesses and the research about diffusion of innovation has blind spots which have not yet been addressed properly. In his book, Rogers mentions these problems with remarkable openness (E. M. Rogers, 2003). The main problem of the diffusion of innovation research is its innovation bias. Innovations are per se regarded as something positive which should be diffused, which draws attention away from research on failures of diffusion, reinvention of innovations, and negative unanticipated effects of innovations. Rogers gives a very impressive example of this bias by reporting an anecdote from one of his very early studies. In his study about the diffusion of hybrid corn in a rural community, one farmer strongly resisted adoption and rather focused on organic farming methods. In the 1960s, he was categorised a laggard, but with today's knowledge he would rather be classified an ultra-innovator, according to Rogers. Another problem of diffusion research is its tendency to side with the innovation agencies (often research activities are funded by them), which often leads to the focus of the non-adoption of the innovation being the fault of the individual adopter, not the innovation or its promotion. Finally, diffusion of innovations often widens the social gap in a society, an effect which has received far too little attention in diffusion research. The analysis of adopter characteristics shows that the already resourceful members of society usually benefit most from early adoption whereas the poorer, less educated people lag behind, disconnecting them even more from progress.

5.2.8 Implications for environmental communication

From an environmental communication perspective, Rogers' diffusion of innovation theory provides numerous interesting entry points. First, it provides the designers of environmental communication with a list of design characteristics that should be acknowledged: the promoted innovation should have a clear relative advantage *for the individual*; it should be compatible with established norms and practices as far as possible, as simple to comprehend and implement as possible, trialable, and observable. The problem is that many environmental innovations do not fulfil these criteria. Often the individual benefit is unclear, the innovation is incompatible with a preferred lifestyle, or it is not observable to a degree that does not integrate it with descriptive norms. This makes many environmental innovations more difficult to diffuse than technological innovations. Furthermore, many environmental innovations are preventive innovations, where the benefit lies in the avoidance of negative consequences whose occurrence in the future is unsure. Such types of innovations spread with a much slower pace.

Furthermore, diffusion of innovation theory outlines who should be addressed in a diffusion campaign. A change agent, which the environmental communicator is, needs to team up with the innovators as pilot users, but even more importantly with opinion leaders in a social system. The change agent needs to know the system and to be able to link with the key members of the system. He or she needs to have a sufficient degree of similarity (homophily) with the target group and take their perspective rather than the change agency's perspective to be successful.

With respect to communication channels, diffusion of innovation theory also makes important suggestions. Mass media channels are helpful to spread knowledge about an innovation, but are less useful in the persuasion stage. Furthermore, they are more useful to address earlier adopters than later adopters. A problem with mass media is that it may not be open to communicating environmental innovation, especially if the innovation is behaviour related. Modern communication strategies involving social media can be an interesting hybrid between mass communication and personal communication, which combine the advantage of a high range and speed of information diffusion with the credibility and persuasive quality of a personal communication.

5.3 Agent-based modelling

ABM is not a theory but a methodological tool that can be applied in various domains that are characterised by a high number of agents (e.g. animals, atoms, persons) interacting with each other in a way that can be put into simplified mathematical rules (Jager & Gotts, 2013). It has become increasingly popular in social science because it implements the single decision-maker perspective in the form of the agent in the model and the decision rules implemented in the agent's behaviour. However, it also covers the complexity of social structures and communication networks where agents are influenced by other agents and situational conditions. A third dimension that is relevant in ABM is time, as such models describe the behaviour of a usually high number of agents over time. The usual unit of analysis is the aggregated behaviour of agents; for example, how the agent's individual decisions in their social and physical context over time lead to the exploitation of natural resources. One advantage of agent-based models is that the unit of analysis can be finetuned; analysis of certain regions of the network or of special types of agents can be performed. Another advantage of an agent-based model is that it not only can reproduce developments over time retrospectively, but it can be used to make predictions about developments in the future, assuming the mechanisms are realistic. An agent-based model can furthermore become a laboratory for testing interventions since the effect of manipulating key variables on the behaviour of the system over time can be simulated.

Probably, the first working agent-based model in the context of social science was presented by Schelling (1971). He programmed a computer simulation which demonstrated that spatial segregation between social groups is often unavoidable if agents apply the simple rule that they choose to live close to a minimum number of equal agents (the percentage of equal neighbours can be manipulated). If the agent is not satisfied (too few equal neighbours), it decides to move. Many demonstrations of this initial agent-based model can be found on the Internet (e.g. http://www.avanderw.co.za/schellings-segregation-simulation/).

5.3.1 Basic assumptions of agent-based models

Agent-based models are computer simulations with three core elements. The first element is the agents. They can be the same agent type or of different kinds. For example, agents can be households, customers, or even companies. The agent has a defined set of rules on how it makes decisions about the behaviour in question, such as buying an electric vehicle. These rules are usually based on empirical experience, gathered by either a theoretically derived questionnaire or expert input (Sopha et al., 2013). The rules can be very simple (Schelling, 1971) or complex, which may include elements of randomness (Sopha et al., 2013). The agent is placed in a simulation of a physical environment that, depending on the type of simulation, may or may not have an influence on their decisions.

The second element of an agent-based model is the social network. The model contains information about how the agents are communicating to each other. Furthermore, the model makes assumptions about which agents are likely to communicate; for example, agents in close physical proximity are more likely to communicate with each other.

The third element of an agent-based model is time. The simulation runs in time frames; each frame corresponds to a simulated amount of real time (e.g. quarter of a year or a day, depending on the model). In each time frame, a certain number of agents make the decision in question based on their decision rules and the status of the variables that go into this decision process in that time frame. Not all agents make the decision in each time frame, depending on the behaviour simulated. At the end of each time frame, the status of the variables in each agent is updated, based on the rules defining the effects of communication with other agents, and a new time frame is initialised.

Since agent-based models are approximations of reality, they are usually calibrated on historical data. If the model is capable of reproducing historical developments reasonably well with the defined rules, it is assumed that the rules are good approximations that can be used to predict future developments or the effects of interventions.

5.3.2 Applications of agent-based models in the environmental domain

Three applications of agent-based models that demonstrate the potential of ABM for environmental research are presented here. The "lakeland study" (Jager et al., 2000) simulated how the effect of agent decisions for fishing or mining affected the quality of a lake, which then in turn affected the choice agents made in the next time frame. Two different sets of decision rules were implemented, one strictly focusing on profit maximising (*homo economicus*) and one also utilising social comparison, imitation, and habitual processes in decision-making (*homo psychologicus*). In the profit-maximising scenario, most agents tried mining because it was more profitable when it was introduced, but many returned to fishing because the competition was reduced and it became more profitable. The model predicted that after the fishers and miners oscillated between extremes, equilibrium would occur between the two professions, which under the circumstances defined in the model also resulted in sustainable use of the lake. In the psychological scenario, very few agents went to mining initially, but more followed, leading to a permanent shift from fishing to mining and an environmental catastrophe for the lake.

As part of a large agent-based simulation project focusing on the water situation in the upper Danube catchment, both everyday water use and the diffusion of water-saving technologies, such as rain harvesting systems, water-saving shower heads, or toilet flushes, were simulated (Ernst et al., 2008; Schwarz & Ernst, 2009). Interestingly, the models were coupled with simulation models of the water-related processes triggered by climate change. The authors used decision-making rules in household agents that were based on psychological models (see Chapter 3) and the diffusion of innovation theory, as well as a segregation of households based on their lifestyles (see Section 7.5.3). They found that attitudes and perceived behavioural control were key variables for the diffusion of water-saving technology; regarding the innovation, characteristics such as perceived performance, costs savings, investment costs, ease of use, and compatibility with existing infrastructure were important. The water-use model was then used to simulate the effects of environmental changes, such as droughts, on household water use and the diffusion of water-saving technology. The authors found that external changes triggered by climate change increased the diffusion of water-saving technology so that households are able to retain their lifestyles.

In a study of the diffusion of wood pellet heating in Norway, Sopha, Klöckner, and Hertwich combined decision mechanisms from the previously described studies (Sopha & Klöckner, 2011; Sopha et al., 2010a, 2011a, 2011b; Sopha et al., 2013; Sopha et al., 2010b). They first conducted a survey to identify the relevant variables for the decision process, and the initial values for variables and their impact on others for agents with different lifestyles. They then calibrated the model on historical data and simulated the impact of different incentive structures and attitude campaigns on the diffusion of wood pellet stoves in Norway. The results of their simulations indicated that technical improvements in the wood stoves and stable wood pellet prices are important to increase adoption rates; under the current market conditions, attitude campaigns would not have a huge impact.

5.3.3 Strengths and weaknesses of agent-based models

The examples presented above clearly show the strengths and weaknesses of agent-based models. Models with realistic decision-making rules for the agents and good calibration can help simulate the effects of different intervention scenarios or environmental scenarios without the need to expose a real population to potentially ineffective or harmful interventions. This makes ABM a valuable policy-making instrument. It can also help researchers in determining the non-linear effects that occur in complex systems with many interactive units.

An important weakness of agent-based models is the tendency to ignore the amount of uncertainty in their predictions. Decision-makers and researchers tend to take the results of an agent-based simulation as certain. However, because predictions are based on simplified decision rules that only incorporate variables known to be important at this point in time, the future might look completely different and even the most elaborate agent-based model might totally fail in its predictions.

Another weakness of many agent-based models is that they lack rules that describe not only how the *value* of a variable (e.g. attitude) in an agent changes as a result of communication with other agents, but also how its relation to other variables changes over time, partly due to communication with other agents. This makes most agent-based models static, since only variable values change over time, and not the structure of variables. But could it not be possible that the impact of, for example, values and norms increases under certain conditions? Norm-activation theory and goal-framing theory (see Chapter 3) would at least predict that. Aiming to model this structural instability might be an interesting endeavour for the future.

5.3.4 Implications for environmental communication

ABM has a strong focus on the relation and communication between agents. This makes the approach also interesting for research on environmental communication. Effects of communication strategies can be studied in vitro and effective communication campaigns can be designed with more options to pilot test them before implementing costly but ineffective alternatives.

5.4 Conclusions

This chapter focused on diffusion of innovation theory and ABM, two approaches (one theoretical, one methodological) that easily go hand-in-hand and combine the individualistic perspective of classical psychological decision-making research with the system perspective of communication networks. Both approaches explicitly model changes over time, with time being a core variable in the models, which distinguishes them from the models presented in the previous chapters. An agent-based research tradition with strong roots in diffusion of innovation research, but also including aspects of the models discussed in previous chapters, seems to be a promising perspective for future research on environmental communication.

Review questions

- What are the stages of the innovation-decision process?
- What kind of communication channels are most effective in which stage and for which group of people?
- What characteristics of an innovation make its diffusion more likely? How can that be used for environmental communication?
- What are different adopter categories and what characterises them? How is that of importance for environmental communication strategies?
- What are the basic assumptions of an agent-based model and which of them are important from an environmental communication perspective?

Suggested readings

Rogers, E. M. (2003). *Diffusion of innovations*. New York: Free Press.

Jager, W., & Gotts, N. (2013). Simulating social environmental systems. In L. Steg, A. E. van den Berg & J. I. M. De Groot (Eds.), *Environmental Psychology – an Introduction* (pp. 281–291). Oxford: Blackwell.

6
Traditional and New Media – About Amplification and Negation

Chapter summary

This chapter analyses the role of media and other actors in defining the perception of environmental risks by the public. First, an introduction to the specificities of different media types, including old and new media, books, and art is given. The basic theories in risk perception are presented, including the psychometric paradigm, the cultural theory of risk perception, the protection motivation theory, and the social amplification of risk framework (SARF). Their importance for risk communication in the environmental domain is discussed. The chapter ends with insights from the newsroom on how media actors select and present news and what their work patterns imply for designing environmental communication. The conclusion presents concrete advice for environmental media campaigns based on the research presented in this chapter.

6.1 Introduction

Previous chapters have outlined how important communication through different channels is for achieving change in environmental behaviour. The diffusion of innovation theory (see Section 5.2) especially emphasised the role of different communication channels for different kinds of actors in the diffusion process. In this chapter, the role of different media channels will be analysed in more detail. First, the different types of media channels will be introduced. The chapter will then draw on theories from risk perception and risk communication, as these psychological disciplines have proven to be especially helpful in understanding the effects of communication through media. The chapter will end with a number of recommendations on how to improve effectiveness of environmental communication through media channels. Many of the theories mentioned in this chapter implicitly include a target group segmentation approach. This, however, will be discussed in detail in Chapter 7.

6.2 The role of media in environmental communication

Nowadays, people have access to a huge selection of media that can have an impact on their beliefs, attitudes, values, knowledge, and other aspects related to environmental behaviour. The essence of media communication is that it is *mediated*, that there is some kind of technology that links the different actors together, such as a printer that produces a newspaper and a distribution system, a computer with an Internet connection, and a TV connected to a satellite network. Usually one of the actors has some degree of power to define and select what is communicated, and usually the number of more passive actors (e.g. the newspaper readers) in the communication activity is larger than the number of more active actors (e.g. the journalists). However, new media types, especially social media, such as Facebook, Twitter, and YouTube, have changed the media world and the roles of the actors dramatically. Starting with "old media" like newspapers, magazines, radio, or TV which have dominated the media world for decades, the focus in this section will shift to new media channels, such as the Internet or smartphone technologies, focusing especially on their implication for social media. The final part of this section will deal with media channels such as books and movies, both documentary and fictional, as well as theatre, visual art, and other forms of communication based on art-related media.

6.2.1 Newspapers and magazines

Newspapers and magazines in their classical form are printed publications that appear with a certain frequency and have both subscribers and single issue sales at newspaper stands. It is important to note that the readers usually pay to read the product. However, newspapers and magazines are far from homogenous; for example, they differ in their release frequency, their target audience, and consequently the length and language level of texts they publish, the amount and quality of pictures they include, the number of copies published, and how much they rely on pre-produced news agency material or produce their own news. A common feature is that a limited number of journalists form the editorial staff of the newspaper or magazine. This group of people, most importantly the chief editor, defines the selection of topics and the way they are presented in the publication. By this selection process, the editorial staff of a newspaper or magazine shapes how the reader perceives the topic and, over time, also which political orientation and worldview the publication will be associated with. As different publications are known to have different political profiles, the reader can choose to select a newspaper or magazine based on this knowledge.

Another common feature is that print publications have a given production time. A daily newspaper will not be able to communicate any news before the next news cycle (the next day). With a production time of several hours, the daily newspapers have been the quickest way to communicate to large groups of people. Nowadays, newspapers already present "old" news when they are published, because the Internet, radio, or TV has already spread the news. To compete with this, the character of newspaper journalism has changed from a mere carrier of news to a carrier of deeper analyses and opinions. Furthermore, under pressure from other media channels, classic newspapers all around the world have struggled in recent years to keep enough subscribers to pay the expenses of newspaper journalism.

6.2.2 Radio

Newspapers and radio productions are similar in that radio programs are also usually produced by the editorial staff, with topics similarly selected through the lens of the journalist. However, there are also important differences between print news media and radio. First, production time on radio programs is much shorter, especially for short news features. The radio can react faster to news events and usually broadcasts 24 hours a day, meaning there is in theory no next production cycle that requires waiting for to present the news. However, most radio channels do not solely present news content or spoken word features. Mostly music is played, interspersed with longer news features or interviews, and a brief news broadcast every hour. During the night-time, the amount of news content is often reduced and many smaller radio channels use pre-produced news. In the case of very special events, however, radio has the possibility to react almost immediately. Another important difference to printed media is that radio can broadcast sound, for example, interviews with the original voice of the interviewees, which has implications for the authenticity of the interview. Unlike printed media, radio broadcasts in their classic form cannot be reheard when something is not understood. Finally, unlike a newspaper or magazine, people usually do not pay directly for a radio broadcast. It is either financed by an annual TV or radio licence, general taxes, and/or advertisement.

6.2.3 Television

Television again has some similarities to both radio and classic print media, including similarly an editorial group deciding what to broadcast and how. Some features are produced by a television company, while others are bought in. Also, most commonly, TV does not present on purely news or thematic features. Much of the time, TV broadcasts series or movies, talk shows, and game shows among other forms of entertainment. However, regardless of the quality of such programs, they should not be deemed irrelevant for environmental communication. For example, environmental behaviours presented as norms in a daily soap might have a stronger influence on the target audience than a documentary feature about the same topic. The Dutch "Center for Media and Health" (www.media-health.nl) implemented a storyline about environmental issues into a Dutch daily soap. The production time for a TV feature is slightly higher than that of a radio feature, but similar to the radio, the level of sophistication can be adjusted so that the TV can also react very quickly to news. "Breaking news" banners allow TV the opportunity to present news bits within other types of broadcasts. A special feature of TV programs is that they combine moving images and sound in their telling of stories and news. This offers options that go beyond both print media and radio broadcasts. However, at least in its classic form, TV is not an interactive communication channel. The recipient watches what the TV channel broadcasts and only interacts by switching the channel. In this form, TV consumption is also limited to a certain space, for example, the living room where the TV set is placed. Recently, both limitations started to disappear as TV broadcasting is merging with Internet technology via additional online features. Finally, most TV channels are free for the viewers and financed by general taxes, an annual fee, or advertisement. Pay TV and pay per view are more common for TV than for radio.

In an interesting paper summarising the experience of a series of meetings between climate scientists and journalists mostly working at the British Broadcasting Company (BBC), Smith (2005) argues that journalists are well aware of their defining role in shaping climate change risk perceptions of the public. Climate scientists, on the contrary, held to a communication model that understood media merely as a channel that transports their information further to the public and, at least in their perception, fails to do so properly. Interestingly, the journalists at the same time embraced the myth that they just source and "transport" the truth, that they are detached from the content of their news. When selecting what is "news", a journalist takes into consideration what he or she thinks the audience expects and likes, and information about what other media is covering.

6.2.4 New media

With the introduction of the Internet and its phenomenal success around the globe, media has changed dramatically. Many limitations of classic media channels have disappeared with the Internet's possibility of easy, cheap, and virtually unlimited publication of content. The introduction of smartphone technology has also removed the space limitations of media channels. Media can nowadays be consumed almost everywhere and almost immediately. The Internet revolution has also removed the interpretative authority that editorial boards of classic media previously had. In theory, almost anyone who is connected to the Internet can publish his or her perspective. The following subsections will discuss some of the implications of new media for environmental communication.

6.2.4.1 Internet

The Internet gives everyone the possibility of becoming the news-producer, offering access to create homepages displaying information, chat rooms, blogs, discussion forums, audio or video streams and downloads, e-mail, wikis, and other formats. The power to interpret reality has been provided to individuals and groups, at least to a certain degree. One has to be aware that Internet-provided communication is filtered, partly by individuals or groups designing and updating homepages or providing media content, but also, and maybe even more importantly, by search engines and meta-sites that filter and rank information sources for the readers to structure the vast amount of available information. This filtering process is less obvious than what occurs in the newsroom of a newspaper, but with a search engine market dominated by a few large companies, people's options to find an alternative perspective are rather limited. The search algorithm and the behind-the-scene filter mechanisms have partly become the undeclared chief editor.

An interesting effect of Internet-based communication is that the boundaries of cosmopolite and localite communication channels become less clearly defined (E. M. Rogers, 2003). Old media, like newspapers, radio, and TV, were cosmopolite and non-personal by covering the non-local. Individual communication was clearly localite and personal.

Internet communication is, on the one hand, cosmopolite because information on the net is usually open to many people in very different social networks, but, on the other hand, is very localite, because the content often does not appeal to more than just a few people. The difference is that the geographical dimension is removed. People with the same interest can connect across large distances. Therefore, localite is not restricted to a certain place anymore but has become more an interest community.

Many classic media channels have now merged with the Internet to a certain degree. This has led to more fuzzy boundaries between different types of media. According to Smith (2005), new developments in the media market that integrate "old" media channels with new features of interactivity and additional information on demand can lead to a better understanding of issues like climate change. By "telling the 360 degrees of a story" (page 1480), stories can be told about climate change in a way that make it easier for people to relate to.

6.2.4.2 Smartphones and tablets

The accessibility of the web has increased through tablets, smartphones, and laptops with their associated applications (apps). In many countries, smartphones have spread so quickly that now a large proportion of the population has access to media almost everywhere at every time. Especially in Asia and Africa, mobile phones have been adopted before landlines were developed. That kind of technological leapfrogging has given people in such countries access to information. It has also changed people's habits of consuming news. The bus trip is used for a quick update on the latest news or checking mails. While children are playing in the playground, their parents are connected to the world via their smartphone. This means also that the presentation of the news has to be adjusted. Short text and short videos suit the smartphone much better than a long essay which can be found in a printed newspaper. However, the availability of information makes it also possible to tailor information to a given situation, which can be very useful from an environmental communication perspective. Never before has it been so easy to get additional information (independent from the seller) about a product you are considering buying while you are in a store.

6.2.4.3 Social media

A special phenomenon within Internet-based communication is social media networks, often coupled with mobile communication devices. Social media connect groups of people and provide a structure to easily keep others updated about the latest developments, usually on a personal level. Social networks have changed communication patterns on the Internet (Kaplan & Haenlein, 2010). Communication matches spoken language more closely, communication pieces are getting shorter, and the information content of each message is often not large and more a social statement than conveying a message (Lantz-Andersson et al., 2013). With this structure, social network communication overcomes the gap between communication through classic media channels and personal face-to-face communication. Thus, social media can be valuable in cases where personal communication has proven a more successful channel (see Section 5.2) but face-to-face communication would be impracticable.

6.2.4.4 Democratisation and exclusion

With its open and decentralised structure, Internet-based communication has many characteristics that make it a very democratic tool. Even if many countries in the world try to censor access to parts of the Internet and their secret services gladly harvest the information that people are providing on the net, the Internet gives individuals the possibility to become newsmakers. This is a phenomenon that has become more and more important in modern conflicts (also of military nature). It has become more difficult to silence undesired perspectives, which has both positive and negative implications. Social networks have been used to organise resistance against undemocratic governments (Eltantawy & Wiest, 2011), such as in the case of the Arabian Spring.

On the other hand, it must not be forgotten that news is also *made* on the Internet; search engines define what is presented, and Internet access becomes a key feature for societal participation, excluding groups of people on both the local and the global levels. People who are not able or trained to use computers, who do not have the resources to buy the equipment, or who are not able to update on the latest development are at risk of being left behind.

6.2.5 Books

Unlike newspapers or magazines, books are non-periodical forms of print media (even if they are published as e-books, they still carry most features of a printed publication). They can come in many forms and are fictional and non-fictional. A classical book has a very long production cycle, often several years (the author of this book knows what he is talking about), but offers, on the other hand, much more space to analyse a topic than other print media offer. Usually books are published by a publisher and paid for by the reader, but exceptions exist. Self-published books or books-on-demand are breaking with some of these assumptions.

For environmental communication, books are a special case because they require that the reader purchases or loans them and invests considerable effort to read them. Fact books, on the one hand, can provide the reader with a detailed background and arguments can be profoundly presented. Fictional books, on the other hand, similar to other forms of fictional work, might provide the reader with the emotional component that seems necessary to engage with an environmental topic (Weber, 2006) by telling a personal story. The potential of communication channels such as this is understated.

6.2.6 Movies

Like books, movies can come in various forms, such as documentaries, pseudo-documentaries that contain a fictional component, or fictional movies. They have the benefit of allowing more time to make a point; however, this time is limited to a small number of hours. Movies are clearly the work of individuals such as the author or director. Since movies are shorter than books, the personal investment for the consumer is smaller and, for many, the visual language can be powerful. There are many examples of both documentary-style movies and fictional films that have an environmental topic. Al Gore's "The Inconvenient Truth" and Jeff Orlowski's "Chasing Ice" are examples of documentary-style movies, whereas Roland Emmerich's "The Day After Tomorrow" is an example of a fictional film. In Chapter 11, research on the effects of such movies will be presented.

6.2.7 Theatre, music, visual art, and other art

Communication channels for environmental messages can be different forms of artistic languages, such as theatre, music, or visual arts like paintings or video art. These channels are largely ignored by the scientific community. Even though many lively environment-related artist groups exist around the world (see Chapter 11 for some examples), the potential of their work for communication is not well understood. Usually, such events or works appeal to a small group of people, and if presented in a fine-art context like a gallery or theatre, this group of people can consist of the already convinced. However, even the convinced might need encouragement to actually act for the environment. If such art-based communication dares to leave the fine-art context, it may appeal to other groups of people and might affect them in ways, especially on the emotional level, that other communication channels have problems achieving. Chapter 11 is devoted to an analysis of such unconventional communication attempts and their potential.

6.3 Environmental communication as risk communication

Many environmental communication problems can be understood as a special case of risk communication. What such communication attempts try to achieve is that people change their perception of an environmental risk and start changing their behaviour to mitigate this risk or its consequences for the individual. This makes it necessary to understand how people perceive risks of different kinds and how they decide to take action when faced with a potential hazard. We will look at how risk communication can be designed to change people's risk perceptions. It is important to note that risk communication can have two fundamentally different aims: (1) increasing the perceived risk in a population, which is common for health or environmental risks that the public often underestimates, or (2) decreasing the perceived risk, which is often the aim with technology-related risks and is mainly driven by companies interested in introducing a new technology.

However, before the topic of risk perception and risk communication is analysed in more detail, we discuss how "risk" is understood in psychology. In her book about the psychology of risk, Breakwell (2007) defines risk as "the probability of a particular adverse event occurring during a stated period of time" (page 2). Risk is therefore more than the hazard it is connected to, containing two defining elements: probability and effects. Probability means that within a certain time frame the adverse event is expected to happen with a certain likelihood. This likelihood can be calculated based on previous experience or estimated based on expert knowledge. The effect dimension of risk refers to the severity: how many people are affected, how severe are the consequences for their lives, health, or property, and so on. This means that the risk of a certain negative event happening and its consequences can usually be quantified. How risk is perceived by the public, on the other hand, does not necessarily relate to this number. People tend to overestimate some types of risks and underestimate others. The next sections will analyse common patterns behind such biases.

6.3.1 Risk perception theories

The two most recognised theories of risk perception are the psychometric paradigm and the cultural theory. The psychometric paradigm was first proposed by a research group including Fischhoff, Slovic, and Lichtenstein (Fischhoff et al., 1978; Slovic et al., 1986; Slovic, 1987). It builds on psychological research methods and aims to identify dimensions connected to a risk that predict perception of this risk. The cultural theory of risk perception, on the other hand, emphasises the cultural dependency of perceived risk (Douglas & Wildavsky, 1982; Sjöberg, 1996; Thompson et al., 1990; Wildavsky & Dake, 1990).

6.3.1.1 The psychometric paradigm

A classical study of the psychometric paradigm used a personality psychology methodology to map the risk that a sample of the public connected to a list of 30 activities and technologies (Fischhoff et al., 1978). The list included examples such as consuming alcoholic beverages, electric power, aviation, nuclear power, motor vehicles, and skiing. For each of these activities or technologies, the participants rated perceived global benefit of the activity, perceived global risk in relation to other activities, and acceptability of the risk. Furthermore, the participants rated the risk connected to each activity on the following dimensions: (1) if the activity is voluntary, (2) immediacy of the effects, (3) knowledge about the risk: the risk is known to the person taking the risk, (4) knowledge about the risk: the risk is known to science, (5) control over the risk, (6) newness, (7) chronic versus catastrophic effects, (8) the risk is commonly known versus dread, and (9) severity of consequences. The authors aggregated and factor-analysed the perceived characteristics for each activity across participants. They found that the characteristics could be reduced to two factors: one that is referred to as dreadfulness and one that is referred to as voluntariness and familiarity.

Furthermore, the authors found that the acceptability of a risk and the perceived risk of an activity can be predicted by the two factors to a large degree (Fischhoff et al., 1978). The more delayed the effects of a hazard are, the less known the risk is to the exposed or to science; the newer, the less voluntary, the more catastrophic, and the more dreadful the effects are, the higher the risk perception and the lower the acceptability are. The more certain fatality is, the higher the risk perception and the lower the acceptability are. It is important to note that the probability of the event is not included in this evaluation, which means that the likelihood of the hazard is not necessarily relevant for the evaluation of its risk. People seem to fear risks that are new to them, have the potential to affect many people at the same time, and are not controllable or are involuntary, whereas the risks connected to voluntary and familiar activities are perceived lower. Additional dimensions of risk characteristics have been discussed in later research. For example, Sjöberg (2000, 2003) argues that "tempering with nature" should be a third dimension. It captures to which degree people perceive a technology or activity to be interfering with the natural way of how things should be. Technologies like gene manipulation or nuclear power score high on this dimension and the risk is perceived to be higher.

The psychometric paradigm has also been applied to understand people's perception of risk connected to environmental pollution. McDaniels et al. (1996) used a psychometric approach to map lays' risk perception of 65 ecological risks (e.g. biodiversity loss, climate change, deforestation, ozone layer depletion) and behaviours that cause them (e.g. refrigeration, hunting, travelling, high consumption) and asked them to rate each on 31 scales describing characteristics of the risk or activity. In a factor analysis of the characteristics, they found five factors underlying ecological risk perception: (1) impact on other species, (2) human benefits, (3) impact on humans, (4) avoidability, and (5) knowledge. The higher the perceived impact on other species and humans, the higher the perceived risk. The stronger the perceived human benefit, the lower the perceived risk. Avoidability was not related to risk perception, but knowledge had a positive impact on risk perception for ecological risks, unlike in the original psychometric paradigm. The more is known about a risk, the *higher* is the risk perception. This factor structure shows that people tend to downgrade ecological risks that are connected to a behaviour that has strong benefits for humans and where the adverse effects for humans and other species are uncertain. What makes this effect even stronger is that the results by McDaniels et al. (1996) show that people tend to have different risk perceptions connected to the ecological outcomes (e.g. ozone layer depletion and climate change) and their causes (e.g. aerosol can use and use of fossil fuels). People seem to dissociate their own behaviours which carry a strong benefit from the ecological outcome, but accept strong effects on other species or the environment.

6.3.1.2 Cultural theory

The main assumption of the cultural theory of risk perception is that the perception of risks is socially constructed and not the result of individual perceptions of risk characteristics. Wildavsky (1993) argues that the prevalent patterns of risk perception in a group of people can be explained by culture, namely that people choose things to fear based on their importance for their way of life (Douglas, 1986; Douglas &

Wildavsky, 1982). The hazards that people fear most are the ones that threaten a group's social and institutional arrangements.

Cultural theory furthermore assumes that there are standard types of cultural biases to risk perception that can be reduced to two underlying dimensions: group and grid (Thompson et al., 1990). The "group" dimension refers to the degree a person is a part of a group with clear boundaries, whereas the "grid" dimension refers to the degree his or her interactions with other people are rule-bound or negotiated. The four possible combinations of the extremes of the two dimensions result in four bias types: (1) hierarchists (high grid, high group), (2) sectarians or egalitarians (low grid, high group), (3) fatalists (high grid, low group), and (4) individualists (low grid, low group).

Hierarchists are characterised as people who are strongly associated members of well-defined groups and comply with strongly hierarchic communication structures. Members of such a culture would be expected to be generally positive to risk factors as technologies, given that experts have approved them. Individualists who are not devoted members of social groups and have a non-hierarchical communication structure should also be positive to technology because they see risks as an opportunity (Breakwell, 2007). Fatalists will not seek risks, but accept them if they are told to, because they have a hierarchic communication structure. Egalitarians finally will be critical towards technology-related risks.

Rippl (2002) related the resulting dimensions to what she refers to as "myths of nature". The results show that hierarchists tend to believe that nature's equilibrium is rather stable and that most human-made events will not disturb it. Opposed to that, egalitarians believe that even small changes can offset nature's equilibrium and have big effects. Fatalists hold the strong belief that nature behaves randomly and humans have no way of controlling it. Individualists had no strong nature-related beliefs, apart from a weak denial of a random nature.

6.3.2 Protection motivation theory

In the previous sections, we analysed aspects that impact human risk perception. However, to perceive an environmental risk as important is not enough to make people change their behaviour. Protection motivation theory (R. W. Rogers, 1975) assumes that both the perception of a threat and the perception of a viable solution to reduce the threat are necessary for people to be motivated to protect themselves from that threat. Figure 6.1 shows an adapted version of the theory (Floyd et al., 2000).

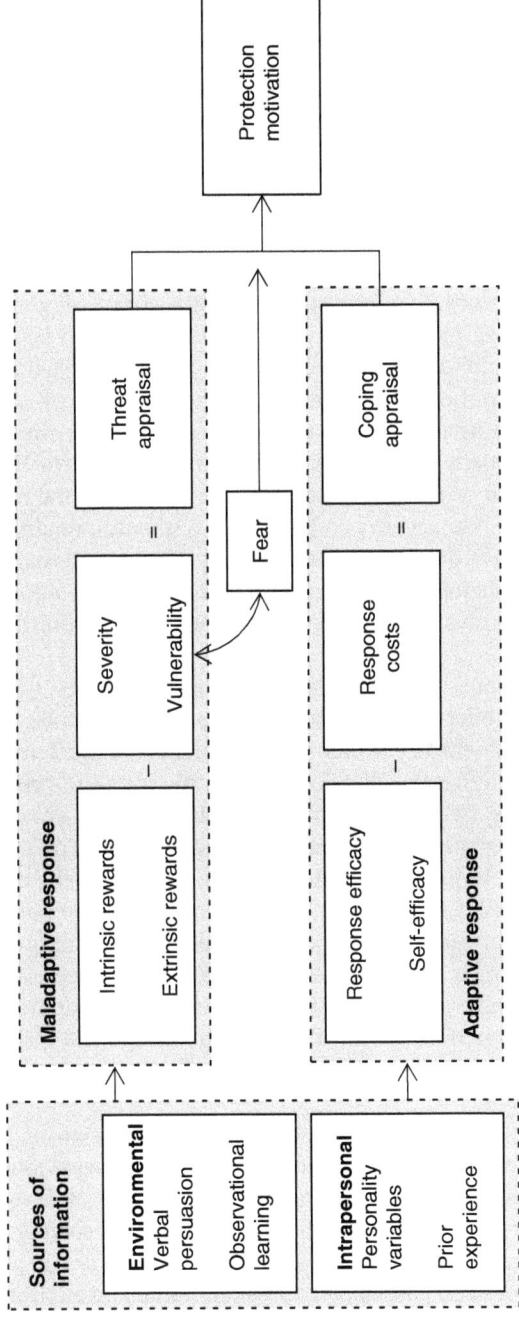

Figure 6.1 The protection motivation theory adapted from Floyd et al. (2000, page 410). Used by permission of John Wiley and Sons

The main assumption in the protection motivation theory is that a motivation to take precautions is dependent on two factors: threat appraisal and coping appraisal. The threat appraisal is the sum of the rewards of a behaviour (either internally or externally) minus the product of perceived severity of negative consequences times perceived vulnerability. To use an example from the environmental domain, driving the car might be connected to a number of internal and external rewards (e.g. comfort and joy while driving, low perceived costs). All those benefits support performance of the behaviour. On the other hand, car use has negative impacts (e.g. health effects, environmental effects). Depending on how severe they are perceived to be and how vulnerable the individual perceives himself or herself or nature to be, the rewards may not outweigh the threat. Then the balance of rewards and threat would become negative which results in a threat appraisal that would potentially trigger a protection motivation. If the balance of rewards and threat is positive, maladaptive responses are the result (e.g. justifying car use). The severity–vulnerability evaluation might also trigger fear, irrespective of the counterbalancing effect of internal rewards. If such a fear-inducing effect occurs, this fear might have a direct effect on protection motivation that resists to some extent the impact of rewards.

The coping appraisal is the evaluation of response efficacy, which is an estimation of the effectiveness of the behavioural alternatives to reduce the threat, and self-efficacy, which is an estimation of one's own ability to perform the alternative behaviour, minus the response costs. In the example of car use, switching to bus use may be perceived as an effective measure to reduce the negative environmental effects. The individual may also perceive himself or herself to be able to perform the behaviour (to use the bus instead of the car), but the costs might be perceived as too high (e.g. monetary costs, effort, and time). If the coping appraisal is positive, meaning if an individual perceives that there are viable alternatives that actually make a difference to the problem and he or she has the ability to perform them, then adaptive responses will become more likely, addressing the problem and not only the negative emotions connected to them.

Homburg and Stolberg (2006) used an adapted version of the protection motivation theory to predict environmental behaviour in the different domains of social engagement, private sphere, and workplace. They found that problem-focused coping like problem solving, expression of emotions, and self-protection acted as a mediator between an abstract feeling of stress caused by a threat appraisal and environmental behaviour. Problem-focused coping is also influenced by collective efficacy which captures the belief that people together are able to make a change against environmental problems.

6.3.3 The role of uncertainty

An essential feature of risk perception and risk communication is that there is uncertainty connected to the occurrence of the negative event. If it was certain when, where, how, and with which effects on whom a negative event would take place, it would no longer be a question of risk. B. B. Johnson and Slovic (1995) studied systematically how different levels of uncertainty affected people's risk perception of health risks and their trust in the information. They found that laypeople were not used to being presented with uncertainty in science. A graphical display of the range of uncertainty increased people's understanding of the uncertainty connected to the estimates, but reduced the trustworthiness of the message for some people. Communication of uncertainty signals honesty to the receivers of the message, but some people also take it as an indication of incompetence.

In another study, B. B. Johnson and Slovic (1998) found that communicated disagreement among scientists about a health risk led to different interpretations by the public. Whereas most people decided to be precautious, choosing to assume there is a negative health effect rather than no health risk, some people also sided with the scientists who did not believe in the threat, a behaviour that reminds a lot about the climate change debate.

Frewer (2004) argues that uncertainty should be differentiated into outcome uncertainty, which is connected to what and with which probability something will happen, and assessment uncertainty, which is connected to accuracy of the estimates. Avoiding the communication of existing uncertainties undermines research findings about the effect of communicating uncertainty towards laypeople which seems to point in the opposite direction: avoiding existing communicating uncertainties undermines the trustworthiness of institutions.

K. M. Kuhn (2000) found an interesting interaction between communication of uncertainty about an environmental problem and the relationship between environmental concern and environmental risk perception. Whereas people with high environmental concern reported high risk perception and people with low environmental concern reported low risk perception if no uncertainty was communicated, both risk perceptions were approaching medium values when uncertainty was communicated.

Patt and Schrag (2003) analysed the effect of using probabilistic language, which is a strategy that the Intergovernmental Panel on Climate Change (IPCC) adopts. Instead of quantifying the likelihood in percentages (e.g. "this is 1–10% likely to happen"), a description of this likelihood is provided in words (in this case "it is very unlikely to happen"). However, the authors show that the understanding of the terms chosen by the IPCC does not match people's interpretation (Patt & Schrag, 2003).

The topic of how to communicate uncertainty is very relevant for environmental communication. Since we have to deal with uncertainty when it comes to environmental problems, we need to plan how to include this uncertainty in environmental messages. Not doing so might impair our trustworthiness, and doing so may lead to people neglecting the problem or doubting our competence. There is no easy solution to this problem; maybe uncertainty should only be communicated to people with low to medium concern.

6.3.4 The effect of contradictory messages

One aspect of environmental risk communication via media is they usually try to contrast what they perceive as opinions, partly because they feel they need to be neutral and partly because they create debate to attract the audience's attention. This makes it likely that media will present several contradictory messages when they report about an environmental problem. Sadler et al. (2004) studied the impact of contradictory messages. They confronted American high-school students with two (fictional) contradictory articles about climate change, both supposedly written by scientists. One article proposed that climate change is the result of human activity and the other proposed that human-made climate change is a myth. They found about 80% of the students were able to identify the data presented in both articles and so have a concept of the empirical nature of science. Most students were furthermore able to identify social influences (e.g. economic interests, religion) on science which expresses itself in the selection of presented results. When asked why scientists could come to such diverging positions based on empirical science, the students identified as probable causes data concerns (other data used, other analysis methods used), different beliefs or opinions of the scientists that impacted their research, and different foci of the research (e.g. more solution oriented vs. basic science oriented). The students were required to explain which of the articles they considered to have more scientific merit. Some students assigned equal merit to both articles, while others judged the articles based on the personal relevance the article had for them, perceived information quality, and previous personal beliefs they had about climate change. Interestingly, 40% of the students did not choose the article that they assigned the higher scientific merits as most convincing. The findings show that contradictory messages about an environmental problem seem to lead to confirming people's positions that they already have. Also in the health sector, it has been shown that contradictory messages are processed with respect to already existing beliefs (Ahn et al., 2011).

Another effect of contradictory messages, more precisely counter-arguments, has been described by inoculation theory (McGuire, 1964). Confronting people with a light version of possible counter-arguments against their attitudes and beliefs makes them more immune against similar but stronger arguments later (see Section 3.3.4.3).

6.3.5 The social amplification of risk theory

It has already been discussed in previous sections how several social processes impact the perception of risk. The social amplification of risk theory (SARF) describes a comprehensive framework of such processes (Kasperson et al., 1988; Kasperson et al., 2003). Figure 6.2 summarises the theory.

The SARF is an attempt to unify the fragmented findings and theories about risk perception in one comprehensive framework. The core of the theory is the processes which lead to either amplification of risk, which means risk is perceived higher by laypeople, or attenuation, the effect that the public underrates a risk compared to the expert judgement.

The SARF identifies five main factors contributing to amplification or attenuation of risk: sources of information, information channels, social stations (which can be translated as social agents), individual stations (which can be understood as intrapersonal processes), and institutional and social behaviour. These processes are not meant to be linear, but dynamically feeding back on each other and iterating back and forth.

Starting at the left-hand side of the figure, a risk is discovered or a risk event happens. How this risk is perceived, how it is given a meaning, depends on aspects within each of the five factors. Either the risk is experienced personally or it is directly or indirectly communicated to other people. The information channels can be personal senses if the risk is experienced personally, informal social networks like friends and family, or professional information-brokers like the media or government agencies. Several social actors with their own agendas are involved in

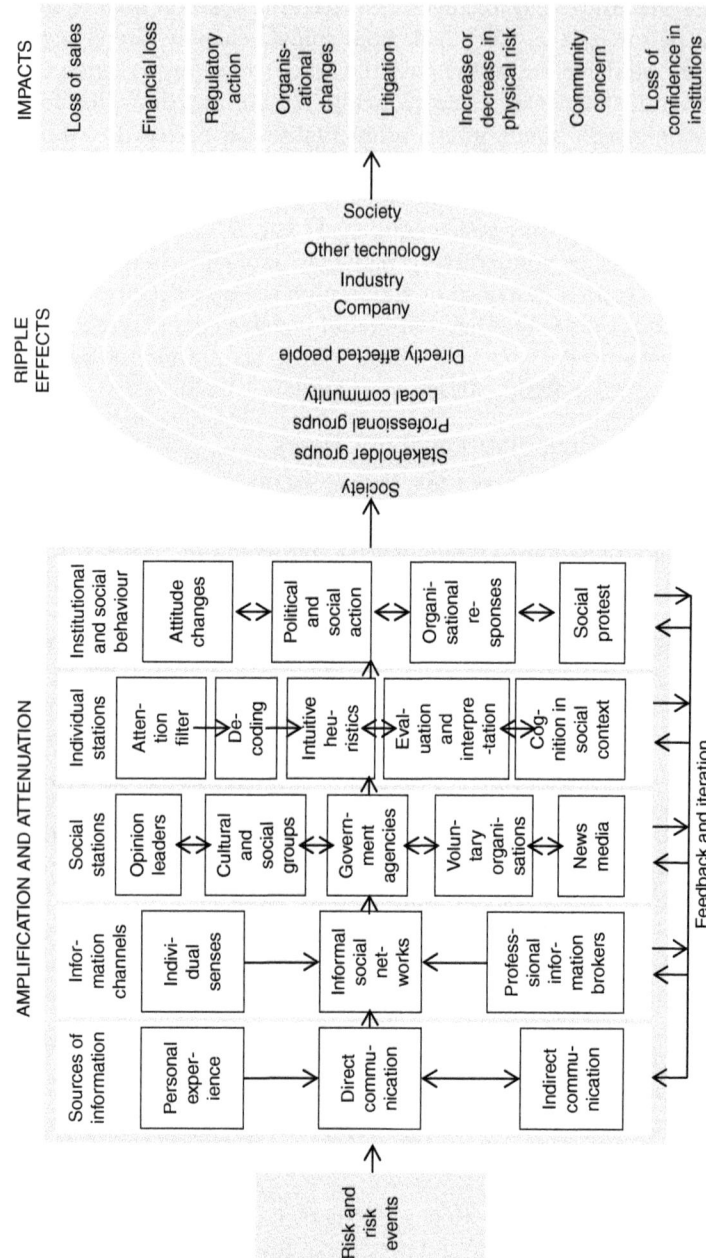

Figure 6.2 The social amplification of risk framework (J. X. Kasperson et al., 2003, page 14). Used by permission of Cambridge University Press

the process of defining the meaning of a risk factor: for example, social groups, opinion leaders, government agencies, NGOs, media. They all may contribute to amplification or attenuation of the risk. Many of the processes in the first three sections can be compared to what has been described in the diffusion of innovation theory (E. M. Rogers, 2003) in Section 5.2. Within the individual, attention and memory-related processes have an impact, but also heuristics and other cognitive functions like decision-making and social cognitions (see Chapters 3 and 4). The last dimension which contributes to amplification or attenuation of risk is what other people, officials, or organisations do in response to the risk.

These processes cause a spreading of the social definition of a risk beyond the people who are directly affected. This is referred to as the ripple effect. The inner layer is formed by the directly affected people, followed in the next layer by the local community, for example, a company involved with the risk. In the next layer are other professional groups, for example, industry representatives who have an interest in the topic. Stakeholder groups form the next layer, for example, producers of other types of technology who might be affected by general scepticism against technology. The outer layer is society as a whole. On the impact level, a whole variety of effects can occur, ranging from loss of sales or financial loss over changes in organisations and regulations, litigation, increased or decreased risks, concern, or loss of confidence in institutions.

Poumadere et al. (2005) used the SARF to analyse why the general tendency of attenuating the risk of heatwaves in France changed to amplification after the summer heatwave from 2003. Before the heatwave, which caused about 15,000 deaths, the risk of heatwaves for French society was not perceived as high. Summer heat was perceived as a natural phenomenon and the victims of heat were perceived as vulnerable for other reasons. This was paired with a strong belief that serious health risks would be addressed by government officials. When the 2003 heatwave hit, officials were soon overwhelmed with rising death tolls and tried to downplay and hide the real number of those affected. However, the disaster was too severe to be neglected by government officials. This led to the opposite effect: the public changed from attenuating the risk to amplifying it because they started to mistrust the government.

6.3.6 Implications for environmental communication

The implications of risk perception and communication research on the design of environmental communication are important. First, the psychometric paradigm and its extensions tell a lot about which risk aspects contribute to higher or lower risk perception. Many environmental risks lack the key features that make people perceive a risk as high: the visible effects of environmental problems are often things humanity has a long experience with (e.g. flooding, storms, or droughts). Many behaviours that lead to environmental problems have strong short-term benefits for people, which reduce the perception of risk connected to them. Furthermore, risk-related behaviours and the risk of the outcomes are often detached, reducing especially the perceived risk of the behaviour. Second, cultural theory introduced the social construction of risk perception. What is perceived as a risk is the result of a social definition process, where people with more power usually have more to say. This aspect is also picked up again in the SARF, which summarises different aspects potentially contributing to denial of a risk or its amplification. Knowing about such processes helps the environmental communicator to utilise such factors and immunise environmental risk communication against attenuation attempts. Third, findings about communication of uncertainty and contradictory messages tell the environmental communicator to carefully find a balance in their communication strategy. Finally, protection motivation theory teaches that creating a feeling of threat is not enough to make people change behaviour, but that their ability for adaptive coping is crucial, including self-efficacy and response efficacy. Both aspects need to be addressed in an environmental communication strategy.

6.4 Strategies of effective environmental communication through media

In her book on risk communication, Breakwell (2007) cites results from a research report about factors that impact the way mass media report risks and hazards (Breakwell & Barnett, 2001). Based on interviews with 24 UK editors and journalists, they identified ten recurring themes that will be applied to environmental communication in the following sections.

6.4.1 "Scare stories" are important

Media in the western world focus on commercial success, which, to a large degree, even applies to state-owned media companies. Since scare stories are considered to sell well, media tend to promote them over less scary news. For risk communication, the best topics for scare stories are those that threaten to affect many people (especially the blameless, defenceless but valuable, e.g. children, pregnant women) and those that are not detectable with human senses until they strike, but have major, deadly consequences. It might thus seem attractive to present environmental threats in a way that fits the character of a scare story to get media attention. To a certain degree, this is a viable conclusion, but an environmental communicator should also have the side effects in mind. Creating a high threat appraisal in the public alone is not enough to make people change their behaviour. If they are not provided with opportunities for adaptive coping, they will rather choose maladaptive strategies. Since scare stories in media often go along with the search for a person to blame (often politicians or other officials), a "scare story strategy" for environmental communication might backfire because it triggers denial of responsibility.

6.4.2 The significance of "infotainment"

Media, including news media, conceptualise themselves as in the entertainment business. Their first aim is to entertain the audience, even in news coverage. This has implications for the way news is presented: the narrative is more like storytelling than presentation of scientific findings and the entertainment effect wears off quickly, so that even serious hazards and threats lose their ability to make it into the news if no new aspect can be found. For environmental communication strategies, this means that if a longer-lasting media campaign is planned, not all information should be presented at once. There needs to be a plan to keep the story alive over several days or weeks, for example, by providing media with a new angle on the topic, a new commentary, a personal story of someone affected, a personal story of someone who managed to cope with the threat in a good way, or something similar after some time. This can prevent media strengthening the entertaining dimension by creating controversy via the presentation of an opposing position (see also Section 6.4.10). It is also important to deal actively with the media's need for controversy. Environmental communication should not neglect counter-arguments, but rather actively work with them. The focus on infotainment also means that media input should be provided in a way that has the entertainment aspect in mind. Personal stories have the advantage of being more entertaining and more engaging than scientific reports, especially stories of people that were faced with the environmental problem and successfully managed to deal with it. Finally, it is also important to select contact people for media campaigns that can spontaneously present the environmental topic in an entertaining way. A stereotypical scientist without communication skills will not get media attention.

6.4.3 The media avoid "real science"

Since most journalists do not have a science background, they do not see themselves as scientists but as mediators between scientists and the public. Scientific reports with a high level of detail will not appeal to journalists who are looking for the "stripped down" version, the simple statement, the headline that summarises it all. This means that environmental communication with media should give a simple and short version of the message alongside the more detailed reports. Since media like original quotes in their journalistic pieces, who is able to give them and who is able to answer follow-up questions should be planned. An environmental communicator should be prepared to give a personal statement: "what do *you* think is most important about this topic?", "are *you* afraid?", "what do *you* do in *your* everyday life about this topic?" An environmental communicator should be able to present clear and simple recommendations adapted to the audience and not hide behind scientific language and uncertainties. This may require either media training for the environmental communicator or adding this particular competence to the team.

It also helps to know how media pieces are structured. Newspaper articles are typically structured according to the "inversed pyramid" (Pöttker, 2003). After the headline that communicates the main message and catches the reader's attention, the lead paragraph needs to answer the following questions concisely in about 30 words: who?, what?, when?, where?, why?, how? This paragraph might also include a "hook" which is a controversial statement, provocative quote, or question to keep the reader motivated to continue reading to the next paragraphs. The body contains the arguments, controversy, story, or issue, which the article is about in more detail providing evidence, background, details, quotes, photos, videos, and audio that support telling the story, dispute the main line of argument, or expand the topic. Often, additional boxes or shorter side articles extend the topic. In the last part of the article, referred to as the tail, less important extra content is provided. Structuring input to mass media in a way that suits their framework will help environmental communicators to attract the media's attention and reduce the problem of getting the message "lost in translation" between the formats.

6.4.4 The importance of individual journalists and editors

The interviewees in Breakwell and Barnett's study (2001) were very aware that the individual editor or journalist has a crucial role in selecting news. Each journalist has his or her own agenda and can be a campaigner. They furthermore said that the individual journalist's agenda is usually well known to the reader and the public due to his or her publication history. This means that the environmental communicator needs to know his or her contact person in the media. Messages should not be sent to "the media" but to very carefully selected people that are likely to pick up the topic and present it in a way that is in line with the environmental communicator's agenda.

6.4.5 The significance of interactions between media

Whereas the interviewees in Breakwell and Barnett's study (2001) recognised the value of a scoop (being the first to report about a topic), they also said that scoops that nobody follows up are not good either. Within that mechanism lies the potential for both amplification, if many other media pick up a story and more feel required to follow, and attenuation, if a report is not followed at all and potentially interested journalists refrain from following up because nobody else does. Therefore, environmental communicators should plan the spread of the news through the media landscape. It may be a good idea to give an exclusive story to a media channel that is known to lead stories that others may pick up on. This is not necessarily the channel with the biggest audience. It can furthermore be good to keep some exclusive information or angle on the topic for other key media that can at a later point in time get their "scoop". The effect of journalists knowing or believing that others are also reporting about the same topic should not be underestimated. For example, planning a press conference at a time, at a location, or with a host that likely attracts many journalists might be a good start.

6.4.6 The absence of investigative journalism and information hunger

Investigative journalism is in decline in most journalistic areas (Breakwell & Barnett, 2001). Modern-day journalists are more open to already prepared stories, with proactive environmental communicators attracting journalists' attention if they present their message in a format compatible with the journalists' needs. Reluctance to provide journalists with information will furthermore create a vacuum that the journalists fill from other sources which might be less accurate.

6.4.7 Length and timing of coverage

It has already been mentioned before that the amount of time a story will get in the media depends on a constant flow of new information. However, timing is also important. It will be difficult to get an environmental topic published on days where other big headline stories make top news, whereas in times of relative scarcity of other stories, the chances of being published are higher. Even the production cycles of the different media types (see Section 6.1) should be regarded in planning media communications, such as scheduling a press conference. For example, to attract the attention of print media, it is crucial that a press conference happens before the editorial meeting. If a news feature is meant to become part of the main television news, enough time for producing the piece and to collect quotes should be planned. It is also helpful to provide media with the possibility of obtaining quotes by several relevant people at the press conference.

6.4.8 Differences between elements of the media

Media are not uniform, and different types of media have different needs. For TV and radio, seconds matter. These media types depend on quick information, often at the cost of not being able to verify each aspect. If an environmental communicator underestimates the need for speed that these media types have, other actors may have already defined the interpretation of the risk before the environmental communicator has prepared their point. Furthermore, TV and radio, but also new media, require pictures and audio. An environmental campaign should plan to provide the media with the material they want them to use, before someone else selects the content for them.

6.4.9 The role of pressure groups

Media are affected by pressure groups, because they are dependent on audience, advertisement, and the goodwill of organisations to cooperate later for other topics. This means that an environmental communicator's agenda will be balanced with the needs of other important pressure groups. Media will measure how publishing a story can trigger audience reactions, impair sale of adverts, or displease valuable partners providing news input. This again underlines the importance to select media channels wisely. In one newspaper, it might be en vogue to create an environmental story that fits the profile of the publication, and it also pleases the pressure groups affecting this paper. In another newspaper, it might be professional suicide by the journalist to propose such a story. Publishing in the first newspaper might be easy; however, the target audience may consist of the already convinced.

6.4.10 Uncertainty and controversy

The interviewees in Breakwell and Barnett's study (2001) reported that uncertainty in itself is not problematic for media to handle, but it is also not newsworthy. With respect to risks, media follow the line that it is better to report about a potential risk even if it might turn out to be less risky than to wait until uncertainty is reduced. For environmental communication, this means that it is reasonable to communicate uncertainty (see Section 6.3.3), but in a way that people can comprehend. Furthermore, communicators can report how uncertainty has developed over time (e.g. the increasing certainty that climate change is human made) and what has been done to reduce uncertainty. Uncertainty can also lead to controversy, which then becomes eminently newsworthy. This effect explains at least partly why climate change critics receive much more media coverage than their number in the scientific community would justify.

6.5 Conclusions

This chapter started with an analysis of different media types and their specific features, before presenting theoretical backgrounds of risk perception and risk communication that can be applied to environmental communication. The protection motivation theory and the SARF are comprehensive theories that describe how people form risk perceptions, including environmental risks. Furthermore, it describes how motivations to act are formed and how risks are socially constructed or amplified or attenuated. Since media have a central place in this process of creating and defining risk and are an important tool in communicating risks, the last section of this chapter applied insights gathered from interviews with media actors on the design of media campaigns in environmental communication.

From this chapter, the conclusions for environmental communication through media are as follows:

- Media channels are very different in their structure, audience, and needs. The most promising channels need to be carefully selected and a successful environmental media campaign needs to be tailored to them.
- New media and social media offer new possibilities that cannot be fully utilised without changing from traditional to new media campaign styles, giving the audience a more active role.
- Analysing the characteristics of an environmental risk helps predict how important people will perceive this risk. Assuming that for most environmental risks the aim is to increase risk perception, characteristics that are known for their relationship to high risk perception should be highlighted.

- People tend to dissociate the risk perceived to their own behaviour from the risk of global environmental problems. Re-linking personal behaviour to the problem should be part of the focus of the campaign, and concrete behavioural advice should be given.
- An environmental risk communicator should be aware that risk perception is socially constructed and risks affecting valued people or things are perceived more important. Furthermore, central actors who claim the power to define the risk should be identified and addressed.
- Increasing people's perception of a threat is not enough to motivate them to change their behaviour. It is necessary to provide them with effective and manageable options for coping behaviour, otherwise maladaptive coping can occur.
- Complex social processes can both amplify and attenuate perception of a risk. Being aware of and monitoring them is crucial to avoid attenuation.
- Uncertainty should be communicated to be trustworthy, but it should be communicated in a way that people can understand. The development over time, the type of uncertainty, and the measures taken to decrease uncertainty need to be communicated.
- Media will pick up on controversy. Environmental communicators should anticipate potential counter-arguments and try to immunise their communication proactively.
- Media campaigns need to be well timed and tailored to specific journalists, who should be selected carefully.
- The message needs to be presented in a way that fits media structures. The need for infotainment should be acknowledged, and people with media experience should develop the communication.
- The need for personal stories should be understood and such stories should be proactively provided, with personal quotes offered.
- For media campaigns that run over longer times, careful planning of with whom to communicate and when to present new pieces of information to whom are necessary.

Review questions

- What are the characteristics of different types of media channels and how can they be utilised for environmental communication?
- What are the assumptions of the psychometric paradigm of risk perception and what are the implications for environmental risks?

- What does cultural theory assume about risk perception? How is cultural theory related to environmental beliefs?
- What are the predictions of protection motivation theory and how are they relevant for environmental communication?
- How does the communication of uncertainty of scientific findings affect people's perception of risks and the risk communicator?
- Which effect does contradictory messages have on the perception of environmental problems?
- What does the SARF tell about environmental risk communication?
- How should environmental media campaigns be designed based on the findings presented in this chapter?

Suggested readings

Breakwell, G. M. (2007). *The psychology of risk*. Cambridge: Cambridge University Press.

Kasperson, J. X., Kasperson, R. E., Pidgeon, N., & Slovic, P. (2003). The social amplification of risk: Assessing fifteen years of research and theory. In N. Pigeon, R. E. Kasperson & P. Slovic (Eds.), *The Social Amplification of Risk* (pp. 13–46). Cambridge: Cambridge University Press.

McDaniels, T., Axelrod, L. J., & Slovic, P. (1996). Perceived ecological risks of global change: A psychometric comparison of causes and consequences. *Global Environmental Change*, 6(2), 159–171.

Thompson, M., Ellis, R., & Wildavsky, A. (1990). *Cultural theory*. Westview Press.

Floyd, D. L., Prentice-Dunn, S., & Rogers, R. W. (2000). A meta-analysis of research on protection motivation theory. *Journal of Applied Social Psychology*, 30(2), 407–429.

7
Target Group Segmentation – Why Knowing Your Audience Is Important

Chapter summary

This chapter argues for the benefits of segmenting the target group in an environmental communication campaign. Based on findings and practices in marketing, different segmentation approaches are introduced and discussed, such as demographic segmentation, geographic segmentation, behavioural segmentation, and psychometric segmentation. Since the focus of this book is primarily psychological, the last approach is discussed in more depth. Different ways to segment based on psychological criteria are presented, such as value-based segmentation, personality-based segmentation, and lifestyle-based segmentation. Finally, a stage model of behaviour change is introduced as a novel tool for target group segmentation. In the last section of the chapter, the possibilities of new information technology for targeted communication with consumer segments are critically discussed.

7.1 Introduction

Psychological intervention strategies and public communication strategies are often unspecific and target the population as a homogeneous group. It is questionable whether such an approach is cost effective and psychologically advisable. Behavioural change is seldom a linear process where improvement in a few predicting variables will directly lead to changes, but rather is a dynamic process with different predictors for different groups of people, or even the same people at different points in time. Designing "one-size-fits-all" communication has the disadvantage that many people receive communication that they are not interested in and that are not suited to their needs at that point in time. In the worst case, this will contribute to a response towards the message and communicator that can negatively impact the reaction to additional messages. It is good practice for environmental communicators to analyse experience with market segmentation from marketing research. Market segments can help identify groups in the population where environmental communication will have the largest effect. In recent years, the search for possibilities to identify the pro-environmental consumer segment has intensified (Ukenna, Nkamnebe, Nwaizugbo, Moguluwa, & Olise, 2012).

Moscardo, Pearce, and Morrison (2001) describe a typology of segmentation approaches and group them into a priori and a posteriori approaches, depending on whether available registry data is used or personal data needs to be collected to conduct the segmentation. Examples of *a priori* approaches are geographical segmentation and demographic segmentation; behavioural or psychometric segmentation are examples of *a posteriori* approaches. Often geographical and demographical approaches are combined (Wedel & Kamakura, 2000), and behavioural and psychometrical approaches overlap to some degree; for example, lifestyle research is rooted in both behavioural and psychometrical methods. The latter two are also especially relevant for the context of this book. Differentiating people according to their actual behaviour can help identify who has the potential for improvement. Taking in the psychometric segmentation (based on, e.g., values, attitudes, or personality) helps to identify people that are most receptive to the message and/or to design a message fitting the target group.

The self-regulation model of behavioural change (Bamberg, 2013a, 2013b) presented in Section 4.9.2 segments target groups according to their stage of behavioural change, which can have implications for the communication interventions assigned to them. The potential of new technologies, such as interactive Internet-based systems, for tailoring interventions based on real-time-identified market segments will be discussed.

7.2 Demographic segmentation approaches

Demographic approaches use information, such as gender, age, income, level of education, disabilities, and mobility, to classify target groups into more homogenous segments (Ukenna et al., 2012). The advantage of such an approach is that the data is usually easily accessible. The demographic variables are not treated as explanatory in themselves but as proxies for other unobservable variables that can predict behaviour (Mowen & Minor, 1997).

Demographic segmentation has become popular due to the relative simplicity of the approach. In a highly recognised review paper, Diamantopoulos, Schlegelmilch, Sinkovics, and Bohlen (2003) analysed 133 publications with data from 1966 to 1995, linking demographic variables to environmental knowledge, attitudes, or behaviour. The paper found that gender is strongly linked to environmental knowledge (males having higher knowledge than females), and attitudes and behaviour (females having stronger pro-environmental attitudes and engage more in pro-environmental behaviour). The effects of marital status were found to be contradictory or insignificant. Diamantopoulos et al. (2003) found that age seems to have no bearing on environmental knowledge, but is negatively related to pro-environmental attitudes. The findings are contradictory with respect to behaviour, which the authors attribute to the fact that younger people are actually more *willing* to show pro-environmental behaviour, but older people have more resources to do so. The number of children in the household seemed to be positively related to knowledge, attitudes, and behaviour. The higher the education level and the social class a person belongs to, the more knowledgeable about environmental topics, the more concerned about environmental problems, and the more engaged in pro-environmental behaviour the person is. More recently, D'Souza, Taghian, Lamb, and Peretiatko (2007) used a demographic segmentation approach to identify subgroups in the Australian population that were different in their use of eco-labels. They found that the dissatisfaction with eco-labels was high in the group of elderly people, whereas satisfaction was high in the young group.

Ukenna et al. (2012) argue that a demographic technique is a good starting point for market segmentation, although it appears that demographic information alone is not enough to identify the "green consumer" reliably. Also Diamantopoulos et al. (2003) argue that demographic approaches need to be supplemented with psychometrical approaches to give a richer picture of consumer segments, which cannot be achieved based purely on demographics.

7.3 Geographic segmentation approaches

The geographic segmentation approach groups the population according to where people reside (Mowen & Minor, 1997). The level of analysis can be countries, regions, cities, neighbourhoods, or any other geographical unit that can be meaningfully identified. Different climate zones can also be understood as geographical structuring. Geographical data is usually easily available, which makes this segmentation approach attractive if access to people is impossible or difficult. The underlying assumption is that people who live in close proximity have common experiences and demographical features and live in comparable structures, but also share, to a certain degree, psychological profiles (Mowen & Minor, 1997).

Often, the pure geographic segmentation approach is supplemented by collecting demographic data in the identified units of geographic segmentation. The result is referred to as geodemographic analysis (Mowen & Minor, 1997) and examples of resulting segmentations from product marketing are the commercial national CLARITAS PRIZM (United States), TAPESTRY (United States), CAMEO (global), ACORN (United Kingdom), or MOSAIC (United States) consumer segmentations.

It appears that in spite of its commercial success, a pure geographic or geodemographic approach to segmentation is not very popular in environmental marketing or research, as few examples could be found where such segmentation techniques have been used. However, Baiocchi, Minx, and Hubacek (2010) used a geodemographic approach to identify regions with different lifestyles in the United Kingdom and then estimated their CO_2 impact. In a similar approach, Collins and Fairchild (2007) used the ACORN segmentation of households in the Cardiff area to find regionally distributed estimates for food consumption.

7.4 Behavioural segmentation approaches

In the behavioural segmentation approach, information about people's purchase behaviour or product use is utilised to segment the target population. A common approach is to analyse what people spend their money or time on and then form clusters of people with similar patterns regarding behavioural dimensions (Ukenna et al., 2012). Also Schlegelmilch, Bohlen, and Diamantopoulos (1996) argue for a use of behavioural data to segment consumers, as they found a close relationship between environmental attitudes and knowledge, on the one hand, and different types of environmental behaviour, on the other.

Sinha and Uniyal (2005) identified six shopper types in an interesting segmentation purely based on observation of consumer behaviour in a variety of shops: (1) choice optimisers, (2) economisers, (3) premeditated shoppers, (4) recreational shoppers, (5) low-information seekers, and (6) support-seeking shoppers. Each type is characterised by specific themes. The choice optimisers are individualistic, are brand conscious, asked for information, were involved in the purchase, and looked for quality and variety. The economisers were looking for bargains or discounts and were conscious of their budget and the price of products. Premeditated shoppers bought large quantities (supposedly for a family), were in a hurry, often had a shopping list, and showed signs of having already made the product decisions before entering the shop. The recreational shoppers were looking for pleasant shopping environments and browsed through the products. They were expressive of their emotional reactions and impulsive in their shopping. Low-information seekers showed signs of being familiar with the shop whereas support seekers actively approached store personnel or consulted with accompanying persons or other shoppers. They showed signs of being uncomfortable in the shop. Often these customers were indecisive. Even though Sinha and Uniyal (2005) did not link their typology of consumers to certain types of purchased products, it can still be helpful to design a communication strategy aimed at pro-environmental purchases for different customer types. Whereas choice optimisers are an interesting target group because of their focus on quality and non-monetary product aspects, economisers would only consider buying a pro-environmental product if it is perceived as a bargain. Premeditated shoppers need to be approached before they enter the shop, while recreational shoppers might be tempted to impulsively buy a pro-environmental product in the store. Low-information seekers as well as premeditated shoppers can be assumed to have a rather high degree of shopping routines, whereas information seekers can be reached through providing (personal) information in the store.

7.5 Psychometrical segmentation approaches

The psychometrical segmentation groups people based on their profiles on psychological variables such as attitudes, values, and personality. The basic idea is that such psychological variables have been shown to determine behaviour. People with similar profiles should have similar behavioural patterns if they face the same situations. Ukenna et al. (2012) present a long, but not exclusive list of constructs that have been used to identify "green consumers" based on their psychological profiles: altruism, political orientation, individualism, collectivism, security orientation, and fun/engagement orientation have been linked to green consumerism, but also perceived consumer effectiveness which is the belief that a person can make a difference by his or her behaviour (Ellen, Wiener, & Cobb-Walgren, 1991).

In the following sections, prominent examples of psychometrical consumer segmentations are presented: value-based segmentations, personality-based segmentations, and lifestyle-based segmentations. They are not mutually exclusive and often overlap with segmentation approaches presented above. In the last subsection, the stage model of behaviour change (Bamberg, 2013a, 2013b) is applied as a segmentation tool based on psychological profiles.

7.5.1 Values

For a value-based segmentation approach, people are divided based on their basic value orientations. Figure 7.1 displays Schwartz's basic value dimensions (2006), which are typically arranged in a circle. More similar values are located next to each other while opposing value orientations can be found in distant segments of the circle. The seven basic values can be further reduced to two underlying dimensions (Schwartz, 1994): (a) self-enhancement versus self-transcendence and (b) openness to change versus conservation. The first dimension scores how much an individual puts oneself before others (self-enhancement) versus how much an individual values aspects transcending beyond oneself (e.g. other people, nature). On the self-enhancement end of the dimension

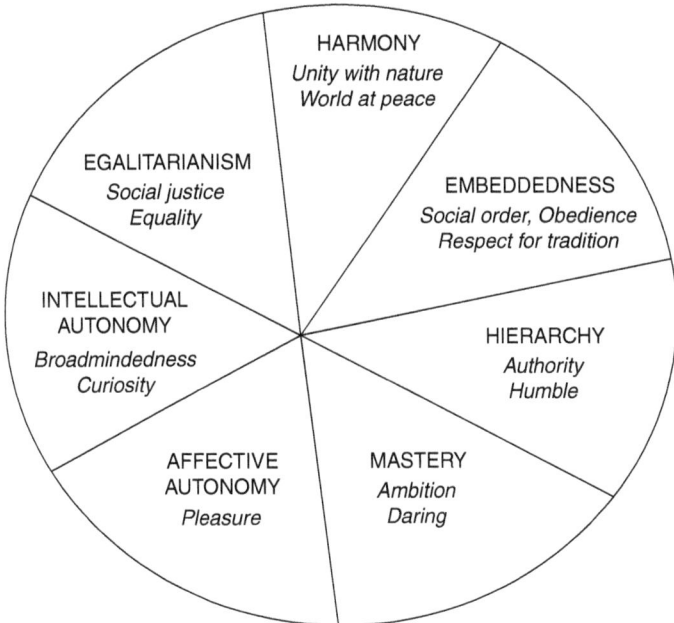

Figure 7.1 Prototypical structure of Schwartz' basic value orientations (Schwartz, 2006, page 142). Used by permission of Brill publishing

are mastery-related values. Harmony and egalitarianism mark the opposing self-transcendence end. The second dimension group values based on conservatism: how open to change would a person that embraces such values be? Intellectual and affective autonomy mark the openness to change end of this dimension, while embeddedness and hierarchy mark the conservatism end.

Inglehart's work (Inglehart & Welzel, 2005, 2010) is based on the world-value survey and groups value orientations in cultures along two dimensions: (a) tradition versus secular-rational and (b) survival versus self-expression. Traditionalist cultures value authority, nation, religion, family, and traditions, whereas secular-rationalist cultures value science and the individual. Survival cultures focus on economic and physical security aspects, whereas self-expression cultures focus on quality of life and individual well-being because the need for basic security is fulfilled. Sometimes, a one-dimensional version with materialism versus post-materialism is also used. Materialistic cultures are more traditional and more oriented towards survival, whereas post-materialistic cultures are rooted in secular-rationalist worldviews and self-expression values.

Another example of a value-based segmentation is the so-called Sinus milieus (Sinus-Sociovision, 2009). Based on value orientations, attitudes, lifestyle, and demographic data, ten distinct segments (milieus) of the German adult population were formed, namely the traditional milieu, the established conservative milieu, the precarious milieu, the new middle class milieu, the socio-ecological milieu, the liberal intellectual milieu, the escapist milieu, the adaptive pragmatist milieu, the high achiever milieu, and the movers and shakers milieu. These ten clusters can be further arranged in a two-dimensional space: social status and basic value orientation with three categories (traditional values, such as order and duty; modernisation including individualisation, self-fulfilment, and hedonism; reorientation including multiple options, experimenting and living with paradoxes).

The Sinus milieus have had a strong resonance in German research on environmental behaviour. For example, Gröger and Bruckner (2011) found that the different milieus have strongly different likelihoods of investing in renewable household heating. The high achievers preferred heating systems based on renewable energy carriers more than the established conservatives. In a market analysis of organic food, it was found that the market potential for organic food differs drastically between the milieus (Sinus-Sociovision, 2002). Whereas traditionalists are anti-organic, the milieus with high social status have a high potential. Interestingly, the reasons differ between the milieus: whereas conservatives value the traditional method of production, high achievers are more interested in the hedonistic aspects of organic food (e.g. better taste).

However, there are also other value-based segmentation approaches. A study about travel mode choice identified six clusters of car users (or non-users) based on a comprehensive collection of value, worldview, norm, and attitude measures (Anable, 2005). Whereas some clusters of car drivers were identified as very unlikely to change their behaviour ("car addicts" and "die-hard drivers"), other car drivers were classified as "malcontented motorists" or "aspiring environmentalists" who had a high potential for behaviour change. Both groups should be addressed in different ways. Furthermore, there were two groups of non-car users, one that is convinced to not use the car and one that is forced to live without a car. The study shows the potential of target marketing and environmental communication activities to the different segments. This helps to save resources by avoiding wasting them on groups which are highly unlikely to show an effect other than negative responses and to make interventions more effective by addressing specific needs of population segments.

Another study segmented students with respect to ecologically conscious consumer behaviour based on a combination of demographic and psychometric characteristics (Straughan & Roberts, 1999). They found that the psychometric characteristics were far more important than the demographic, especially perceived consumer effectiveness and altruism.

7.5.2 Personality

Segmenting the consumer population based on personality variables has been used in marketing research since the 1940s (Engel, Kollat, & Blackwell, 1969). Personality traits in psychology are defined as "more or less stable, internal factors that make one person's behaviour consistent from one time to another, and different from the behaviour other people would manifest in comparable situations" (Child, 1968, page 63). One of the most widely used personality trait categorisations is known as the "big five", a five-dimensional system of basic personality factors (P. T. Costa & McCrae, 2008). The five dimensions are neuroticism, extraversion, openness to experiences, agreeableness, and conscientiousness. Neuroticism is a tendency to experience negative emotions such as anger, anxiety, or depression. High neuroticism thus can be referred to as emotional instability. Extraversion is connected to sociability, high energy, positive emotions, or talkativeness. Openness to experiences is related to curiosity, adventure, and seeking variation. Agreeableness is the tendency to be cooperative, trusting, and helpful. Conscientiousness is a tendency to be organised, structured, dutiful, and self-disciplined.

In a number of studies, these personality variables have been related to environmental concern and behaviour. Higher agreeableness and openness to experiences relate to stronger environmental concern (Hirsh, 2010; Hirsh & Dolderman, 2007). Also neuroticism and conscientiousness showed a weak positive relationship (Hirsh, 2010). Markowitz, Goldberg, Ashton, and Lee (2012) found a relationship between openness to experiences and pro-environmental behaviour. Similar results were reported by Luchs and Mooradian (2012) who found significant impacts of agreeableness, openness to experience, and conscientiousness on the perceived importance of sustainability and a significant impact of agreeableness on sustainable consumer behaviour. The link between personality and pro-environmentalism is clear: especially openness to experience and agreeableness, but also conscientiousness, reappear across several studies as predictors of pro-environmental behaviour and its determinants. This can be applied in campaigns as a tool not only to identify the best targets, but also to tailor information in a way that suits the different personality types.

7.5.3 Lifestyles

The concept of lifestyles has become relevant to market segmentation research (Lazer, 1963). "Life style as used in life style segmentation research measures people's activities in terms of (1) how they spend their time; (2) their interests, what they place importance on in their immediate surroundings; (3) their opinions in terms of their view of themselves and the world around them; and (4) some basic characteristics such as their stage in life cycle, income, education and where they live" (Plummer, 1974, page 33). The basic components of the lifestyle concept cover demographic and geographic information, and also behavioural preferences and values, and world views. Often they are described in terms of activities, interests, and opinion (Plummer, 1974; Ukenna et al., 2012). The potential of the lifestyle concept is demonstrated by the next two examples.

Nie and Zepeda (2011) used a food-related lifestyle segmentation of US food shoppers to predict the purchase of organic and local food. The following variables were used in the lifestyle segmentation: ways of shopping (specialty shops used, farmers' market used, member of the community to support agriculture, recognition of organic food labels), importance of food quality aspects (freshness, taste, healthiness, safety, convenience, brand, cost, organic production), cooking methods (enjoying cooking, cooking often), and purchasing motivations (someone in the household keeps a diet because of an illness, fitness, vegetarianism, religion). With these 18 criteria, they identified four distinct consumer types: (1) rational consumers, (2) adventurous consumers, (3) careless consumers, and (4) conservative uninvolved consumers. Whereas the last two categories purchased organic or local food only to a small degree, the first two categories were much more interested in both types of food but for different reasons. The rational consumers were interested in taste and healthiness of food. The adventurous consumers were more often interested in food safety and more often had a religious motivation for their food choice.

In the domain of mobility behaviour, Lanzendorf (2002) developed a mobility-style categorisation. The resulting lifestyles were based on the scores of ten leisure-related dimensions (e.g. going out and friends, recreation in nature, high culture, sports, family, and children) and eight dimensions of mobility orientations (e.g. preference for bicycle, preference for bus/rail). The resulting mobility styles were FAMOS (family oriented who enjoy non-motorised travel, who enjoy the pleasure or exercise of walking and cycling and are not interested in going out), MULTIS (multiple activities and modes, who are in favour of many travel modes and have many leisure activities), CARCULTS (interested in high culture and highly favouring the car), STROLLERS (value family and travelling, strolling, and shopping), QUICKFITS (favour speed and low price in transportation, interested in fitness, going out, travelling, and family), DOMOS (interested in watching TV, favour public transportation), and SELFCULTS (prefer cycling to walking, and believe speed is important, cultural events are important, but less high culture). Obviously, the mobility styles not only explain the choice of travel modes to a high degree, but also link travel patterns to leisure preferences.

7.5.4 The stage models of behaviour change as segmentation tool

In Section 4.9.2, a stage model of behaviour change (Bamberg, 2007, 2012, 2013a, 2013b) was introduced. This stage model is also relevant for consumer segmentation because it provides a new angle on attempts to tailor environmental communication activities along the lines of consumer segments, namely by stage of change a person is in. As was presented in the earlier chapter, the model groups people into one of four distinct stages: predecisional, preactional, actional, and postactional. People in different stages of behaviour change benefit differently from different interventions. Interventions focusing on inducing negative emotions for the unwanted behaviour or positive emotions connected to the wanted change are especially successful for people in the first or predecisional stage. Interventions that make social norms or a possible mismatch between personal norms and one's own behaviour salient are also relevant for people in the first stage. Interventions focusing on attitudes and perceived behavioural control (see Chapter 4) match the needs for people in the preactional stage. In stage three, or the actional stage, people need support in planning and overcoming obstacles of implementation, whereas in the last stage, the postactional stage, support against fall-backs or relapse is the main issue. Recent research showed that when people are presented with a website that offers all types of such interventions at once, they try to self-tailor the information to their needs according to their stage of change (Prugsamatz et al., 2014a). Furthermore, a second study by the same authors shows that information-based interventions tailored to the stage of change people are in lead to more stage progression than providing all information at once and leaving the participants to self-tailor (Prugsamatz et al., 2014b).

Interestingly, Bamberg (2013b) also proposes a simple instrument to detect the stage of change a person is in with respect to the behaviour analysed (see Box 7.1). New technology that screens the consumer for the stage of change and then tailors the information accordingly is relatively easy to implement and much easier than, for example, personality or value measures.

Box 7.1 A measurement instrument to detect an individual's stage of change

Bamberg (2013b) introduced a measurement instrument to detect the stage of change people are in with respect to a given behaviour. The instrument is built on a description of the state of mind that goes along with having passed the relevant previous transition point (hence, having formed a specific type of intention), but not reaching the next. This instrument has been adapted and refined by Prugsamatz et al. (Prugsamatz et al., 2014a; Prugsamatz et al., 2014b). A prototypical version looks like this:

> Which of the following statements describes your current state best with regard to Behaviour X?
>
> a) I am happy with my current level of Behaviour X and have no intention of changing it. (predecisional stage)
> b) I would like to change my level of Behaviour X but see no way to do that at the moment. (predecisional stage)
> c) I have the goal of changing my level of Behaviour X but I have not decided yet how to achieve that. (preactional stage)
> d) I have already made concrete plans, how, when, and where to start with my change of Behaviour X, but I have not implemented it yet. (actional stage)
> e) I have already reduced/increased my level of Behaviour X. I intend to keep it on that level or even reduce/increase it further. (postactional stage)
>
> Statements (a) and (b) are both placed in the predecisional stage, although for different reasons. Whereas a person selecting statement (a) is not even thinking about changing the behaviour (and thus lacks, e.g. perceived negative consequences of the own behaviour or ascription of responsibility – see Section 4.9.2), a person selecting (b) favours a change, but feels completely incapable of implementing that change (and thus lacks perceived goal feasibility).
>
> It might be advisable to present the items in reversed order since statements (a) and (e) sometimes lead to confusion because people who have already changed their behaviour can select (a), because they might also be happy with the level of behaviour they have achieved and are not planning any further change.

7.6 New technology and targeted approaches

The previous sections have established how market segmentation might help to save resources or use limited resources. Furthermore, it has been argued that non-tailored interventions might even have negative effects. Recipients can be overloaded with information so they cannot identify the relevant information, or they might give negative responses if they receive a communication attempt that does not match their mindset. The benefits of new technologies like dynamic webpages, smartphones, or tablet PCs for tailored environmental communication are discussed in the next paragraphs.

Dynamic webpages offer the possibility to tailor the information that is presented to a user at a given point in time. This makes it easy to reduce the information load and to confront the users with only the pieces of information that they would need in the given situation. For example, in an electronic tourist guide, information can be tailored to the preferences of the reader (by extracting them from previous search activities) and the location a person is in (Cheverst, Davies, Mitchell, & Smith, 2000). Also web shops can be dynamically personalised to become simpler to use and tailored to the user's anticipated needs (Ardissono & Goy, 1999).[1] In combination with mobile devices including smartphones or tablet PCs, such dynamic technologies can get even closer to the point of decision where consumers select a product or behaviour. Such mobile devices usually have a GPS tracker that makes it possible to adjust information according to the geographic location, which makes a match to geographic segments easy. Furthermore, latest technological developments like "near-field communication", which is the short-distance wireless communication between a mobile unit like a smartphone and a stationary unit providing information, make tailoring communication within a small environment possible. Consumers can receive information very specific to their preferences regarding the products offered in a very specific section of a store (Wiedmann, Reeh, & Schumacher, 2009). Less technology-demanding solutions exist, such as quick response codes (QR codes) that can store large amounts of information in a visual pattern which become accessible when scanned with a mobile device.

All types of segmentation can be combined with dynamic information technology: geographic segmentation can be easily integrated with the GPS functionality of devices, and demographic segmentation can be linked to data that users of the mobile devices provide while using their device (e.g. in social networks). For behavioural segmentation approaches, the user behaviour of such a device leaves a trail which is often utilised to profile users and their preferences. The psychometric segmentation approach is dependent the most on user cooperation to provide the necessary input to link the segmentation to the user of a particular device.

However, especially with the recent renaissance of data protection issues, consumers may be suspicious of the far-reaching possibilities that these kinds of marketing/communication activities have (Wiedmann et al., 2009). Even though there is no reason for environmental communication not to employ such techniques, it is important that environmental communication campaigns do this in a credible way, informing the user about the use and combination of data sources and giving them the chance to decide how data is going to be handled. There is in fact a trade-off between ease of use in this domain and protection of privacy for the user and related third parties. Overstretching the possibilities might undermine credibility and lead to negative reactions.

7.7 Conclusions

In this chapter, it has been argued that consumer segmentation, which is popular in marketing, may also have advantages for designing environmental communication campaigns. Although environmental communicators might be reluctant to employ techniques that are associated with commercial activities to increase consumption, there are good reasons to do so. Usually the resources for an environmental communication campaign are limited, which means that resources are best used for target groups where the effect is going to be largest. For example, if you plan to increase bus use in a region in Norway, start with the people living in areas with good access to the bus system in the large city and try to identify people there who are willing to try the bus. Do not waste time on the people living in a remote small town where the bus goes only twice a day, if at all. A combination of geographic, demographic, behavioural, and psychometric segmentations can be very helpful for this task. Identify geographic sections of the area where bus use is feasible, then demographic segments within this region that might be interested and able to change. Then, based on the current behaviour and psychological profiles, identify the groups that are likely to respond to the interventions and then start with the communication, in the best case tailored to subgroups within the identified prime targets for the campaign.

Following such a strategy has the advantage that people, whose time and interest for your communication attempts are limited, will not be overwhelmed with huge amounts of information. They will be provided only with information that they hopefully find useful or interesting since it has been tailored to match their specific needs. This should decrease negative reactions or ignorance of your campaign.

Smartphones have become an essential part of people's lives in many countries, a reality which environmental communicators can make use of. The use of modern communication technology can help to provide information at the point of decision when it is actually needed and in a form that matches the recipients' behavioural patterns. It is essential that this is done with the necessary amount of transparency to protect consumers' privacy and to retain credibility of the environmental communicator and their campaign.

Review questions

- Why is consumer segmentation important for designing environmental communication?
- Which segmentation approaches can be found and what are their advantages and disadvantages?
- Give an example of a value-based segmentation approach and discuss how it can be useful in environmental communication.
- Give an example of a personality-based segmentation approach and discuss how it can be useful in environmental communication.
- Give an example of a lifestyle-based segmentation approach and discuss how it can be useful in environmental communication.
- How can the stage model of behaviour change be used for segmenting target groups?
- In which ways are new technologies useful in communicating with segmented target groups?

Note

1. And the company's sales interests.

Suggested readings

Bamberg, S. (2013). Applying the stage model of self-regulated behavioral change in a car use reduction intervention. *Journal of Environmental Psychology*, 33, 68–75.
Haustein, S., & Hunecke, M. (2013). Identifying target groups for environmentally sustainable transport: assessment of different segmentation approaches. *Current Opinion in Environmental Sustainability*, 5(2), 197–204.
Inglehart, R., & Welzel, C. (2010). Changing mass priorities: The link between modernization and democracy. *Perspectives on Politics*, 8(02), 551–567.
Mowen, J. C., & Minor, M. (1997). *Consumer behavior* (5th ed.). New Jersey: Prentice-Hall.
Ukenna, S., Nkamnebe, A. D., Nwaizugbo, I. C., Moguluwa, S. C., & Olise, M. C. (2012). Profiling the environmental sustainability-conscious (ESC) consumer: Proposing the SPP model. *Journal of Management & Sustainability*, 2(2), 197–210.
Schwartz, S. H. (2006). A theory of cultural value orientations: Explication and applications. *International Studies in Sociology and Social Anthropology*, 104, 33.

Part III

8
An Overview of Communication-Based Intervention Techniques

Chapter summary

This chapter presents an overview of environmental psychology intervention techniques with a special focus on techniques that are based on communication. In this context, the chapter introduces well-established intervention techniques, like environmental education, information packages, commitment, goal setting, prompts, social models, block-leaders, foot-in-the-door, feedback, competitions, and rewards and punishment, which all can be understood as communication-based. They are contrasted with other intervention types, such as structural changes that do not build on information, and are evaluated concerning their effectiveness based on research results from environmental psychology. A typology of interventions based on their timing and the effort necessary to implement them is developed.

8.1 Introduction

This chapter provides a structured overview of a number of intervention strategies that have been analysed in environmental psychological studies. Most of the strategies used and researched by environmental psychologists are based on means of communication. The first section of this chapter presents the most prominent communication-based strategies and links them to key constructs in the psychological models presented in Part 2 of this book. Empirical findings on the efficiency of a technique and the conditions in which it is most effective will be discussed. Some intervention types that are not based on communication are briefly introduced and contrasted to the communication-based interventions. A section on environmental education will discuss peculiarities of an educational approach, even though it is obvious that environmental education is more than a single intervention. In the last section, a classification system of the interventions is proposed.

8.2 Communication-based intervention techniques

The communication-based intervention techniques in this section start with the most conventional "providing information", progressing to more advanced techniques that make use of psychological principles described in Part 2 of the book.

8.2.1 Providing information

Providing information is probably the most common environmental communication strategy. Activists, politicians, or agencies often print brochures, run information campaigns, and use lectures, TV broadcasts, interviews, and other means to inform people about behaviours with high negative environmental impacts and possible alternatives. The provision of information is built on the assumption that knowledge about negative environmental effects and alternatives will make people change their behaviour. In fact, Hines et al. (1987) identified environmental knowledge as a key factor in environmental action.

Providing information might furthermore be understood as a technique of attitude change. If we take into account that attitudes (see Section 4.2) are the sum of all activated beliefs about a behaviour and its alternatives, then changing attitudes at a given point in time can be achieved via two different processes. (a) The set of beliefs could be changed by trying to add more positive beliefs to the pro-environmental behaviour and more negative to the environmentally damaging alternatives. Alternatively, negative beliefs about the pro-environmental behaviour could be removed, while removing positive beliefs about its alternatives. Keeping in mind that beliefs have both a valence (an evaluative dimension) and a probability dimension, such changes could try to target perceived probabilities of outcomes as well as their evaluation. Most traditional information campaigns make use of this category of interventions. For example, people are confronted with new information about the positive effects of cycling (e.g. "cycling is twice as fast in the morning rush hour") or the negative effects of car use (e.g. "car use contributes to local air pollution"). All mechanisms of persuasion described in Section 3.3.4 are relevant to understanding this approach to attitude change. (b) A second strategy to change attitudes makes use of the assumption that attitudes are dynamic and generated based on the set of beliefs that is activated at a given point in time. This means that people do not always make use of all their beliefs when they generate an attitude. Making beliefs salient via communication measures is therefore another possibility to change how an attitude is generated and make sure that pro-environmental beliefs are represented in the generated attitude. A technique that can be used here is prompting (see Section 8.2.2). Since perceived control (see Section 4.2) is the sum of all control beliefs, changing the set of (activated) beliefs in parallel with the approach described for attitudes can be chosen. Furthermore, knowledge and skills related to the desired behaviour are relevant aspects of perceived behavioural control. Educating people about how to enact the desired behaviour on a procedural level ("How exactly do I do it?") reduces perceived difficulty and thus increases perceived control.

A typical example is a public information campaign via mass media to communicate the greenhouse effect to the Dutch public which was launched by the Ministry of the Environment in 1990. An evaluation of the effects of this campaign showed that it did indeed increase knowledge about the problem of climate change, but did not lead to higher environmental concern, perceived seriousness, more climate-saving behaviours, or more support for most climate change-related political measures (Staats et al., 1996). These results, which are rather typical for information campaigns, show a dilemma of mass media campaigns. Even if people's knowledge increases, information provided is often too non-specific to generate behavioural effects. Another problem with providing information is that people are different and lack different pieces of information at a given time. Putting together a campaign that addresses at once a general lack of information easily leads to information overload.

8.2.2 Prompts

Prompts, also referred to as point-of-decision prompts, are small signs that are placed in close proximity to where people are supposed to perform the behaviour in question. They contain a short message that tells people what they should do and often also why. Examples can be the "switch off the light when you leave the room" signs often found in public buildings. One study analysed the effects of two short informative prompts on people's participation in a waste separation scheme in a university (Austin et al., 1993). The prompts were two types of signs, one stating "recyclable materials" and giving examples of such materials and one stating "no paper products". The latter was positioned above the ordinary trash container, while the first one was placed above the paper recycling container. Since most people already have a positive attitude towards paper recycling, it can be assumed that recognising the prompts in a situation when you are about to throw away paper activates the relevant beliefs and thus creates a positive attitude. This would result in higher rates of the desired behaviour, because people act more in accordance to their beliefs. In fact, the study found an increase of more than 50% recycled paper as compared to a baseline without prompts (Austin et al., 1993). However, they also found that the positive effect of prompts depends strongly on their positioning. If the prompts were posted four metres away from the recycling bins, the effect was reduced to only 17% improvement.

In general, it can be concluded that prompts are an effective intervention strategy in cases where people already have positive attitudes towards the behaviour but do not activate them in the decisional situation. Prompts are effective when they are placed in close proximity to the location of the behaviour, when they include concrete instructions of what to do (or not to do) in a simple message, and when they are easy to see (Bell et al., 2001). A disadvantage is that the effect of prompts "wears off" when people get used to seeing them. More dynamic prompts (e.g. on electronic displays) may be a way to avoid this problem.

8.2.3 Rewards and punishments

Classical behavioural psychology in the behaviouristic tradition suggests that people increase the frequency of behaviour that is reinforced (rewarded) and decrease the frequency of behaviour that is punished (Skinner, 1938). Reinforcement can be either introducing a positive outcome of a behaviour (a reward) or removing a negative outcome. In parallel, introducing a negative outcome is a positive punishment and removing something that is regarded as positive is a negative punishment. The positive and negative outcomes can be anything from money or other materialistic gains to social appreciation.

Most policy strategies build on reward or punishment schemes by connecting either pro-environmental behaviours to incentives (e.g. tax reduction and the opportunity to drive on bus lanes for electric vehicles) or environmentally damaging behaviour to fees (e.g. for littering). Rewarding or punishing behaviour is usually effective if the reward or punishment is regarded as substantial enough and provided in close temporal proximity to the behaviour (Bell et al., 2001). The downside of providing external rewards or punishments as interventions is that they reduce the intrinsic attribution for the behaviour (see Section 3.3.3), which means people that were intrinsically motivated to save the environment transfer the motivation to the external motivator. Once the external reward/punishment scheme is taken away, people tend to stop performing the behaviour. Furthermore, running large-scale reward or punishment schemes can be very costly in terms of monetary resources and man-power, for example, when punishments need to be enforced (Bell et al., 2001; Steg et al., 2012). An interesting variant to reduce the costs of reward schemes and reduce the negative effect on attribution is to provide the reinforcement in a lottery scheme, so that not every occasion of a behaviour is rewarded. The Norwegian system, where you can write your name and address on the milk cartons returned for recycling to participate in a lottery, is an example.

8.2.4 Feedback

The effects of individual behavioural change are hard to detect for many environmental behaviours. Thus, people need information about potential effects before they perform a behaviour and about real effects afterwards. They need that feedback in a form that is useful for them. In the domain of energy conservation, it has been frequently shown that giving people feedback about the savings they achieved had a positive effect on their achievement of energy-saving goals. This was especially the case if the feedback was individually tailored, given frequently, and in close temporal proximity to the behaviour (Abrahamse et al., 2007; Hutton et al., 1986; Van Houwelingen & Van Raaij, 1989).

Feedback-based techniques can also be helpful to increase awareness of consequences (see Section 4.3). Here, the information provided must be focused on the personal contribution a person can make to the environmental problem at hand. A personal carbon footprint calculator and energy audits are good examples. Mallett, Melchiori, and Strickroth (2013) showed that confronting people with their personal carbon footprint increased their feelings of guilt. This is a clear sign of an activated personal norm (see Section 4.3), most likely triggered by increased awareness of consequences of their own behaviour. Support for pro-environmental groups was also higher after this confrontation. Another study confronted car drivers with individual feedback about the effects of their driving activities and showed that the awareness of consequences increased considerably (Taniguchi et al., 2003).

8.2.5 Increasing awareness of need

An intervention to increase awareness of need, one of the triggering variables in the norm-activation theory (see Section 4.3), could provide information about an environmental problem with the focus of an urgent need to act. This aims to give a feeling that there is a problem that needs immediate attention (Klöckner & Ohms, 2009). Interestingly, interventions in the norm-activation model context do not specifically focus on the awareness of need beyond the recommendation to communicate a problem. However, general findings on how to create environmental awareness can be utilised here. One study used an interesting technique based on mobile phones (Uzunboylu et al., 2009). The study asked participants to document environmental pollution in their local environment for a period of six weeks with their mobile phones and to share the pictures with other participants. The result was a highly increased awareness of environmental problems. Another technique that has proven to impact on awareness about behaviour and its consequences is writing a diary (e.g. a travel diary or a food waste diary). By observing one's own behaviour, actions that often go unnoticed become salient. In the domain of changing diets, food diaries have been very effective, especially in the form of photo diaries (Zepeda & Deal, 2008). Smartphones can be a useful resource to easily provide people with such opportunities.

8.2.6 Goal setting

Goal setting is an intervention technique where the target person either chooses a goal himself or herself or an external person sets this goal. Energy-use reduction goals are an example: save 10% electricity within the next year. Often, goal setting is combined with other techniques such as feedback or commitment. A study on using washing machines found that the combination of an ambitious goal and feedback was effective in reducing people's energy use, whereas either technique alone was not successful (McCalley & Midden, 2002). The study also found another interesting effect. For people who were more self-oriented, a self-set goal was more effective than an externally set goal, whereas for pro-social respondents the result was reversed.

8.2.7 Competition

In some contexts, the element of competition can also increase pro-environmental behaviour. This element seems particularly effective if groups of people can be constructed to "compete" against each other, like neighbourhoods, employees of several companies, or students of several universities. In a group-based intervention program, competition between several teams was studied (Staats et al., 2004). However, since different interventions were used at the same time, it could not be concluded which contribution the competition element made. In general, evaluations of comparative feedback between groups or individuals are inconclusive (Abrahamse et al., 2005).

8.2.8 Commitment

Commitment is an intervention technique where people are asked to either privately or publicly state their willingness to perform certain behaviours within the future, usually within a defined time frame (e.g. "I commit to take the bus on at least two days when I travel to work next week"). This statement can be given in writing or orally and the commitment can be personalised ("I commit") or a group commitment ("We commit"). A meta-analysis showed that commitment is a successful intervention strategy when used alone, as well as when combined with other techniques (Lokhorst et al., 2013). In a literature review, Abrahamse et al. (2005) highlighted that commitment is one of the more powerful intervention techniques and that public commitment is more effective than private commitment. Personal commitment is usually more effective than group commitment, and written more effective than oral (Bell et al., 2001). Commitment is assumed to be a technique that triggers personal norms, and it is also assumed to be particularly effective over longer time periods where other intervention strategies' effects are reduced. Matthies et al. (2006) found that the combination of habit-deactivating techniques (see Section 8.3.1) with commitment was the only intervention that showed effects after the intervention period was over.

8.2.9 Social models

Social models that behave in the desired way can strengthen social norms. Descriptive norms (see Chapter 4) can be made salient by communicating what other people do, and people who are important to the decision-maker can communicate to them what kind of actions they expect (thus creating injunctive norms).

One study analysed the effect of social models on participation in a composting scheme in a cafeteria (Sussman et al., 2013). The study found that people participated more often if they observed two other people also composting. Interestingly, the effect did not occur if only one other person was observed. They also found that the effect of two models was much stronger than the effect of prompts alone.

An interesting experiment manipulated hotel signage that promotes the reuse of towels (Goldstein et al., 2008). Signs that usually say "please help us save the environment and reuse your towels" were changed to "the majority of guests reused their towels". This made a descriptive norm salient, and the reuse rate increased by 10%. In a second experiment, they changed the text slightly to "the majority of guests who stayed in this room reused their towels" and found an additional increase in reuse rate of about 5%. Even if there is no other connection to the people than that they used the same room, the effect became stronger: people *in the same situation as me* do this or that. The effects descriptive norms can have on people's behaviour should also be recognised when communicating about the undesired behaviour, as stating that many people perform something with negative environmental effects creates an unintended descriptive norm to perform that behaviour (Cialdini, 2003). Another case of interesting side effects of communicating descriptive norms is described in D. L. Costa and Kahn (2013): whereas liberals in the United States reacted with substantial electricity savings when they were informed on their electricity bill that their personal electricity use is above average in their neighbourhood, conservatives did not save energy. If the personal electricity use was reported to be below average, conservatives increased electricity use, while liberals did not. This shows that value orientations have an impact on how descriptive norms are framed.

A common way of communicating injunctive norms is to use celebrities or other recognised people to make a pro-environmental statement and promote a desired behaviour. This is supposed to increase the perceived subjective norms for people. A study found that the use of a credible celebrity (the basketball player "Magic Johnson") increased the effectiveness of an HIV prevention message (Flora et al., 1996). Sahin and Atik (2013) argue that celebrities have a growing influence on especially young consumers' decisions due to widespread new media. However, since subjective norms are only effective for people that are *important* to the deciding person with respect to *this specific behaviour*, the use of celebrities might also have no effect at all. I could be very fond of a singer and her music but at the same time not care at all about her environmental engagement.

Legal regulations, fees, and punishments can also be understood as a communication of injunctive norms, namely what kind of behaviour is officially sanctioned. In health promotion, banning certain types of behaviour (e.g. smoking) was shown to be related to a change in social norms (Procter-Scherdtel & Collins, 2013).

8.2.10 Block-leaders

The "block-leader" approach has been proposed as an approach to communicating injunctive norms through a person closer to the target person (Hopper & Nielsen, 1991). Here, an important person in a neighbourhood acts as a promoter for a recycling program and approaches their neighbours personally. Potential opinion leaders in a neighbourhood were recruited to inform their neighbours about the recycling scheme and motivate them to participate. Compared to prompts, information leaflets, and a control condition, the group that were visited not only displayed the strongest increase in recycling behaviour, but also was the only group with an increase in the level of personal norms. It should, however, be recognised that not all cultures consider being approached by neighbours about a private behaviour appropriate. The risk for causing negative responses can be high. Furthermore, block-leader approaches are highly costly.

8.2.11 Foot-in-the-door

Another technique that can be assumed to work via personal norms is described in a paper by Katzev and Johnson (1984). They refer to the technique as "foot-in-the-door" and it works as follows: first the participants are asked to do a small favour for the environment, something that people are usually willing to give, for example, a signature on an environmental petition. Then in a second step, assuming that the first step activated personal norms to be environmentally friendly, participants are asked to make a change in their behaviour, which is a larger step that people would be more hesitant to commit to without the first step. A variation of the technique was tested, where not one, but two initial requests were presented with the second being a little more demanding than the first, before the big third step was introduced (Souchet & Girandola, 2013). They found this technique to be more effective than the single foot-in-the-door.

8.2.12 Making self-discrepancies salient

Self-discrepancy theory (Higgins, 1987) asserts that people gather motivation to change behaviour from realising that their perception of their actual self (who they are at the moment and how others see them) differs from the ideal self (who they want to be) or the ought self (who others think one ought to be). Making this discrepancy salient is a technique that can motivate people to change their environmental behaviour. If they find out that they would like to be environmentally responsible and others think they ought to be, but in reality they are not (or might not be perceived that way), they perceive a self-discrepancy. To make the discrepancies salient, people can be asked to first describe the person they want to be with respect to the environment (ideal self), then the person who they think they should be with respect to their sense of responsibility and moral rules (ought self). Finally, they are asked to describe the person that they really are (actual self). This intervention is not well researched in the environmental domain, but similar interventions in the domain of school absenteeism (Oyserman et al., 2002) or health-related behaviour (McNally et al., 2005) have been successful.

8.2.13 The hypocrisy paradigm

A technique that can have an effect on ascription of responsibility or reduce the likelihood of responsibility denial (see Section 4.3) is the so-called hypocrisy paradigm (Aronson et al., 1991). The technique is a two-step procedure. First, people are asked to publicly commit to performing an environmental behaviour. Then, in the second step, they are asked to recall instances when they did not act according to that commitment. The technique builds on dissonance theory (see Section 3.3.4.1) that predicts that people try to avoid a mismatch between different cognitions they have at the same time (Festinger, 1962). The technique has been applied to the environmental domain in a study that induced a feeling of hypocrisy in visitors to a public pool with respect to water conservation (Dickerson et al., 1992). After using the two-step procedure, it was found that the group took shorter showers than a control group. However, in an intervention study to reduce plastic bag use with supermarket customers, it was found that when there is a time delay between hypocrisy induction and performance of behaviour, the effect did not show (Rubens et al., 2015).

8.2.14 Providing experience

Personal experience with a pro-environmental behaviour during a trial period might contribute to correct unrealistic perceptions about behavioural difficulty. For example, people often perceive using public transport as more difficult when they have no experience as compared to after experiencing a trial period (Bamberg, 2006). This correction of control beliefs does, of course, assume that the experiences made during the trial period are positive. Furthermore, it has been shown that positive general experiences in nature increase the likelihood of an individual acting out pro-environmental behaviour (Klöckner et al., 2010a, 2010b; Wells & Lekies, 2006).

8.2.15 Providing everyday problem-solving abilities

In the domain of health-related behaviour, it has been shown that analysing and acknowledging possible obstacles beforehand and preparing with possible solutions, a procedure referred to as "everyday problem solving", increases self-efficacy (Artistico et al., 2013). In this procedure, participants are encouraged to generate possible obstacles towards the target behaviour and find solutions to overcome them in a theoretical exercise based on their previous experience. A list of possible strategies is compiled and solutions generated by participants are collated. These are then given back to the participants after strategies that they already tried and failed at are excluded. Participants are then encouraged to identify the root causes for the obstacles and match causes with strategies to overcome them. In a final step, participants are encouraged to recall as many solutions to their initial problem as possible without looking at the list.

8.3 Intervention techniques not based on communication

Whereas the intervention techniques reported in the previous section employ communication, the following two approaches do not rely on communication.

8.3.1 Structural changes

Chapter 2 underlined the importance of structural context for environmental behaviour. It is not surprising that structural changes consequently can have the most fundamental effect on behaviour. This effect will be partly mediated by perceived behavioural control: removing barriers will have a strong effect on perceived control (Klöckner & Blöbaum, 2010), but also other psychological variables like attitudes will indirectly benefit from structural improvements (Steg & Vlek, 2009).

Structural changes are also important when behaviour is highly habitualised and thus connected to a specific context (see Section 4.8). Verplanken and Wood (2006) suggest a differentiated intervention approach depending on habit strength. Whereas for behaviours with low habit strength, information and education-based intervention techniques as described above are effective, they need to be combined with a context change for habitualised behaviours. This suggestion is based on the link between situational cues and the behaviour that the habit constitutes. If this link can be deactivated, for example, because the context of behaviour is changed or the habituated behaviour substantially fails due to changed conditions, people re-enter a mode of deliberate decision-making and become more receptive to information. Several studies have shown that residential relocation or other important life events like child birth or retirement are such disruptions that can be utilised to change habitualised behaviour (Bamberg, 2006; Klöckner, 2004). More subtle events such as receiving a free public transportation ticket or a road closure have also been shown to temporarily deactivate the impact of habits (Fujii & Gaerling, 2004; Fujii & Kitamura, 2003; Matthies et al., 2006).

8.3.2 Product bans

Another form of structural change is to ban certain products or behaviours completely. Whereas banning behaviours can always be undercut (people break speed limits or drive without a seat belt even if it is forbidden), product bans on the producer level might have a powerful effect. As soon as it is illegal to produce or sell a certain product in a country, its numbers will decrease (although mostly not to zero, as some people always find ways to circumvent the ban and illegally import or home produce). However, such measures usually meet a strong resistance since they are perceived as impairing personal freedom and are most likely only accepted if there is a safety issue connected to the product.

8.4 Environmental education

Environmental education is a wide field that cannot be comprehensively addressed in a short paragraph. Furthermore, environmental communication is an overarching concept that might include many of the more specific intervention strategies mentioned above. However, since environmental education is mostly focused on providing knowledge and trying to change attitudes, it is probably most related to providing information as discussed in Section 8.2.1. Some selected findings of environmental education programs or environmental socialisation are presented here.

Environmental education programs have been linked to more environmental awareness and better knowledge about environmental concepts (Fisman, 2005), which can consequently increase the likelihood of identifying an environmental problem as needing attention. The effect of environmental education can also be relevant to increasing awareness of consequences. A study showed that the awareness of consequences of primary school children to not recycle or reuse paper was dependent on how much their parents communicated with them about this topic (Matthies et al., 2012).

As ascription of responsibility is a critical step in activating personal norms (see Section 4.3) and denial of responsibility is a common exit strategy from the norm-activation process, increasing responsibility ascription is crucial. Few studies have actually addressed this issue specifically. Schweizer et al. (2013) analysed how environmental education programs about climate change implemented in American national parks can affect how visitors feel responsible for their climate-related actions. They concluded that the attachment people have to a place like a national park can be utilised to increase their feeling of responsibility by creating an emotional and localised connection to the problem.

Boyes and Stanisstreet (2012) are rather critical of the effectiveness of many environmental education programs. They found in an empirical study that environmental education had hardly any effect when believed effectiveness of an action and willingness to act are only weakly linked. When there is a stronger link, environmental education might have stronger effects. These findings are in line with what has been presented above for the effectiveness of providing information: for most behaviours, the barrier is not a lack of knowledge.

A case study in school environmental programs concluded with the following recommendations for effective environmental education (Ballantyne et al., 2001). (1) That the students enjoy an environmental education program does not necessarily mean that it succeeds in providing a deeper understanding. (2) Environmental education programs need to be carefully tailored to the age group targeted. (3) The individual characteristics of the teachers matter and can make a difference even in standardised programs. (4) Environmental education programs should liaise with parents. (5) Students need to be engaged emotionally through providing evidence for an environmental problem, its effects, and the efforts needed to solve it. The study concluded further that environmental education programs are especially effective if they (a) combine research activities, environmental experiences, and class discussions; (b) focus on local environmental problems; (c) provide positive experiences which demonstrate that the students' actions can have an effect; (d) involve the students' parents in activities; and (e) involve community members in activities (e.g. surveys) (Ballantyne et al., 2001).

8.5 A classification system of intervention techniques

In total, 18 different intervention strategies have been introduced in the previous sections. To structure this large number, this section will provide a more systematic overview. A common segmentation is into antecedent and consequent intervention techniques, placing them either before performance of a behaviour (antecedent) or after (consequent) (Abrahamse et al., 2005; Bell et al., 2001). Logically, consequent techniques can affect behaviour through their anticipation before the behaviour and through their impact on subsequent occasions of the same behavioural choice. Of the techniques mentioned before, the following are antecedent: providing information, environmental education, prompts, increasing awareness of need, goal setting, commitment, social models, block-leaders, foot-in-the-door, making self-discrepancies salient, providing experience, providing everyday problem-solving abilities, structural changes, and product bans. Consequent techniques are rewards, punishments, feedback, competitions, and the hypocrisy paradigm.

In Table 8.1, the techniques are furthermore placed into groups according to their resource consumption with respect to man-power or money. This categorisation depends on how each intervention is provided, as the same intervention can be provided in many ways. As soon as some face-to-face interaction is included, the resource demand increases as compared to mass media communication or use of Internet or smartphones. A crude estimate of the technique's efficiency is presented based on the results reported above. This table is meant to provide the reader with a structured overview, not as a shortcut to selecting intervention techniques. It is by no means always most appropriate to choose the technique that has the best balance of resource needs and efficiency, because an intervention package always needs to be tailored to the real-life case.

8.6 Conclusions

This chapter introduced many intervention techniques that are common among environmental psychologists. It also introduced some that are less common, but are interesting to include due to their

Table 8.1 A structured overview of intervention techniques

	Antecedent	Consequent
Rather high resource demand	• Commitment (++) • Block-leaders (+) • Foot-in-the-door (+) • Providing experience (−) • Providing everyday problem-solving abilities (?) • Structural changes (++) • Product bans (++)	• Rewards (++) • Punishments (++) • Feedback (++)
Medium resource demand	• Environmental education (−) • Social models (++) • Making self-discrepancies salient (?)	• Hypocrisy paradigm (?)
Low resource demand	• Providing information (− −) • Increasing awareness of need (+) • Prompts (+) • Goal setting (+)	• Competitions (−)

Note: ++ = empirical evidence for high efficiency; + = empirical evidence for some efficiency; − = sometimes inefficient; − − = often inefficient; ? = empirical evidence missing.

unique approach, like the hypocrisy paradigm, providing everyday problem-solving ability, or making self-discrepancies salient. What works well for some people does not work at all for others; some techniques have strengths under some conditions which turn into weaknesses in other conditions. The bottom line here is that interventions need to be tailored to specific situations and target groups; and they need to be pilot tested. Most likely, a combination of different techniques is most effective if matching the demand a person has at a given point in time. This again underlines the importance of knowing the background of environmental decision-making as described in Part 2 of this book when designing a strategy. Being able to identify variables that need to be addressed, being able to see structural and psychological barriers, and being able to address and remove them is crucial in this process. Hopefully, this chapter contributed to linking the tools from the environmental psychological tool box together with their theoretical background. In most cases, an intervention strategy based on theory and empirical analyses will be more efficient than an ad hoc strategy.

Review questions

- Describe different communication-based intervention techniques, give an example and discuss their effectiveness and challenges.
- Describe some characteristics of non-communication-based interventions.
- Discuss effectiveness and challenges of environmental education.
- How can intervention techniques be structured?

Suggested readings

Abrahamse, W., Steg, L., Vlek, C., & Rothengatter, T. (2007). The effect of tailored information, goal setting, and tailored feedback on household energy use, energy-related behaviors, and behavioral antecedents. *Journal of Environmental Psychology*, 27(4), 265–276.

Bell, P. A., Greene, T., Fisher, J. D., & Baum, A. (2001). *Environmental psychology* (Fifth ed.). Orlando: Harcourt College Publishers. (Chapter 14)

Steg, L., van den Berg, A. E., & de Groot, J. I. M. (2012). *Environmental psychology: An introduction*. Oxford, UK: Wiley-Blackwell. (Part 3)

Verplanken, B., & Wood, W. (2006). Interventions to break and create consumer habits. *Journal of Public Policy & Marketing*, 25(1), 90–103.

9
Promoting Pro-Environmental Behaviour in Groups and Organisations

Chapter summary

This chapter focuses on special characteristics of groups as targets for interventions. Groups can be found in families, at the work place, in education settings, and in leisure activities, among other arenas. It discusses the differences between individual, household, and group behaviour, drawing on social psychological findings about group processes such as establishing social norms, group polarisation, diffusion of responsibility, majority and minority influences, risky shift, in-group/out-group phenomena, and group competition. The chapter presents group-centred intervention strategies that target the behaviour of people in organisations and presents evidence for their effectiveness. Strategies steered by external actors as well as participatory intervention strategies that include the target group in the design of the intervention program are discussed with their advantages and disadvantages. The chapter also looks at how an organisation both provides a structure to the individuals within it and itself is a construction of the individuals forming it.

9.1 Introduction

The previous chapters have focused on individual behaviour, which is typical for a psychological approach. However, people are members of many groups in very different constellations throughout their daily lives. People live in households, which often are more than one individual; they are part of the company they work for; if they are studying they are part of the university or school; they are member of a fitness club, a book club, a theatre group, or even a board game community.

Nowadays, people are also members of many virtual groups, such as Facebook groups. This makes it necessary and interesting to look at the differences between individual behaviour and behaviour in different kinds of groups.

Some core findings from group psychology, which are important in understanding how environmental communication impacts groups, will be presented, before specific group-centred intervention techniques are outlined. Some of them mirror similar techniques for the individual, but are nevertheless different because the group adds a layer of complexity. In the following section, an analysis will be presented on how the organisation has a twofold function: on the one hand, it provides structures and frameworks for the individuals engaged in it, but, on the other hand, it is also constructed by the individuals.

9.2 Differences between individual, household, and group behaviour

People make decisions either alone, in the household they live in, in groups where people physically meet, and also in virtual groups. The following section will briefly look at the characteristics of each type of decision context.

9.2.1 Individual decision-making

Some decisions are made by individuals. It is actually not so easy to come up with good examples of decisions that are really taken at the individual level alone. Maybe a person living alone and deciding what to buy in the supermarket for dinner does make such an individual decision. That the decision lies on the individual level does not mean that there is no social context to the decision. Anticipated reactions from other people will always be part of such a decision, represented by variables such as subjective norms or descriptive norms, and also values and "culture" in the models described in earlier chapters. The key here is that there is no immediate other individual included in the decision-making; the social perspective is exclusively represented in the head of one decision-maker. That makes individual behaviour relatively simple to analyse (as compared to the behaviours described in the following sections), even if the complexity described in decision models is already high. In theory, it is enough to know the mental representations a person has about behavioural alternatives to predict the behaviour and to target them by means of environmental communication as described in the previous chapter. The social context of the decision becomes a variable on the individual level in the decision model (Klöckner, 2013a).

9.2.2 Household decision-making

Most decisions are not made on the individual level. Consider a person living in a household with more than one member. In this case, most decisions are jointly made, be it the dinner shopping in the supermarket together with the child or the decision of which new car (if at all) to buy by the couple running the household. It has been shown that children have a very active role in food shopping at the supermarket, influencing the purchases to a large extent (Pettersson et al., 2004). In the case of car purchase, interesting results from a study in India show that investment decisions in a context traditionally ascribed to the male head of a household actually are to an increasing degree being made jointly by males and females (Srivastava & Anderson, 2010). This makes it obvious that understanding decision-making on the household level is more complex and demanding than on the individual level. The decision is made by a system of individual actors who are dependent on each other, know each other very well, have established communication structures, and also (as a household) have a social context around them.

In this process, the roles of different household members need to be understood. Depending on culture and socialisation, male and female heads of a household take different roles with respect to decision-making depending on the topic. Children in the household also have different roles and abilities in decision-making, depending on their age, the topic, and the culture they are raised in. Other household members, such as grandparents, may also have an impact on decision-making, again depending on the topic and the general role a senior household member is ascribed in a given culture. A study about vacation purchase decisions analysed different strategies employed by spouses to convince each other of their own preferences for a vacation destination and how the choice of strategy is influenced by marital power (Bokek-Cohen, 2011). The study showed that more objective marital power, hence more material resources on which the partner depends, leads to more use of coercive influence strategies in male spouses, meaning that males threaten to "take revenge" and make the female spouse's life difficult if their preference for a vacation is not accepted. If a partner has more subjective marital power because they are less satisfied with the relationship and thus have the power to withdraw an emotional resource from the other, males and females tend to use more emotional influence strategies such as crying or withdrawal from the relationship. Males that have high subjective marital power also use more coercive influence strategies and more reward strategies, such as promising the female partner some kind of reward for following their preferences.

Su et al. (2003) propose a model of dynamic spousal family purchase decision-making, based on the assumption that with growing egalitarian gender roles, family decision-making is less consensual and more characterised by bargaining, coercion, and compromise rather than spontaneous or forced consensus. Thus, decisions also impact each other. Giving in on one occasion is a good bargaining argument for the next time a conflict occurs in decision-making. In an empirical analysis of three sequential purchase decisions, namely a family vacation, a family dinner, and a family music event, the authors found support for their predictions.

Table 9.1 gives an overview of influence strategies spouses employ when they try to convince each other of their point of view as reported in the above studies (Bokek-Cohen, 2011; Su et al., 2003). The influence

Table 9.1 Overview of influence strategies spouses use in marital decision-making (based on summaries by Bokek-Cohen, 2011, and Su et al., 2003)

Strategy	Explanation	Example
Expert influence strategy	One partner uses their access to specific information relevant for the decision to influence the other partner	One partner collects information about a new car they want and presents that information, influencing the decision of the spouse
Legitimate influence strategy	One partner plays on values concerning role expectations shared with the other partner	One partner argues that they both agreed that decisions regarding purchase of clothes fall into his/her domain, so he/she should be the one deciding
Reward influence strategy	One partner offers rewards to the partner for agreeing with him/her	One partner offers to include some of the other partner's favourite activities in the vacation plans if the other partner agrees with him/her on the destination

Identification influence strategy	One partner utilises the feeling of "being one" with the other partner	One partner references that they are always both wanting the same thing, which is why he/she expects that they will also agree on the car purchase
Coercive strategy	One partner punishes the other for not agreeing with him/her. The punishments can be psychological or material	One partner emotionally or physically withdraws from the other partner when they do not agree
Information management strategy	One partner carefully tailors the persuasive communication, sometimes arguing that there are external forces making a decision in his/her favour necessary	One partner argues that a certain holiday destination (the one he/she prefers) should be chosen, because there is such a good bargain (which is an external cause)
Emotional influence strategy	One partner puts emotional pressure on the other partner	One partner starts crying when he/she does not get his/her way
Triangulation strategy	One partner draws in a third person to argue for his/her cause	One partner invites a friend to talk about their fabulous holiday at the same location he/she prefers
Reciprocity strategy	One partner uses his/her compliance last time as an argument for the other partner's compliance this time	One partner argues that last time the other partner got to pick the holiday destination, so this time it is his/her turn

strategies of children and adolescents are not discussed due to limited space, but many of the strategies fall into similar categories. The dynamics of household decisions have implications for environmental communication because it should be taken into account that a communication can change or convince one individual of the household, thus influencing the negotiation process. It might also be beneficial to identify and target the household members who have the largest impact on a decision. More often than expected, this household member is a child (the advertisement industry is very aware of this).

9.2.3 Group decision-making

Before looking at the specific characteristics of decision-making in groups, "group" needs to be defined. Obviously, a group consists of more than one person; many researchers define people as a group from two members upwards (Mills, 1967). However, a group is also characterised by some shared patterns of experience. In their book on group theory, D. Johnson and Johnson (2013) describe a group as a number of people joining together to achieve a goal, who are dependent on each other to a certain degree, have interpersonal interaction, a perception of group membership, a structured relationship, mutual influence, and a motivation to stay in the group. Since humans are, most of the time, part of one group or another, understanding the essentials of group dynamics, group decision-making, and group behaviour is very relevant also from an environmental communication perspective.

As we have already seen from the example of the household or family, groups are characterised by a structure. This structure is constructed by the group through establishing group roles and group norms (D. Johnson & Johnson, 2013). A role is an expectation of what this person should do in the group related to others, for example, the role of an organiser or creative idea producer. Group norms are common beliefs about all group members' appropriate behaviour, attitudes, and perceptions (D. Johnson & Johnson, 2013). They can be implicit or explicit. Over time, each member of the group ascribes himself or herself a role or is ascribed a role by the group. Roles can change, and situations and group members can have several roles at once.

This kind of structuring makes the decision-making process different from individual decision-making. Here a decision is reached on the group level, with members of the group contributing to decision-making within the boundaries of their roles and the group norms. In Section 9.3, some very important lessons about group decision-making are summarised. These can help understand how environmental interventions on an organisational level differ from individual-centred interventions.

9.2.4 Virtual groups

Virtual groups, for example, Facebook groups, are in many respects comparable to groups that meet physically. They consist of a number of people that share a common goal or interest, that are motivated to be and stay in the group, have a perception of group membership to some degree, and have a structured relationship to other group members and mutual influence. However, there are also differences. In virtual groups, being in or out of the group is more obvious since the group membership is marked electronically. Roles are often more balanced, with group members participating to varying degrees and communication structures defined by the medium used. Mutual trust and liking can be more difficult to establish in virtual groups, but if transparent rules are established, they develop more easily (Walther & Bunz, 2005). Some negative effects of groups on decision-making seem to be less prominent in virtual groups, but, on the other hand, perceived barriers for norm violation are lower and common understandings of norms develop slower (Graham, 2003).

9.3 Important insights from group psychology

Group psychology has analysed the behaviour of groups for a long time, identifying when they perform more efficiently than individuals and also when they have characteristic shortcomings. The following section will briefly introduce some of the findings that are relevant for designing effective environmental communication in organisations.

9.3.1 Establishing norms in groups

Common norms are an important characteristic of functioning groups, but they do not exist from the first day the group meets. Group norms make the behaviour of group members predictable, thereby reducing uncertainty (Feldman, 1984). They are likely to be enforced if they facilitate the group's survival, make the group members' behaviour more predictable, help avoid interpersonal problems, and if they express central values of the group and clarify the group's identity (Feldman, 1984). Mechanisms of enforcement are, for example, peer pressure or social exclusion.

According to Feldman (1984), norms in groups develop mostly in the following ways. (1) A powerful member of the group makes an explicit statement about a norm (e.g. about the unacceptability of being late). This is often the case if one group member formally has power over other group members, but may also happen if some group members are strong and explicit even if they formally do not have the mandate to define the rules. (2) Norms are set and defined by the group after a critical event, when the group realises that a norm has to be set to prevent the same critical event from happening again. (3) An effect referred to as primacy also sets norms. The first behaviour pattern that emerges in a group defines the standards for later occasions. (4) Members of a group have a toolkit of group experiences from before, so they carry over their behaviours and expectations from previous groups which has an impact on defining norms in the new group. For environmental communication, this means that this process of establishing norms needs to be understood for a group. Who are the group members setting the norms and what is the toolkit of experiences the individuals and the group carry?

Tuckman and Jensen (1977) describe the development of a group in five stages: forming, storming, norming, performing, and adjourning. In the forming stage, relationships between group members are formed, first ground rules are established, and boundaries are tested and established. The storming stage is a phase of intergroup conflict where the roles and rules are still not well defined and are questioned. During the norming stage, group cohesion develops and more binding roles and norms for the group and its members are established. The in-group feeling develops and people aim to maintain the group. Conflicts are avoided. In the performing stage, the group is finally able to work on the tasks it is given and the roles of the members are well defined and work together. The group can afford to handle roles and norms more flexibly. The final stage describes how the group is dissolved after its task is completed.

Even if the Tuckman and Jensen model has been criticised for its oversimplifying linearity (Bonebright, 2010), it is still helpful to realise that groups of people can be in different stages of their development. From an environmental communication point of view, it makes a difference to communicate to a group which is in their storming stage (and thus hardly receptive to any outside input because the group is taken up in internal conflicts) or a group with clear norms and roles, where it is relatively easy to identify who should be addressed.

9.3.2 Group polarisation and the risky shift

When discussing a topic in a group, it often happens that the group decision is more extreme than each individual member's decision would have been. When the group members on average tend towards a risky decision, the group's decision becomes even more risky; when the group members initially are cautious, then the group's decision is even more cautious (Stoner, 1968). A group polarising towards a more risky decision is often referred to as the "risky shift" (Breakwell, 2007).

The reasons for a risky shift, and to a lesser degree also the cautious shift, have been debated in the risk psychology community (Breakwell, 2007). A possible explanation for the willingness to take bigger risks as a group can be diffusion of responsibility (see also the next section) (Wallach et al., 1962). When a group of people can be held responsible for the outcomes of an action, people tend to take more risks. However, also other more subtle explanations have been proposed, for example, that in discussions people are forced to defend their position, which provides arguments also for others. The arguments provided tend to be biased towards a risky solution (Nordhøy, 1962). Another important mechanism in the risky shift seems to be that leader personalities who tend to have more influence in groups also tend to be more on the risky side and thus influence the other group members more strongly than the other way around (Wallach et al., 1962).

The "persuasive argument theory" assumes that group polarisation occurs because people selectively respond to new arguments that support their own view, thus becoming more extreme in their view (Burnstein & Vinokur, 1977). The "interpersonal comparison theory" claims that people want to be accepted by the group and thus shift their opinion towards what they perceive to be the dominating view (Jellison & Arkin, 1977). Hogg et al. (1990) propose a social identification perspective, assuming that group polarisation is the result of conformity processes. As people in a group construct a representation of themselves as being part of a group that has a certain position distinct from the position of out-group members, they tend to make the difference between their in-group position more distinct from the out-group position, thus more extreme. A group confronted with a risky out-group would polarise to more caution, and a group confronted with a cautious out-group would polarise to more risk taking.

No matter which explanation for group polarisation is favoured, an important lesson to learn is that groups tend to shift their positions to more extreme positions, especially when confronted with an out-group (see Section 9.3.5). When an environmental communicator approaches a group and is perceived as out-group, even more extreme anti-environmental positions in the group may result. It has, however, been demonstrated that the group polarisation effect disappears when the decisions have real, binding, and costly consequences for all group members, so making the personal consequences of group decisions salient can be a way of preventing the negative effects of group polarisation (Baron et al., 1974).

9.3.3 Diffusion of responsibility

Another effect that makes group decisions different from individual decision-making is the diffusion of responsibility in groups. Whereas an individual will always feel, to a high degree, responsible for his or her actions (unless responsibility is attributed to circumstances or structural forces), in groups it is unclear who bears the responsibility for the actions taken. The diffusion of responsibility was first described in cases of helping, or not helping, people who were in an emergency (the "bystander effect"). It was found that the tendency to help the victim of an epileptic seizure was higher when only one potential helper was present as compared to many (Darley & Latane, 1968; Fischer et al., 2011). This is interpreted to be an effect of the feeling of responsibility diffusing on too many people. Wallach et al. (1964) propose diffusion of responsibility as one explanation for the risky shift effect described in the previous section. When many people in the group decide collectively, the responsibility for failure is shared and does not feel as big, which leads to more risk taking. Voelpel et al. (2008) demonstrated the group size also influenced diffusion of responsibility effect in virtual groups.

An important implication is that when communicating environmental issues to groups, there will be a tendency that each member of the group will feel less responsible than if the communication would be directed at individuals. A study that framed environmental behaviour in terms of pro-social behaviour found that the non-action in environmental domains bears the same characteristics as shown in the bystander effect studies where people do not help when too many others are present (Anker & Feeley, 2011).

9.3.4 Majority influence and minority influence in groups

When groups discuss topics and form group opinions, the majority of the group members often have the largest impact and determine which decision the group takes, especially when the stronger group members are part of the majority. Research on majority effects has shown that the group can even repeat mistakes if the majority of the group had made them before. A famous study by Asch (1951) demonstrated that people who were answering questions about which of three lines matched a comparison line (a simple and easy to solve task which individuals manage to answer correctly to almost 100%) were answering wrongly if other people in the room consistently did so (people who were colleagues of the researcher and were instructed to give wrong answers). Even members of a group that was formed just before the experiment adjusted their answers to the answers of the others. However, this can indicate two things. It can indicate either that the person still knows that the answer is wrong but answers consistently with the other people to not obviously deviate. Or it can indicate that the person really believes that the wrong line matches the comparison line. In follow-up experiments, it was found that most people returned to the correct answers when questioned individually later. Interestingly, this majority effect disappeared if the participant had one ally who also gave the correct answer.

A similar study demonstrated the opposite effect, namely that a minority answering consistently wrong also had an impact on the majority (Moscovici et al., 1969). In this case, six people in a room were shown 36 pictures of light blue and asked which colour it was. Two of the people in the room were colleagues and either consistently called the colour green in all trials or gave false answers in two-thirds of the cases. In the case where the colleagues consistently answered wrong, 8% of the answers the participants gave were also wrong. As opposed to Asch's experiment (1951), Moscovici et al. (1969) were convinced that they really changed people's perception and not only their compliance. In a test after the experiment, the participants from the group with the consistently false answering confederates changed the threshold between blue and green so that more colours in between blue and green were interpreted as green.

Minority and majority influences have been analysed from the perspective of the dual-process theory of persuasion (see Section 3.3.4). Maass and Clark (1984) analysed research literature since Moscovici et al.'s initial minority influence experiments and have proposed that majority and minority influences follow different cognitive mechanisms. Whereas majority standpoints lead to conformity (public compliance in order not to be excluded from the group but not necessarily a change of attitudes), minority standpoints lead to private acceptance. This is due to the different routes minority and majority influences take in the dual-process model of persuasion (Petty & Cacioppo, 1986). Majority influence tends to be processed along the peripheral route, which leads to only superficial attitude change or public conformity, whereas minority influence triggers active thinking and permanent attitude change.

This line of argument is very interesting for environmental communication attempts. If one (or better two) members in a group can be convinced to consistently behave and argue for the environmental cause, their impact can be strong and lasting even if the majority is against them in the beginning. This is also in line with the diffusion of innovation theory (E. M. Rogers, 2003), which predicts that innovations are first adopted by very few people with special characteristics (see Section 5.2) and only over time reach the majority.

9.3.5 Social Identity: In-group/out-group phenomena

Groups are important entities for humans and we attempt to protect groups against intruders. As soon as we attach ourselves to a group, the other members of the group become in-group and outsiders become out-group. Social identity theory (Tajfel, 2010) describes how humans derive an important part of their self-concept, their identity, from membership in groups. Being a member of a group is of high value to the individual, especially if it is a group with a high status. That leads to processes where in-group members start to be perceived as more positive and more alike oneself, whereas out-group members are perceived as less positive and less alike. The in-group/out-group difference is becoming more distinct, and positions by out-group members tend to be less accepted. Prejudice against out-group members grows.

Ashforth and Mael (1989) argue that organisations such as workplaces are groups, and membership to such a group creates an aspect of identity for its members. This means that the principles of social identity theory should also apply to organisational settings and in-group/out-group phenomena are to be found there also. Within the context of environmental behaviour, it was shown that those identifying with a group of local farmers that engaged in sustainable agricultural practices were more willing to implement such practices (Fielding et al., 2008).

The findings related to social identity theory are very relevant for environmental communication. When communicating with groups, especially groups with a high status, outsiders trying to propose an environmental topic will be treated as out-group, making their arguments less acceptable to the group and leading to the potential for the group to defend itself against the communicator. A way around this problem could be to recruit group members as confederates that then pursue the environmental communication from the inside. Participatory intervention planning as described in the next section is partly based on this assumption.

9.4 Group-centred intervention techniques

The group psychology effects described above make it obvious that groups are not comparable to individuals when it comes to decision-making, which means that environmental interventions based on environmental communication that address groups also need to be specifically tailored. Interestingly, not much research is done on group-based interventions compared to individual interventions in the environmental domain. Four perspectives will be presented in the following sections. First, competition between groups (as opposed to competition between individuals) and feedback to groups will be introduced as intervention instruments. Then the additional benefit of using local knowledge that resides in organisational groups is discussed, before a social practice perspective on environmental behaviour in organisations will be explained.

9.4.1 Group competition

Group competition is an intervention instrument that builds on the idea that social identity process will fuel the commitment of group members to outperform other groups, in this case in performing pro-environmental behaviours. Groups of higher status are more attractive (Tajfel, 2010), and being better than other groups in a competition increases the status of the group. Compared to individual competitions, the gain factor is not a direct individual increase of status, but an increase of the group's status which then makes it even more attractive for the individual to be a member of this group. Furthermore, being committed to the group's goal may motivate the individual more than competing alone against others. For example, observing the contributions of others in a group makes individuals more hesitant to withdraw from the competition.

Interestingly, no scientific papers could be found that tested group competition as an intervention instrument in the environmental domain. Tilyard (2011) discusses the potential of group competition in environmental interventions and concludes that the intergroup processes might enhance the efficiency of interventions. However, the positive effects of group competition are documented well in other domains. Erev et al. (1993) showed that group competition reduced significantly the amount of social loafing, which is the tendency in groups to reduce engagement and benefit from the work of the others. Bornstein et al. (2002) demonstrated that group competition enhances the efficiency of group work, and Bornstein and Erev (1994) found a positive effect of group competition on intra-group cooperation. Another study showed that group competition had a positive influence on group creativity, if the competition was not too strong (Baer et al., 2010). Conclusions from this research are encouraging for environmental interventions. It appears that medium levels of group competition (e.g. between teams in a work environment, neighbourhoods, or school classes) can reduce the degree of freeriding, increase cooperation between the group members to reach the environmental goal, and increase creativity in finding solutions.

9.4.2 Group feedback

In Section 8.2.4, the positive effects of individual feedback on environmental behaviour were introduced. Feedback can also be provided to groups of people. Group feedback has in one way the same effects as individual feedback; it provides the acting person with a confirmation of the outcomes of their behaviour. However, this information is now no longer traceable to the individual's behaviour, which reduces the efficiency of the feedback intervention because the individual's effort is hidden in the group result. This disadvantage of group feedback can be counterbalanced by the positive effects a feedback has on the group. Receiving feedback, especially in comparison to other groups, stimulates group competition, even if there is no extra reward. This then creates the positive effects of group competition described above. Group competition is usually including some form of feedback, but feedback can also be given at intermediate stages of the competition to motivate the groups.

A study compared individual feedback and goal setting as intervention in a company with a group that in addition received their feedback in comparison to another group (Siero et al., 1996). They found a long-lasting effect of the group feedback on energy consumption. It appears that this effect was achieved without changes in attitudes or intentions of the participants, simply because of the effects of group membership and comparison as described in social identity theory (Tajfel, 2010). Abrahamse et al. (2007) found that group goals and group feedback (the group being a city) had an additional motivating effect on energy saving in households on top of the effects of their other interventions.

9.4.3 Participatory intervention techniques

Groups of people in organisations possess knowledge about the peculiarities of the setting and the group of people itself, which can be used to tailor interventions to the local needs and conditions. A study by Matthies and Krömker (2000) illustrates the approach. They were interested in reducing the amount of wrongly disposed garbage in a student residence. To do so, they chose a participatory approach:

(1) observing the setting, (2) activating the target group, and (3) supporting participation. In the first step, the researchers visit the setting consisting of the spatial situation, the target group, and the behaviour in question. They form a first impression based on observations and informal conversations with members of the target group. Also interviews or questionnaires might be used in this stage. In the second step, as large a group as possible from the target population should be motivated to (a) see the need for change and (b) participate in planning an intervention package that afterwards is to be provided to the whole population. A suitable method for this is workshops. In the workshops, it makes sense to provide information to the participants about potential intervention strategies to open up more possibilities. In the last step, the members of the target group design the interventions and implement them on their own (hence, from the in-group). The researcher provides support in this implementation. From a group psychological perspective, an advantage of participatory intervention planning is that the resistance of the group against an external intervention is reduced. Furthermore, individuals from within the group have a better chance of becoming an influencing minority than externals because they are part of the group and have a higher likelihood of being consistent. The study found a substantial reduction of wrongly disposed waste by the intervention group following a participatory approach compared to the control group.

9.4.4 A social practice approach

Social practice theory (Shove et al., 2012) is useful for analysing, explaining, and changing behaviour on the group level (see Section 1.2.3). Hargreaves (2011) used social practice theory to analyse the change of environmental behaviour in the head office of a large construction company in the United Kingdom. A team of "environmental champions" was recruited from within the organisation that first conducted an environmental audit and then designed a campaign through a series of planning meetings. This design followed the recommendations of participatory intervention techniques described in the previous section and potentially counteracted problems arising from out-group resistance. After the campaign, which lasted for a couple of months, a second audit was conducted by the "environmental champions". The "champions" were recruited in line with diffusion of innovation theory principles (E. M. Rogers, 2003), meaning that environmental pioneers were recruited that had good social standing within the company. None of the leaders was included in the team.

Even if the process so far can also be understood as participatory planning, Hargreaves used social practice theory to go beyond this approach. What makes this approach interesting is that the process of changing a company's behaviour is not understood as changing the determinants of pro-environmental behaviour of individual employees. On the contrary, it is a change of social practices within the company, which are constituted by an interplay of people, structure, and behaviour and are thus more than the sum of individual behaviours. Hargreaves (2011) describes the initial audit as a process of looking at the practices in the office from a distance, enabling the "champions" to question those practices. In the planning meetings, the meanings of the practices were discussed, analysed, and challenged. New practices were coupled to existing meanings, such as efficiency or cost saving. Environmentalism as a meaning was mostly excluded. Furthermore, it was discovered that many practices, for example, disposing of waste in the under-desk-bins, carried more than just one obvious meaning. If the meanings of practices go unnoticed, it may be hard to change them.

9.5 An organisation as structuring framework and construction of its members

An interesting characteristic of organisations is that they are both a context for their members and a product of their members' constructive processes. In other words, an individual member of a group is impacted by the norms, values, role expectations, and structural conditions of this group. On the other hand, the members of a group constitute its structure and rules, and even minorities and individuals can have an impact that changes a group (as analysed above). This makes groups and behaviour in groups more complex than individual behaviour because the group is re-creating and redefining itself based on its members' behaviour. Figure 9.1 visualises some of the important relationships in this process.

9.6 Conclusions

This chapter started with an analysis of how individual decision-making; decision-making in dyads, families, or households; and decision-making in groups differ. The essence of this chapter is that decision-making that involves more than one person is more dynamic than individual decision-making. One partner in a relationship tries to influence the other by various techniques; members of a group are impacted by the

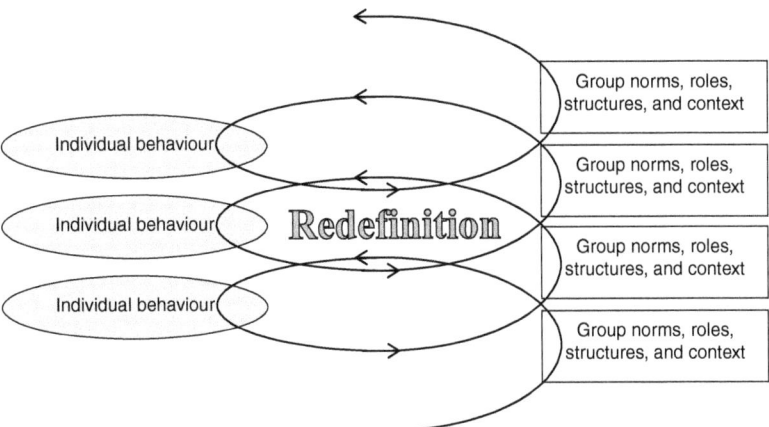

Figure 9.1 The process of groups shaping group members' behaviour which in turn shapes the group

group and have at the same time an influence on the group. Groups are powerful entities and influence human behaviour more than we like to admit. Humans are "programmed" to strive for group membership and do much to achieve this, especially when the group is ascribed high status. This offers many opportunities for group-based environmental communication which utilises group psychology, for example, by stimulating group competition, which motivates group members and stimulates cooperation and creativity. On the other hand, groups tend to defend themselves against external threats. This makes an external communicator who approaches a group a potential threat, which can have negative effects. Therefore it is a good strategy to align with individual group members before starting the group intervention campaign, so that they can become the carriers of the message. The message then comes from within the group, which protects against rejection because of in-group/out-group processes, as long as the internal group members are not expelled from the group because they stretch group norms too far with their statements in favour of the intervention. Since most human behaviour occurs in groups, it makes sense to address the impact of groups from psychological and scientific perspectives.

Review questions

- What are the characteristics of household decision-making as opposed to individual decision-making?

- What are the influence strategies spouses use in marital decision-making?
- What are the characteristics of a group?
- Describe the important group psychological effects and their relevance for environmental communication.
- Describe environmental communication interventions utilising specifically the effects occurring in groups.

Suggested readings

Hargreaves, T. (2011). Practice-ing behaviour change: Applying social practice theory to pro-environmental behaviour change. *Journal of Consumer Culture*, 11(1), 79–99.

Hogg, M. A., Turner, J. C., & Davidson, B. (1990). Polarized norms and social frames of reference: A test of the self-categorization theory of group polarization. *Basic and Applied Social Psychology*, 11(1), 77–100.

Johnson, D., & Johnson, F. (2013). *Joining together: Group theory and group skills*. Boston: Pearson.

Maass, A., & Clark, R. D. (1984). Hidden impact of minorities: Fifteen years of minority influence research. *Psychological Bulletin*, 95(3), 428.

Mynatt, C., & Sherman, S. J. (1975). Responsibility attribution in groups and individuals: A direct test of the diffusion of responsibility hypothesis. *Journal of Personality and Social Psychology*, 32(6), 1111.

Siero, F. W., Bakker, A. B., Dekker, G. B., & Van Den Burg, M. T. (1996). Changing organizational energy consumption behaviour through comparative feedback. *Journal of Environmental Psychology*, 16(3), 235–246.

Su, C., Fern, E. F., & Ye, K. (2003). A temporal dynamic model of spousal family purchase-decision behavior. *Journal of Marketing Research*, 40(3), 268–281.

Tajfel, H. (2010). *Social identity and intergroup relations* (Vol. 7). Cambridge: Cambridge University Press.

10
Playing Good? – Environmental Communication through Games and Simulations

Chapter summary

Game scenarios are increasingly being developed with an aim to influence people's pro-environmental behaviour, by either changing their attitudes or their understanding of complex environmental phenomena. This chapter presents selected examples and analyses how they might affect people's behaviour, mediated by psychological mechanisms presented in earlier chapters. The selected games are computer games, board games, and role plays. In this context, the importance of personal experience of environmental phenomena, behaviour related to them, and their consequences is summarised. Empirical evaluations of the games' impact are presented. The second part of this chapter deals with conclusions about human behaviour based on the analysis of people's behaviour in the so-called social dilemmas. The contribution of game theory to the analysis of human environmental behaviour is outlined and the potential of simulations based on game theory for learning pro-environmentalism is discussed as well as the limits of that approach.

10.1 Introduction

This chapter discusses the usefulness of a playful approach to communicating environmental issues. Games that focus on more than entertainment are often referred to as "serious games" (Susi et al., 2007). Selected computer-based games with an environmental message are presented, including games for tablets or smartphones. Three classic board games and games based on role playing are also discussed. Recently, many environmentally based games have addressed climate change, and so this topic was selected as a focus for the first half of the chapter, but the conclusions drawn can be generalised to other environmental topics.

The environmental games scene focusing on climate change developed drastically in the last 25 years (Reckien & Eisenack, 2013). The majority of the games, which were computer games (mostly online), board or card games, and role play or management games, were initiated or developed by academic, governmental, or non-governmental organisations. In recent years, there has been an increase in more professional game developers joining the ranks and developing environmentally focused games. The games mainly addressed mitigation of climate change (thus trying to find actions as a player to reduce the negative effects of climate change); basic knowledge about the climate, climate change, and its effects; climate change policies; impacts of and adaptation to climate change; and energy issues (Reckien & Eisenack, 2013).

These games are first of all games, meaning they are designed to entertain people. The environmental topic, message, or educative approach comes as an addition, although it is part of their design. They must be able to compete for the players' attention, in competition with other games on the market without an environmental topic. This means that they must first of all be entertaining to be played and to consequently deliver their message. As an anonymous member of the board game community once put it: "CO_2 is a very good game, in spite of its topic."

10.2 Computer games as a means of environmental communication

In the popular science book *Reality is broken – why games make us better and how they can change the world*, McGonigal (2011) elaborates on the hypotheses that games have the potential to help solve real-world problems. She formulates a number of assumptions about characteristics of modern games that can lead to such positive effects (see Section 10.2.3). However, first, two examples of climate change-related computer games will be presented in some detail to get an idea of how such games compare to "ordinary" games.

10.2.1 Example 1: Fate of the World

The computer game "Fate of the World" by the software company Red Redemption (http://www.fateoftheworld.net/Home) published in 2010 is a commercial computer game that simulates societal and environmental impacts of global climate change over a time period of 200 years.

The player acts at the level of global governance, working on different missions, such as improving living conditions in Africa, as the head of the newly founded global environmental organisation (GEO), an environmental pendant to the United Nations. Via agents in the different regions, the player can influence decisions in those regions, selecting strategies that are described on "cards" the player can play. Thus, "Fate of the World" is a virtual card game in a highly dynamic simulation of the world with a changing climate. Underlying the game are rather accurate models of the climate system resulting in more than 1000 potential effects of climate change and more than 100 realistic political instruments to tackle the challenges. It teaches the player the complexity of the climate system and its interaction with societies around the world and decisions made by their leaders. The difficulty of the game is high and often decisions lead to disasters.

10.2.2 Example 2: Energy Saving Game

As an example of a very different computer game from the quiz type, the Energy Saving Game (http://www.olliesworld.com/club/gamehouse.htm) focuses on younger school children as the target group, building on providing knowledge about the climate impact of energy use decisions in the household by relatively simple multiple choice questions. Correct answers reduce the visualised energy use of the virtual household and the game ends when the energy bill has been reduced considerably. The complexity is very low and the playing time is short.

10.2.3 Potential mechanisms through which computer games may be effective

Comparing the two presented game types is very difficult and the mechanisms they address are also very different. The Energy Saving Game, as a slightly more advanced version of a simple quiz game, primarily aims to communicate procedural knowledge (what is it that I as a school child can contribute to save energy at home). The Fate of the World simulates political, social, and climate systems with high accuracy, giving the player a simulated and emotionally engaging experience of the decisional pressure political decision-makers are under. The advantage of the latter game is clearly the potential for simulating an emotional relationship to the necessary decisions and being able to experiment with effects in an environment that behaves to a large degree natural. This provides the player with knowledge about the system components and their relationships, but also provides them with relevant feedback about success. This can then impact the perceived efficacy in environmental domains. In the best case, experiences from such computer games can increase acceptance of or lobbyism for other kinds of policy measures. In the worst case, however, the experiences in such games might also reduce the perceived significance of individual action, as compared to high policy making on the world level. In other words, it might be easy to leave the topic of climate change to big politics after playing as the head of the GEO.

10.2.4 Evaluations of computer games in environmental communication

Interestingly, the effects of playing the described types of computer games are not often evaluated. There is of course substantial literature on computer- and game-based learning in schools which demonstrates that a combination of traditional teaching with computer-based teaching creates the best results (Krotoski, 2010), but very few of these are about the environment. What makes interactive games effective in the classroom are that they utilise rewards (and thus motivate the children), allow for individual pathways to deal with obstacles, and allow for failure in a safe place.

One study evaluated the effects of a mobile phone-based computer game for teenagers called "Power Agent" (Gustafsson et al., 2009) on a family's energy use. The study concluded, based on a small sample of participating families, that the game's elements of information at the right place and competition against other families were highly effective. Energy consumption was drastically reduced during the period the game was played, but the authors explicitly said that they were not able to make any conclusions about the post-game period. The game succeeded furthermore to stimulate social interaction about energy use between the family members and increased their knowledge, especially procedural knowledge (what to do).

McGonigal (2011) asserts that a main advantage of computer games is the number of people participating and interacting. Whereas the examples above were games with unconnected players, more and more simulation games build on connectivity between players. This makes it possible to make more use of the social features of computer gamers' networks. The increasing collaborative character of modern complex computer games also offers some potential for the future design of unorthodox environmental campaigns. Smartphone and app technology offer exciting new possibilities, with elements within apps often blending with the other functions.

10.3 Board games as a means of environmental communication

Three board games are presented that have sustainability or climate change as a central focus of their gameplay. They received positive evaluations by the users of one of the leading board game player forums (www.boardgamegeek.com) and can thus be assumed to be "real" board games rather than board games that have been developed for educational purposes only and are not taken seriously by the gaming community. The three selected games are the Settlers of Catan Oil Springs Scenario, the board game CO_2, and the business simulation Green Deal. They are very different in their complexity and realism with respect to the economic and natural mechanisms simulated. Neither is the selection of games complete nor should it be understood as a promotion of the selected board games.

10.3.1 Example 1: The Settlers of Catan Oil Springs Scenario

Settlers of Catan is one of the top-selling board games in the world, published by Teuber in 1995 (www.catan.com). The game is a relatively simple simulation of a rural economy where a small number of natural resources (e.g. clay, wheat, sheep, wood, and ore) are used to build and develop small societies on an island of limited size. The original version of the game has no obvious sustainability dimension in the gameplay, but it includes scarcity of resources and space as well as trading resources as central gameplay elements. Over the years, many variants and scenarios of Settlers of Catan have been published, one of them adding a crucial resource for modern societies and its impacts on sustainability to the game: the Oil Springs Scenario.

In 2011, Assadourian and Hansen published their Oil Springs Scenario as an add-on to Settlers of Catan (http://www.oilsprings.catan.com/). In this scenario, a sixth resource is added to the gameplay, namely oil. This new resource is a very powerful resource in the game as it can be converted into two other resources of the player's choice and also helps develop a city owned by the player into a metropolis. Thus, each player is highly motivated to gain and use oil in their gameplay. However, using oil comes at a cost: for each fifth oil resource used, a natural disaster caused by climate change hits the island. Either the coast is flooded, which affects all players with settlements at the coast, or one of the resource-producing fields on the game board is permanently "ruined" and will no longer produce resources. In other words, using oil in the long run reduces the sustainability of the island community because it reduces the flow of other resources, but this will not necessarily affect the player(s) who use the most oil. However, the player might also decide to sequester (to "destroy") oil during the game instead of using it, thus giving up on the benefits of oil use. This personal sacrifice is rewarded by an "environmentalism" token, with the player with most such tokens winning the game in the case when a total environmental collapse occurs before the game is ended. The rulebook also contains a short concluding educational section about climate change and the effects of uncontrolled use of non-regenerative resources.

In total, the mechanisms in the game are relatively simple. There is a simple relationship between use of oil and the occurrence of disasters; the benefits of oil use are big for each individual player which makes it highly attractive to "overlook" their negative consequences. Often, a strategy of excessive oil use will make a player win, even if the island world would have collapsed shortly after. However, experiencing this inner drive to sacrifice the island community for the short-term win is educational in itself, as the author can report from own experience.

10.3.2 Example 2: CO_2 – The board game

In 2012, Lacerda published "CO_2 – the board game" that gives a very complex economic simulation in the global context of climate change and CO_2 emissions (http://www.giochix.it/scheda.php?item=3205&lingua=0). The player takes the role of a globally active energy company building power supplies in different continents. The choices made by the players have an impact on the CO_2 levels in the atmosphere, which again affects the likelihood of natural disasters potentially destroying the different countries and industrial installations in them. If the CO_2 level in the atmosphere reaches a certain level, the process becomes irreversible and the system collapses completely and all players have lost.

The players develop their level of expertise in energy technologies and need to plan their construction work in much detail to satisfy the energy demand of a selected continent. They benefit personally from supplying power to continents in need. Regenerative power sources help reduce the CO_2 problems, but demand more knowledge and resources. The central mechanisms of the game are the economic aspects of financing and building the power plants, developing the knowledge by investing in scientific research to build less polluting power plants, and emission trading in a world with permanently increasing energy demand. Forestation and recycling are also treated as a type of "power plant" in the game. Also, elements of lobbyism have been integrated into the game to simulate its effect on climate change policies.

The game, which can also be played as a single player game, is highly complex and simulates the intertwined mechanisms of energy supply, CO_2 emissions, energy demand, and scientific progress. Interestingly, the game's difficulty has not been adjusted to make it more player-friendly so that in most games, especially with inexperienced players, the simulated world collapses because of too high CO_2 levels at one point of the game. Nevertheless, the players have the tools to prevent this negative outcome, as almost all effects are caused by the decisions of the players.

10.3.3 Example 3: Green Deal

The third example of a board game with an environmental topic, or in this case sustainability, was published in 2014 by Al-JouJou. The players in this business simulation manage companies that compete on the worldwide market. What makes the game interesting is that the sustainability of the company, with its dimensions of ecology, economy, and social standards, is important in winning this game.

The central mechanisms in this game are investment decisions about different kinds of projects with more or less sustainable potential. The decisions build on not only different dimensions of sustainability, but also the dividends that the company is able to pay its investors. Investments in sustainability can also be used to increase the company's public image. Three components determine the winner of the game: good public relations work, the real scores on the sustainability dimensions, and finally the financial evaluation of the company. The sustainability scores have the highest potential for victory points.

An interesting twist in the game is that the investment projects are also localised on a world map and effects are influenced by neighbouring projects. These neighbouring projects may cooperate and thereby reduce costs or compete against projects of other owners.

10.3.4 Potential mechanisms through which board games may be effective

If we look at the board games presented here, the obvious effect they may have is the increase in knowledge. Knowledge about mechanisms in complex systems has been shown as an essential prerequisite for engaging in pro-environmental decisions (Ungar, 2000). What is striking though is that all three games build on an approach that uses today's economy of growth as an unquestioned model. The target and winning move in all three games is to become the most economically successful of all players. Further interesting research could explore if playing such games increases the belief of people that problems like climate change can be addressed by means of making the right decisions in companies in a society that needs economic growth as its central driver. However, in games such as CO_2, the player may start questioning this assumption when confronted with the almost exclusive series of failures of such a system: in most cases all players lose, because the climate system collapses before the greener economy's effects kick in.

A second interesting effect of the games is that the players become decision-makers that are emotionally involved in solving a pressing environmental problem – even if that problem only exists for the time the board game is played, and the games have a defined end point (unlike reality) beyond which the players do not have to plan. This decision-making not only provides the players with knowledge about important mechanisms of economy and climate, but also teaches them how it *feels* to be a responsible person for making such decisions. Emotional involvement is a central aspect when trying to engage people in environmental topics (Weber, 2006). The possibility of compressing many decades into one or two hours of a game makes it possible to experience failures and to try interventions whose success in reality would only show after many years. Furthermore, the game can be started again after a failure, which makes it possible to see the effects of different strategies.

A third effect of board games is that they are usually played in groups of two to five players (even if CO_2 can also be played as a solitary game). Playing a game is a social situation, and communication about the negative effects of other peoples' or your own actions on the environment during the gameplay establishes how the topic is framed in this group. Maybe these games can contribute to establishing the environment as a topic in a social group. Green Deal especially incorporates some elements of social dependency of actions and their effects, which also strengthens the perceived importance of socially coordinated actions.

A fourth effect that board games can have is the experience of efficacy, which in itself is rewarding for people (Bandura, 1982), especially in domains such as climate change where the outcomes of actions in reality are often hard to detect. Board games where the effects become visible almost immediately can provide people with a valuable experience: I am able to do something about the problem, my actions count. These experiences may be generalised to real life to a certain degree.

10.3.5 Evaluation of board games in environmental communication

Scientific evaluations of board games with an environmental topic are even rarer than evaluations of computer games. One study evaluated a board game developed to include farmers in the participatory design of future life stock systems, concluding that the game was very helpful in motivating the target group (Welp et al., 2006). Eisenack (2013) describes the benefits of the board game "Keep Cool" that he helped develop. He concluded that the game was successfully used as a communication tool (a) to communicate science across different disciplines, (b) as a means of public relations for the producing institute but also for the topic (since a game received more media coverage than just another press release about climate change), and (c) for science communication to the public. He evaluated the game qualitatively and found many positive effects: mainly shifts in problem framing, structuring already existing knowledge, and deep discussions about mechanisms behind the game and thereby also reality. Thus, the communicative character of board gaming provides the potential to discuss rules and their background, making them especially interesting in creating discussion about a topic like climate change.

10.4 Role plays as a means of environmental communication

A substantial fraction of climate change-related games are role plays and management simulations. These are simulations of decision-making or negotiations in a large group of people, usually played in an educational setting like a university course on climate policy negotiation (Reckien & Eisenack, 2013). Two simulations are briefly presented, before their potential effect mechanisms are discussed with an evaluation of such approaches.

10.4.1 Example 1: Climate Diplomat

Climate Diplomat is a role play developed by Craig Hart in 2009 that simulates the Bali Action Plan negotiations for eight participants. The material for the role play can be downloaded at http://www.iucnael.org/en/documents/doc_download/648-climate-diplomat-negotiation-simulation.html.

All participants receive not only common background information, but also confidential information that describes their particular role. The players go through a 90-minute negotiation session that aims to come to an agreement on four topics: (a) developed country mitigation commitments, (b) developing country mitigation commitments, (c) technology transfer to developing countries, and (d) financial contributions to adaptation measures. The role players are provided with extensive background information. Each representative is provided with confidential information that gives them an overview of the impacts of potential scenarios on the specific party, preferred pathways of development, opinion polls in the country, and so on. All material is rooted in positions stated by the partners in the real world.

10.4.2 Example 2: Mock Environmental Summit

In their paper about the effects of an innovative role play-based university course, Rebich and Gautier (2005) present their approach in the context of constructivist pedagogy. Based on the assumption that people have prior knowledge which they bring to new situations and thereby will impact their understanding of new situations, they question the efficacy of educational programs that try to tackle climate change just by providing new information to people without dealing with their prior concepts and mental models.

The Mock Environmental Summit consists of several parts: first, students listen to a limited number of lectures about the scientific background of climate change. Second, they engage in a number of role plays drafting and negotiating international agreements similar to the Kyoto protocol. They act as representatives of selected countries. The role plays stretch over several weeks and part of the play is that the students acquire information on the Internet that they utilise in their negotiations. The students receive both group feedback and individual feedback and support in their roles.

10.4.3 Potential mechanisms through which role plays may be effective

In addition to the mechanisms discussed above for computer games and board games, role plays are often characterised through their high degree of pre- and post-role play input. In role plays, the players are usually instructed extensively on the background and their role, something that is missing to a large degree in the other game types. Role plays usually include a debriefing discussion, which can deepen the experience further, and they take place over longer time periods. They also include more players than board games and the players have predefined roles.

These characteristics open up some new possibilities. Through the predefined role profiles, players can be "forced" to experience opposing perspectives, which can increase their willingness to explore others' experiences and compromise. The opportunity for long instructions and debriefings allows the embedding of an experience in a larger context, and consequently reflection. The downside is that role plays usually happen in educational contexts, such as universities, and are not necessarily transferred to the private sphere.

10.4.4 Evaluations of role plays in environmental communication

Rebich and Gautier (2005) were also interested in documenting the effects of their role play, conducting a concept-mapping study where they asked the students prior to the course and after completion to draw maps of the central concepts related to climate change. Almost all students' post-course maps were more complex, contained more concepts and propositions, and contained less misconceptions or weak conceptions. Thus, the authors concluded that the role play was effective in increasing the structural quality of the students' knowledge.

10.5 Social dilemmas

Another popular role-play game is about behaviour in social dilemmas. This research started with a paper named "The Tragedy of the Commons" (Hardin, 1968). A social dilemma is a case in which an individual's interest conflicts with the collective interest. For example, if an individual's interest to use electricity for increasing personal comfort conflicts with the collective interest to save electricity, this situation might be called a social dilemma. Social dilemmas are characterised by two criteria: (a) each individual receives a higher payoff (e.g. money) if the individual acts in self-interest as compared to a cooperative strategy, but (b) all individuals together will receive a lower payoff when all act in self-interest and do not cooperate (Borgstede et al., 2013). The next section will give some examples of such social dilemma games and findings based on them.

10.5.1 Social dilemma research

The classic social dilemma studies confront participants with a decision game where uncertainties about the collective costs and social willingness to cooperate are varied systematically. A typical example is the experiments by Wilke (1991) which led to the GEF hypothesis: whereas rational choice theories assume that maximising personal utility is the only driver of behavioural decision-making, leading to greed (G) as the steering principle, the GEF hypothesis states that efficiency (E) and fairness (F) are also important principles of human behaviour that are effective under certain conditions. Greed is stronger when the stakes for a decision are raised and when the uncertainty about the negative collective outcome is higher (Borgstede et al., 2013). Efficiency motivations, which means to maximise the total outcomes while keeping the common resource intact, are strongest when fairness is understood as equity, which means that people should be rewarded proportionally to their input (Borgstede et al., 2013). Fairness can be perceived according to three principles: the equity principle (people receive in proportion to what they put in), the equality principle (people receive all the same share), and the need principle (people receive according to their need) (Borgstede et al., 2013).

One study investigated if travel mode choice bears the characteristics of a social dilemma situation (Van Vugt et al., 1996). They assumed that choosing the car over public transportation is at least partly determined by an individual gain–common loss situation. The individual gains comfort and probably a shorter travel time at less perceived costs, but the collective pays via the costs for maintaining the infrastructure and bearing the negative effects of car use (e.g. emissions, noise, health risks). They found that individuals that had a pro-social self-concept preferred public transportation more.

A number of factors have been identified that increase cooperation in social dilemma situations (Borgstede et al., 2013). In small groups (three to five members), cooperation tends to be higher than in large groups (more than ten members). Communication between the group members about the structure of the dilemma before decision-making reduces selfish actions. Higher perceived response efficacy, meaning the feeling that the individuals' or group's action can resolve the common resource problem, increases willingness to cooperate. Social and environmental uncertainty decrease willingness to cooperate, which means that people act more selfishly if they are unsure about the negative collective effects of their actions or about how other people are going to decide. Social norms and common values are guiding principles that tell people how other people will most likely behave, thus reducing social uncertainty.

10.5.2 Game theory

Closely related to the study of social dilemma is game theory. Modern game theory was initiated by von Neumann's research in the early 20th century (Von Neumann & Morgenstern, 2007). Game theory studies strategic decision-making, especially in cooperative games with two or more players. Three classic examples are the prisoner's dilemma (Rapoport, 1965), the ultimatum game (Thaler, 1988), and the dictator game (Kahneman et al., 1986).

In the prisoner's dilemma, two prisoners who have conducted a crime together and are now imprisoned separately from each other are offered the following choice: (1) testify that the other person committed the crime or (2) not say anything. The prison sentence depends on the combination of answers from the two prisoners. If both remain silent, they will receive a minimal sentence (e.g. one year). If one prisoner betrays the other and the other remains silent, the betraying prisoner goes free and the other is sentenced to a long sentence (e.g. three years). If both prisoners betray each other, both are sentenced to a medium sentence (e.g. two years).

In the ultimatum game, two players decide how to divide a given sum of money. One player makes a proposal on how to divide the money (e.g. 50:50 or 70:30) and the second player decides if he or she accepts or rejects the proposal. In case of rejection, both players receive nothing. A rational choice for player one would be to maximise his or her share by offering a small amount to player two and a rational behaviour for player two would be to accept everything that is above 100:0. However, in most cultures, the first player tends to offer an even split or something close, demonstrating experienced fairness is much more important for acceptance than economic rationality (Sanfey et al., 2003; Oosterbeek et al., 2004).

The dictator game is a variation of the ultimatum game where the opportunity for player two to reject the offer and thus cause a loss for player one is removed. In other words, player one decides how the money is split and player two just has to take his or her share. Even if there is no way player one would be punished for taking everything, many participants reduce their outcome by sharing the money with player two (Kahneman et al., 1986). The ultimatum game, and even more so the dictator game, demonstrates that humans have a tendency to include fairness and kindness considerations into their economic decision-making.

Fairchild (2008) analyses companies' investment decisions from a game theory perspective, concluding that costly environmental investments in companies are not only dependent on fiscal instruments implemented by governments (the rational choice approach), but also the "green awareness" of the public. If the societal norm is that green decisions are good decisions, the companies follow that directive to a certain degree even if it does not pay off economically.

10.5.3 The contribution of dilemma research and game theory to environmental communication

In a study about the effects of a mass media campaign to promote climate friendly behaviour among Dutch citizens, Staats et al. (1996) frame their discussion of the findings from a social dilemma perspective. They argue that the campaign did succeed in making the seriousness of the collective problem salient. What made the campaign less successful was that it did not rule out the uncertainty connected to when and where which negative effects of climate change would affect the Dutch citizens. Even more importantly, the campaign did not address the social uncertainty, meaning that after the campaign people would be convinced that climate change is a serious problem that might affect them collectively, but they remained unsure about how other people thought and if they were willing to cooperate to resolve the issue. Thus, insights from social dilemma research can be of great value for designing communication campaigns in situations where the individual (short-term) benefit overshadows the negative collective (long-term) effect.

Another conclusion that can be drawn from social dilemma research for environmental communication is the aspects that trigger cooperative behaviour. People should be acting in smaller groups, meaning it makes sense to address people not as a whole group but in smaller units to reduce the negative effect of the large group. Communication between people should be fostered to suppress selfish behaviour. Both aspects can be implemented in modern computer-based communication, for example, via groups in virtual social networks. Increase of response efficacy is further crucial for increasing cooperation; people only cooperate if they assume that the action is going to make a difference. Whereas reducing environmental uncertainty may be difficult, reducing social uncertainty can be an option by giving feedback about cooperative behaviour of other people. Highlighting social norms that are in favour of pro-environmental actions are one way of acting.

10.6 Conclusions

The first part of this chapter was dedicated to exploring the potential of games for communicating environmental topics. A growing number of such games have been developed and they seem to have some advantages that more conventional environmental communication does not have. The main advantage seems to be that games offer the opportunity to try management strategies first hand in a protected space. The experiences are more direct than when mediated via media communication, and they lead to a more emotional response which again can become a driving force for generalising them to the real world. However, the protected space and the unusual role individuals take in such games are also a problem for their generalisation. Most of us are not world leaders, and returning from the game board or the computer screen to our ordinary lives can disconnect the experience we made as (simulated) world leaders in the game from our lives. Furthermore, it should be asked who is attracted to playing games with an environmental topic? Are people who are already aligned to environmental protection and pro-environmental behaviour playing? However, even these people can benefit from the emotional component and the experiential learning the games offer. Some games and simulations are also used in controlled educational contexts where participants can be "forced" to play. On the one hand, this may reduce the effect the games have by increasing negative reactions, but, on the other hand, the target group increases beyond the already convinced which can be a promising strategy. Modern communication technologies via apps that blend game aspects, such as competition, with serious aspects can provide fodder for future games in environmental communication. An example is the app eco-challenge.

The second part of the chapter briefly analysed the contribution that research on social dilemma and games in the game theory context make to environmental communication. It showed that some conclusions from this line of research may help in addressing relevant aspects in communication strategies that can have a positive influence on cooperative behaviour (e.g. segmenting the target audience into small groups within which the members have the chance to communicate with each other, or highlighting the response efficacy of the behaviour).

Review questions

- Give examples of computer-based games and how they can be used in environmental communication.
- Give examples of board games and how they can be used in environmental communication.
- Give examples of role plays and how they can be used in environmental communication.
- Give examples of social dilemmas and how they can contribute to understanding people's relationship to environmental problems.
- Explain what kinds of interventions reduce the overuse of common resources according to social dilemma research.

- Give examples of typical games analysed in game theory research and how they might be relevant for environmental communication.

Suggested readings

Borgstede, C. V., Johansson, L.-O., & Nilsson, A. (2013). Social dilemmas: Motivational, individual and structural aspects influencing cooperation. In L. Steg, A. E. Van den Berg & J. I. M. De Groot (Eds.), *Environmental Psychology – An Introduction* (pp. 175–184). Chichester, UK: John Wiley & Sons.

Eisenack, K. (2013). A climate change board game for interdisciplinary communication and education. *Simulation & Gaming*, 44(2–3), 328–348.

Reckien, D., & Eisenack, K. (2013). Climate change gaming on board and screen: A review. *Simulation & Gaming*, 1046878113480867.

Susi, T., Johannesson, M., & Backlund, P. (2007). *Serious games: An overview.* Skövde, Sweden: School of Humanities and Informatics, University of Skövde.

11
Rock Festivals, Sport Events, Theatre – Some Out-of-the-Ordinary Means of Environmental Communication

Chapter summary

This last chapter of the book describes alternative approaches to effectively communicate pro-environmentalism. It addresses how conservation appeals can be placed in settings where people primarily focus on enjoyment. How can big events like rock festivals, culture festivals, sport events, or fun fairs be utilised to promote "saving the planet"? How do implementation strategies look? What is known about the psychological background of humour in such communication? Can lessons learned in advertisements be transferred to the context of environmental protection? What are potential obstacles (e.g. commercial interests, potential intoxication of the target group, or lack of attention)? The aim of alternative measures can be to improve the ecological footprint of the festival or event itself, but they can also aim at changing people's attitudes and behaviour beyond that. Such spillover effects will be contrasted against a possible trade-off of behaviour in one domain against behaviour in another.

11.1 Introduction

In this last chapter of the book, the perspective of communication arenas will be broadened by exploring two case studies the author was

---

Parts of this chapter, namely the description of case one, are adapted from the chapter "Nye måter å fremme miljøvennlig atferd på – kan miljøvernbudskap tilpasses en rockefestival", written by the author of the book "Norsk Miljøpsykologi – Mennesker og omgivelser" (Klöckner, 2012). The text is used with kind permission of SINTEF akademisk forlag.

involved in. Whereas environmental communication is often used in settings where the recipients are expected to be in the mood for making pro-environmental decisions in a deliberate way, this chapter looks at the potential for environmental communication at large events, such as rock concerts, music or culture festivals, sport events, theatre, or carnivals. People visit these festivals to relax, so why should we bother them with environmental messages? Would the messages even have a chance of being perceived? On the other hand, festivals have been an arena for social change throughout history (Sharpe, 2008), with the setting of a festival offering the chance to build social bonds between audience members, artists, and the organisers that can contribute to effective communication. In Chapter 4, the impacts of social norms have been described, and in a festival context social norms can become particularly strong.

The next section introduces the difference between using environmental communication to make the event itself less polluting and using the event as a means of environmental communication. Some dilemmas of implementing environmental communication in big events will be discussed, before the role and effect of humour in communication is analysed. Two case studies are explored: (1) the collaboration between the author of this book and a local rock festival in Trondheim, Norway, and (2) the collaboration between the author and an international film festival in Trondheim. Since the main assumption of this approach builds on a spillover of pro-environmental behaviour from one behavioural domain to another, a brief summary of research findings on how likely it is that the wanted behaviour spreads is given. The final section of the chapter will conclude some of the lessons learned from the two cases.

11.2 Improving the environmental impact of a big event versus changing people's mind sets

When thinking about big events like a rock festival, environmental protection is probably not the first thing that comes to mind. Festivals and similar events are about sports, music, art, being social with other people that have similar interests, forgetting about your ordinary life, and having a good time. However, since big events and particularly rock festivals often take place in natural or semi-natural environments, they have a close connection to nature, both in a positive sense by utilising nature to create a pleasing and restorative environment for the audience and in a negative sense by potentially harming nature. Furthermore, such events are visited by tens of thousands of people who generate substantial resource use and waste.

The environmental impact of a big event is difficult to calculate and many factors play a role in determining what the main contributions are. Several festivals and similar events have therefore conducted life-cycle assessments to develop an understanding of the material flows caused by their event (Jones, 2014; Roig et al., 2011). Table 11.1 outlines seven domains in which a big event, such as a festival, might impact the environment and suggests some strategies that could be taken by

Table 11.1 Possible contributions of organisers and audience to reduce the negative environmental impact of a big event

Aspect	Event organisers' contribution	Audience's contribution
Transportation of equipment, professionals, and audience	– Use local catering and equipment – Include free use of public transportation in the ticket – Provide good connection to local and long-distance public transport – Provide a guarded bike park – Provide support for carpooling on the festival website – Use environmentally friendly travel modes in the event administration during the year – Compensate for CO_2 emissions of transportation that cannot be avoided	– Choose environmentally friendly travel modes – Use carpooling
Energy and water use	– Use low-energy lighting (LED) – Use low-energy cooling equipment – Use regenerative energy supplies – Minimise water use – Use sustainable waste water treatment	– Do not waste water

Table 11.1 (Continued)

Aspect	Event organisers' contribution	Audience's contribution
Waste	- Reduce packaging in the event arena - Use environmentally friendly alternatives if packaging is needed - Ban flyers as they are a substantial source of littering - Control at the entrance for unnecessary waste but inform the audience before the event - Use waste separation systems - Use reusable or recyclable material wherever possible - Use token systems for beer glasses, catering, and so on - Use environmentally friendly sanitary systems - Use recycled products in event promotion (posters, T-shirts, etc.) - Make waste bins easily accessible (both placement and number of bins are important)	- Do not litter in the event arena and the entrance area - Take part in waste separation - Take part in token systems - Do not bring own food/drinks - Do not bring one-way products that produce extra waste (e.g. one-way rain coats)
Protecting nature in the festival arena	- Fence off/guard vulnerable areas - Cover grass in front of the stages - Use less damaging stage/catering constructions - Avoid driving with heavy machinery in sensitive areas - Provide enough and easily accessible toilets - Take care of animals living in the area	- Develop a mental connection to the area, and feel responsible - Do not destroy plants or buildings - Do not urinate outside the sanitary facilities - Do not litter

Catering	– Use organic food/drinks – Use local food/drinks (if the environmental impact is lower) – Use seasonal food – Use fair trade products	– Do not bring own food/drinks
Noise	– Limit maximum loudness – Use decentralised PA systems – End the outdoors part of an event early, if there are neighbours – Invite the neighbours	– Avoid noise while travelling to and from the event – Avoid unnecessary noise in the event arena
Other	– Cooperate with environmental interest groups – Develop a communication strategy that emphasises the environmental aspect of the event, also in the marketing campaign	

Source: Translated from the Norwegian version with kind permission of SINTEF akademisk forlag.

the organisers and the audience to minimise that impact (see Laing & Frost, 2010, for more suggestions).

However, environmental communication connected to big events can be more than a contribution to reducing the environmental impact of the event itself. The experience of positive emotions during a big event can spill over to conservation activities carried out under the same circumstances, motivating the audience to perform these behaviours in the long run. Such spillover effects have been demonstrated for emotions such as shame and fear to unrelated subsequent behaviour (Zeelenberg et al., 2008) and might work in favour of pro-environmental behaviour at the festival and afterwards.

11.3 The dilemmas of environmental communication at big events

Whereas event organisers are a natural target for communicating environmental improvements, one might conclude that the audience of an event is not a preferable target group. People might be non-receptive to messages, even intoxicated, and not willing to react to your ideas in a positive way. However, a deeper analysis reveals that blending big event experiences and conservationism may be useful. First, the direct environmental problems potentially caused by a big event are large enough to justify not only taking action by communicating with the organisers, but also trying to impact the audience to contribute. Second, many big events have a tradition of being an arena for social and political discussion (Sharpe, 2008). In some contexts, the audience has been willing to engage in pro-social or pro-environmental actions even during a festival. The key lies in how to blend the message into the overall hedonistic leisure activities at such an event. Sharpe (2008) concludes that festivals have had a history of "resistance and social protest" which makes them a natural arena for trying new, pro-environmental thinking in a secured and confined space. Many music or cultural festivals all over the world have a clear pro-environmental profile, some of them being genuinely motivated to convey conservation, others being motivated by reducing costs for cleaning up the festival arena afterwards, a marketing advantage, or satisfying requirements to receive access to vulnerable natural areas for the festival (Laing & Frost, 2010). Third, festival-goers usually have at least some financial resources available, since festival tickets in many countries are expensive. In Rogers' theory about diffusion of innovations (see Section 5.2), the fraction of the population with available financial resources has a high probability of including the early adopters of new technology and new social developments (E. M. Rogers, 2003). The probability of this group adopting lifestyle changes is higher, leading to the probability of a spread of new behaviour through the population.

11.4 Humour in environmental communication

Humorous messages can fit better into an event context than moralising messages. In a meta-analysis, Eisend (2009) found that the use of humour in advertising increased positive attitudes both about the advertisement and about the brand that it advertised. Humour also increased attention and purchase intentions but decreased the credibility of the communicating source. A literature review of the effect of humour on learning concluded that it is a very efficient means to gather attention but has less favourable effects on information acquisition and retention (Banas et al., 2011). A study about smoking prevention found that especially young people reacted negatively to judgemental or moral messages in social marketing campaigns but preferred humorous communication (Hicks, 2001). Adolescents reacted positively to humorous anti-smoking adverts because they were distinguishable from the normal fear-inducing adverts they were already habituated to (Messerlian & Derevensky, 2006). Also in the domain of pro-environmental behaviour, adolescents and young adults reacted positively to humorous messages and strongly supported pairing pro-recycling messages with something the target group valued, such as music (Prestin & Pearce, 2010).

Although the effectiveness of humour or entertainment in communicating pro-social messages is disputed, such a communication strategy seems to be very well suited to the context of an event for several reasons: (a) gathering attention of the audience is a major barrier in communicating pro-environmental behaviour, and strategies that have a higher probability of achieving this should be preferred. (b) Young people who form the main target group for rock festivals react positively to humour and negatively to moral, fear-inducing, or judgemental campaigns. However, for events with different target groups, the effects might be less positive. (c) Humorous messages can easily be adapted for the tone of the event and have a higher probability of being accepted by the audience. This seems very relevant in contexts where the reaction to serious messages could easily be negative.

11.5 Case one: Environmental communication at a rock festival – Ecorock

In 2008, the author and the PSTEREO festival in Trondheim (www.pstereo.net) engaged in a collaboration to bring some of the ideas presented in this book into practice. After a start-up workshop for the project, two surveys were conducted providing data about the attitudes of rock audiences towards the environment and environmental messages at rock festivals. The rationale behind that was to explore how much support for pro-environmental communication could be expected in the context of a rock festival. Selected results from this project are presented in the following paragraphs.

11.5.1 The start-up workshop

A workshop with 20 students aimed to develop ideas on how to connect positive aspects of being at a rock festival with communicating environmental protection. This was based on the assumption that pro-environmental communication only has a chance of being positively accepted if it links or even contributes to the positive atmosphere. The aspects displayed in Figure 11.1 were identified as the most positive aspects of being at a rock festival. Interestingly, the mind map shows a combination of hedonistic aspects, concepts related to group experience, references to disconnecting from ordinary life, and also, promisingly, aspects referring to engagement and social action. That the latter are named as positive aspects of a festival at least by some of the participants of the workshop makes the approach of implementing such action into a festival promising.

11.5.2 Pilot study one

A questionnaire was administered to analyse the openness of concert attendees to environmental messages and the role group processes play at rock concerts (for more information see (Klöckner, 2012)). Questionnaires were distributed at four rock concerts in Bergen and Trondheim before the performances of two Norwegian bands. The participants of the study agreed very much that a concert constitutes a group experience. Furthermore, the participants agreed moderately that they feel part of a group that is sharing the same values. The importance of an ecological conscience of organisers, the artists, or the audience was rated rather low. Only 14% agreed to the statement that their decision to attend a concert or a festival depended on its ecological profile. However, even if the importance was rated low, the idea of sustainable concerts or festivals received support. It seems that environmental messages are perceived, but the environmental profile of an event is not prioritised in deciding where to go. However, participants gave support for green festivals. Depending on the bands playing, people report a moderate to strong group experience during the concerts.

11.5.3 Pilot study two

A second study was conducted with festival attendees to explore the perception of environmental aspects at the festival by the audience more directly. The aim was to map out the image of the festival and the perception of environmental priority domains. Immediately after the PSTEREO festival, a link to an online questionnaire was posted on the festival's homepage. First, it asked what was perceived as constituting PSTEREO's profile. Environmental protection was among the least agreed aspects. This shows that the festival had room for improvement in the public perception of their environmental efforts. Second, most of the people answering the questionnaire were able to name some

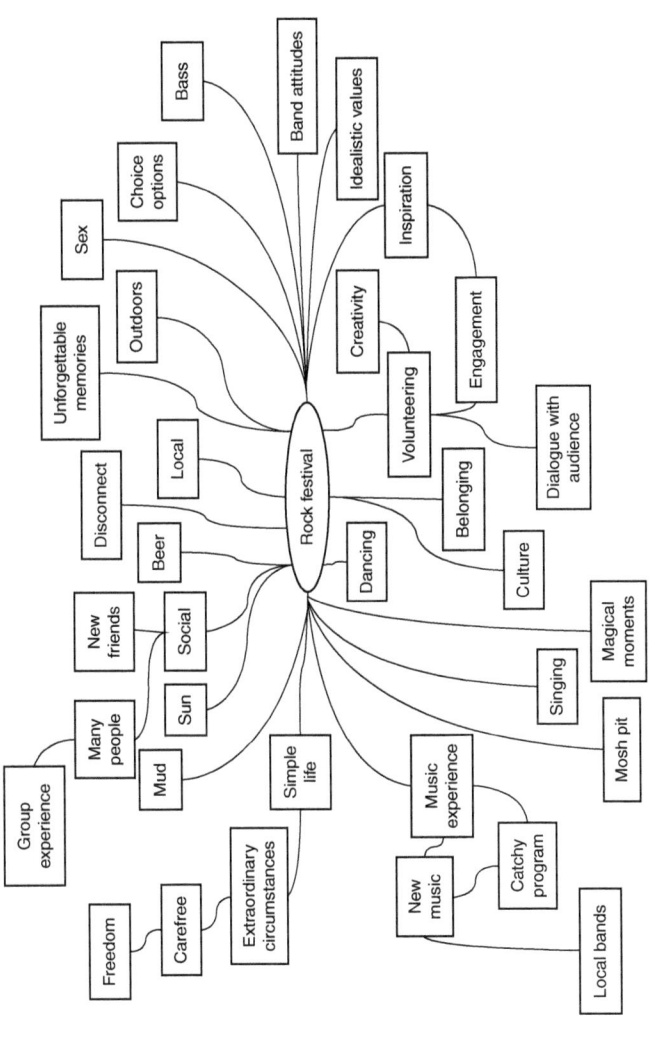

Figure 11.1 Positive aspects of a rock festival as identified during the workshop
Source: Translated from the Norwegian version with kind permission of SINTEF akademisk forlag.

of the environmental actions the festival takes, most prominently that people were constantly picking up waste in the festival arena, that there were many waste bins, that ecological food was served, that the grass was protected by a cover, and that the festival organisers were using an electric car. By far, most of the participants thought that waste causes the largest environmental impact of the festival, followed by energy use, transport of artists, and transport of the audience. Only few considered the environmental impact of food and drinks served at the festival a relevant contribution. A life-cycle analysis of the festival showed, however, that transport of people and material and vending were the two sections that contributed the most to the environmental impact of the festival (Johannessen et al., 2010). Waste and energy use were relatively unimportant. This mismatch between public perception and calculated impact can be explained by the high visibility of waste and the low visibility of the impact connected to food production. However, it poses a challenge for the communication strategy of the festival. The suggested priorities by the participants for the organisers of the festival reflect the perceived areas of the largest impact described before. The participants wanted the organisers to use local providers, to protect nature in the festival arena, to provide waste separation systems, and to reduce waste. By far, the lowest priority nominated was reducing the noise level which seems to be perceived as interfering with the festival experience. People declared that their most likely contribution to a green festival is to not litter, to protect nature in the festival arena, and to participate in waste separation. Avoiding noise on the way to the festival was less popular. Summarising the findings of pilot study two, people recognised some of the environmental efforts PSTEREO had made and were willing to participate. However, they held false beliefs about which aspects of a festival have the largest environmental impact and suggested actions to the organisers and themselves based on these faulty assumptions.

11.5.4 Project ideas

For three years, students of a course taught by the author worked in 13 groups on the topics of quantifying the impact of a rock festival, comparing different waste management options, developing waste handling strategies during the festival, developing strategies for waste reduction, developing tools for communicating environmental thinking to the audience, developing strategies for litter reduction, promoting reuse and recycling, promoting use of public transportation, and promoting saving energy. Four of the resulting projects will be briefly outlined as examples in the remainder of this section.

The smoothie bike (Gajic et al., 2010). This project aimed to raise awareness about the use of energy in everyday life. A bicycle-driven smoothie blender that the audience of the festival could use for free to produce their own smoothies was built. The group referred to similar ideas circulated on the Internet. The activity of cycling a bike to produce a smoothie was fun for the audience and therefore perfectly fitted into the tone of the festival.

Switch off the light (Andresen et al., 2011). Since Norwegians have a reputation for leaving the lights on, this project aimed to sensitise festival attendees towards the topic of energy use. Light switches could be installed on trees all around the festival arena that activate fun effects when the switch is triggered (e.g. a spotlight on the person pushing the switch or a sound effect). In addition, a large switch could be placed at the exit with the slogan "switch off the light when you leave". This switch could be connected to a counter display which is placed outside the exit to show how many people switched off the light in order to create a feeling of common norms and for the aggregated effect.

Waste voting (Fardzadeh et al., 2010). One of the most visible problems of a festival is that many plastic cups are discarded. The idea of this project is to turn the beer cups into the currency of a vote for the best band performance. The group suggested starting a fun competition between the bands regarding who gave the best performance. Votes could be placed by putting a beer cup into specially designed containers placed next to the stages, one representing each band. The project idea revolves around playful competition between fan groups and the fun of participating in this rather nonsensical activity. Ideally, the area would be cleaned of beer cups as a result.

Power failure (Suppipat et al., 2009). This project aims again at sensitising for energy use by staging a fake power failure while one of the main acts is playing. The idea is based on a real power failure that occurred at one of the stages during the festival the year before. Shutting down the music and light on the main stage should be combined with a sound landscape specifically designed for the purpose (a "powering down" sound created by the group) and a light installation, which could include the trees and the display of subtle energy-saving messages in the area. After a few seconds, the show on stage is resumed. The event is meant to create irritation and confusion by breaking out of the ordinary festival experience and then to trigger thoughts about the importance of energy and how it is used.

11.5.5 Conclusions of case one

To conclude this section, some critical reflections should be presented. The theoretical background presents pertinent arguments for attempting new methods of communicating environmental protection to young people by blending unobtrusive events and messages into a rock festival that attracts thousands of young people every year. Why this demographic is an interesting target group and why more and more festival organisers have an interest in greening their events have been outlined. However, the success of such an approach is dependent on the engagement of all participating parties and their cooperation. Not all ideas can be implemented at any time. For example, sometimes economic considerations or respect for the needs of sponsors, artists, or interests groups make it difficult to realise promising innovative projects. Much could be achieved if the group developing communication ideas was integrated into the planning stage, making it possible to tailor the projects even more to the needs of the festival. One thing should not be forgotten: neither the organisers nor the audience will have the environmental aspect of the festival highest on their priority list.

11.6 Case two: Environmental communication through visual art at a film festival

The second case study explores a different setting with a very different audience: a film festival. In recent years, more artists and artist collectives engage in producing artworks that focus on environmental problems, such as climate change, air pollution, or overconsumption (Buckland, 2012). Often, such artistic approaches receive a strong positive response in the artistic community and among well-educated people. Claims are made about what can be achieved with such alternative approaches of attracting attention to environmental topics. At the same time, traditional methods of communicating environmental problems via providing information have often been shown to be of limited success (Steg & Vlek, 2009). It might therefore be that an artistic approach to environmental communication offers a new and promising method of creating attention for environmental problems, but so far very few studies have systematically evaluated the effects of such approaches.

11.6.1 Visual communication of environmental problems through art

Art-based approaches to communicate environmental topics through films, video installations, sculptures, paintings, or other media have been discussed as an approach in its own right, not just as a tool to accompany traditional campaigns (Chiu & Arreglo, 2011). One study explored the potential of visual art as a new and more powerful carrier of environmental messages by analysing the contemporary art exhibition "Weather Report" by 51 artists in Canada as a case study (Dunaway, 2009). The messages of the artworks were about such abstract problems as climate change. The study argued that the aspects the artists added to the domain were the emotional links between people's personal spheres and local experiences, on the one hand, and the global problem, on the other. Furthermore, artwork served as the link between doomsday scenarios, inspiration to change, and visions for the future. However, environmental art also does have its pitfalls. In a review of the film "Manufactured Landscapes" about the work of the environmental photographer Edward Burtynsky, Cammaer (2009) raises an important question about the role and principles of visual environmental art, namely the clash between the aesthetic dimension and the ethical dimension, or in other words, the tension between creating something beautiful and aesthetically pleasing and conveying the (ugly) message of environmental destruction.

Very few studies have actually analysed the effects of such art pieces, beyond the individual reflections about art by the authors of scientific papers in a number of papers or books (Doyle, 2011; Dunaway, 2009). Probably the most intensively researched pieces of artistic environmental communication are the films "An Inconvenient Truth" and "The Day After Tomorrow". One study found that people who had recently watched "The Day After Tomorrow" were more worried about climate change, expected more dramatic consequences, were more likely to accept that the climate is a fragile system that might tip at some point, stated more willingness to act personally, and ranked climate change higher on the list of political priorities (Leiserowitz, 2004). In line with these findings, Nolan (2010) presented results from two studies that indicated people who had seen "An Inconvenient Truth" reported a higher degree of knowledge about climate change, concern about the problem, and willingness to act. However, a month later, no significant changes in people's behaviour could be detected.

11.6.2 The art pieces

The art pieces analysed in this case study were created by groups of students who had highly diverse cultural and educational backgrounds. All four pieces will be presented in the following paragraphs.

11.6.2.1 The waste sculpture

Inspired by shadow art by artists such as Tim Noble and Sue Webster, one student group created a sculpture made of cinema waste (popcorn cartons, beverage containers, etc.), so that its shadow resembled characteristic features of the skyline of Trondheim when illuminated by a strong spotlight. The sculpture itself looked like a large pile of typical cinema waste and the skyline was not to be recognised without the spotlight. The sculpture was presented in a central location at the film festival and the spotlight was connected to a motion sensor which triggered the lights when someone approached the sculpture.

11.6.2.2 "Butterflies to waste" video installations

A second group chose a subtle approach to visualise the effects of global environmental changes on animals, more precisely, butterflies. They produced a large number of artificial butterfly wings of endangered species living in Norway. They then used a high-speed camera to create a number of short video loops of the butterfly wings, each loop making the wings disappear or pile up in a large trash-like pile. Different versions of the butterfly loops can be found at the following webpages and should be watched before proceeding to the next sections: "short loop" – http://vimeo.com/64994743, "resurrection" – http://vimeo.com/64995468, "the vortex" – https://vimeo.com/64994745. The message "Hope to see these this summer?" was presented in the "short loop", projected on a screen in one of the main gathering areas of the festival.

11.6.2.3 "Environmental karma" short film

The third group created a two-minute short film about two young men who like to attend the Kosmorama film festival together with their girlfriends. One of them makes the right environmental choices (not wasting water, switching off the light, cycling, etc.), but the other behaves with environmental ignorance. Whereas the environmentally friendly guy reaches the festival cinema happily with his girlfriend, the other guy is stuck in a traffic jam and his girlfriend leaves the cinema before he arrives; his environmental karma played out unfortunate for him. The tone of the video is humorous with a catchy soundtrack. The short film was presented on the film festival's website and as a trailer before selected movie screenings. The short film can be seen at http://vimeo.com/64995946.

11.6.2.4 "Food waste" video installation

The last group produced a 1.5-minute short film that visualised the amount of food wasted over the course of different meals. The group shot the film using actual food waste that was found in waste bins at the university and student dorms. The film was presented in a redesigned standard household waste bin where a small projector was installed screening the film as a loop on a screen mounted on the top of the waste bin. The bin was placed in the gathering area of the festival. The short film can be seen at http://vimeo.com/64994741.

11.6.3 The quantitative evaluation at the film festival

A quantitative survey was conducted at the festival to evaluate the effects of the art pieces on the festival audience. A more comprehensive description of the study can be obtained from the author of this book on request (Klöckner, 2013b). The survey consisted of several parts: (1) the participants were presented with a list of 22 societal challenges and were asked to rate the level of priority that should be given to each of them. Five factors emerged:

- Priority area "human well-being"
- Priority area "safety and security"
- Priority area "environment"
- Priority area "animal rights"
- Priority area "global threats"

The priority area with the highest average importance was "global threats", followed by "human well-being", "environment", "safety and security", and "animal rights".

(2) An instrument was then used to measure basic value orientations following Schwartz's value system (Schwartz, 1994) with the following dimensions:

- Value orientation "self-enhancement and traditionalism"
- Value orientation "self-transcendence"
- Value orientation "creativity"

The participants scored on average highest on the "self-transcendence" value dimension as is typical for Scandinavia, followed by "creativity" and "self-enhancement and traditionalism".

(3) Afterwards the participants were asked if they recognised each of the four art pieces at the festival.

(4) Finally, socio-demographic variables, like gender, age, education, employment status, and place of residence, were recorded.

On average, 65.7% of all participants in the survey did not see any of the installations at the festival. The proportion of people who did not recognise a single piece dropped from 69% on day one to 47% on day seven because many people had been to the festival for a number of days.

When analysing the effects of exposure to the art pieces on the perceived importance of the political priority areas, no significant main effect of exposure to the art pieces could be found, but interesting patterns of interaction with value orientation occurred. In the animal rights priority area, exposure to the butterfly installation, the food waste installation, and the environmental karma short film made the topic of animal rights more relevant for people who scored high on self-enhancement values. However, people who score high on self-transcendence values showed the opposite effect, perceiving animal rights *less* important after exposure to these art pieces. Exposure to the food waste installation seemed to have a positive impact on the perceived importance of environmental problems among people with strong self-enhancement values. It appears that being confronted with the art installations had a positive effect for people who value their personal gain more than other people, but no or even negative effects for people who already embraced self-transcendence values.

11.6.4 The qualitative evaluation after the film festival

In-depth interviews with 12 members of the audience were conducted after the festival to gain a deeper insight into the associations and thoughts triggered by the installations. The results presented below are based both on reactions to what was remembered and on statements triggered by the presentation of the clips as well as pictures during the interview situation.

Although many of the aspects associated with the three butterfly clips are similar, they also triggered a number of different associations. The short loop presented at the festival mainly led to two responses in almost all participants: "this is beautiful to look at" and "the butterflies are dead". The visual beauty of the clips was also connected to a positive image of butterflies as representing both freedom and fragility. The aspect of death was connected to a number of associations: extinction of species, environmental pollution, but also falling leaves in autumn. The butterflies' resurrection piece, where the wings started to lift up again about halfway into the clip, triggered some of the same thoughts, but also some different. Again, death was one of the main associations. The resurrection was mentioned by almost all participants and triggered different associations; some interpreted it as a sign of hope, that something can be done, some as a literal resurrection (they already have been saved and live again), but some interpreted that as the ultimate disappearance, some even with a religious connotation: the way into butterfly heaven. The final and most different butterfly clip (the vortex) triggered very different associations. The most prominent response was "chaos", which made it stressful for many to look at the clip and created feelings of dizziness. It also made it difficult to make sense of what was going on, some interpreting it as panic. On the other hand, the high degree of motion created an impression of living butterflies, which some perceived as a sign of them being in a good place that was sustaining them, and some as fighting for their lives or dying. The emotional responses were dominated by the uneasiness caused by the chaotic motions, but some also described sadness and some positive emotional reactions.

The associations triggered by the food waste clip are more complex. Most participants immediately entered a discussion about responsibility for food waste problems, often with a tendency to deny their own responsibility. Reflections about what the actors were doing while they ate and the unhealthy habits of eating were also common. Other prominent associations were a feeling of too much food wasted by too many people and reflections about overconsumption in Norwegian society. These reflections were often contrasted to starvation in other countries and ethical problems connected to that. Many participants reported strong emotional reactions to this clip, ranging from disgust to anger to a guilty conscience. Many participants were able to identify with the actors or their activities which led to impulses to reduce food waste.

For the waste sculpture the main type of association was "this is beautiful, skilful or creative". Many participants were impressed and noted that something very beautiful had been created from something ugly. For some, this created an interesting friction which triggered thoughts and reflections, while for others it reduced the ugliness of the waste.

People reflected immediately about the high amount of waste and overconsumption in general. On the other hand, the emotional response to the sculpture was limited compared to the other pieces. The familiar skyline and waste pieces created a recognisable identification, which consequently triggered thoughts about responsibility. For many, the responsibility lies with other people, which led to only a few participants feeling an impulse to act. The surprise effect of the installation with the motion sensor created a moment of reflection.

The environmental karma video prompted three main reactions, which were reflections about health behaviour, reflections about environmental behaviour, and impulses to act. The most prominent reaction was about health, triggered by the "bad guy" eating cheese doodles with ketchup. This was a distraction in the clip, which also framed other activities as health-related. However, many participants also understood the environmental message, with showering and cycling versus car use, the two behaviours mentioned the most. Many perceived an impulse to act although this was often weakened by a denial of responsibility (other people are worse). The variety of actions mentioned in the film made it easy for people to find instances where they thought they were already behaving environmentally friendly. The most positive aspect mentioned by the participants was that the clip was easy to understand and had a humorous approach which made it easier to take the message in. Furthermore, the clip showed what to do with actions that were easy to implement, reducing the feeling of helplessness.

Finally, the participants were asked to describe the characteristics of a piece of visual art communicating environmental topics that would have an impact on them. Most participants preferred film or video as a medium. However, pictures, photographs, or posters and paintings were also named. The participants were then asked to formulate rules for designing the pieces, with responses including the use of simple, understandable messages; connecting everyday behaviour to its usually unseen effects; creating emotions; using a variety of sensual modes; providing an aid to understanding the artwork when necessary; creating points of identification for people by either places, behaviours, or actors that are familiar; using humour and positive messages to reduce negative reactions; contrasting the good and the bad scenarios; presenting solutions; creating something beautiful; and presenting in public or unusual spaces. With respect to emotions, the participants disagreed if the messages should be drastic or not and to which degree people might get scared away by strong emotions.

11.6.5 Conclusions of case two

The attempt to systematically evaluate the effects of an artistic intervention to communicate environmental messages has demonstrated several things. First, many of the film festival attendees reported not recognising a single art installation although at least two of them were presented in exposed locations. This effect might be even stronger in contexts where people are not expecting any artistic communication.

Second, even if art pieces are perceived, their effect on people's evaluation of what is important or not may be limited. However, the few effects that could be shown are interesting: people who are already motivated to act because of their own values do not feel the reinforcement of their actions by art pieces, whereas people who have more selfish value orientations may benefit. What seems to work for one group of people can have opposite effects on people with a different value orientation. For some people with high creativity values, the aesthetic aspect of art might draw attention away from the message.

The qualitative analysis extends these conclusions by offering deeper insights into the thought and associative processes that were triggered by the different pieces. Abstract artistic visuals, such as the butterfly video clips, trigger deep reflections in some people whereas others felt irritated. On the other hand, more concrete approaches, such as the environmental karma or food waste clips, demonstrated the potential to inspire reflection in people but were also understood by a broader audience. However, their interpretation was more restricted. Visual beauty and artistic creativity and skill contributed to catching attention but drew attention away from the message for some people. This underlines the problem raised by Cammaer (2009). Many of the installations failed to create strong impulses to act. Even if some art pieces made people reflect about responsibilities, much of the reasoning after the initial trigger was about why the people themselves are not the main bearers of responsibility.

Furthermore, it appeared that stronger negative emotional messages enhanced the likelihood of some people reflecting, but it also disconnected others that were not so engaged in the topic. The humorous approach of the environmental karma clip appealed to them more. It also clearly showed that offering people points of personal identification in an art piece made it much easier for them to understand and accept the connection to their own lives.

Finally, it became obvious how small unintended distortions can affect art pieces and the way they are comprehended. The cheese doodles scene in the environmental karma clip framed the whole video as a health promotion video. In the food waste clip, the international cast drew attention to the global dimension of inequalities in food distribution. The lesson learned from this is that art pieces should be pilot-tested and discussed with the potential audience prior to final implementation.

In their concluding recommendations for designing environmental art, the participants identified many of the aspects that also shine through in the analyses of the associations connected to the individual pieces and the quantitative analysis. These analyses can be condensed into the following ten design rules for effective environmental art:

1. Use a (visual) medium people are accustomed to. Many people prefer film to other media due to what they habitually consume.
2. Appeal to several senses; accompany vision by sound and other stimuli.
3. Create surprise and the opportunity to stop and reflect. Create an unexpected experience and a comfortable environment within which to engage with the art.
4. Place the artwork outside the walls of the gallery. Try to approach people in their everyday life. This will extend the target group beyond the art-educated audience, a subset that is more likely to be engaged with the issue.
5. Connect to people's everyday lives by providing identification points, a familiar point of reference that people can relate to.
6. Create art pieces that work on an emotional level and provide an outlet by directing the audience to information about ways in which individuals can be part of the solution. Be aware not to create negative reactions by overplaying emotional drivers.
7. Carefully consider how to avoid denial of responsibility, which is one of the main threats to effective environmental communication through visual art.
8. Consider the use of humour and how it might enhance engagement with the target group, but balance this so as to avoid trivialising the subject.
9. Consider what kind of guidance (parts of) your audience might need to understand the artwork.
10. Consider and engage the audience when creating and testing the works. Piloting will give important insights into unexpected side effects.

However, one should not assume that experiences of environmental art pieces alone will change people's behaviour. What they seem to create in the best case are moments of reflection, attention to a problem, and personal emotional involvement. According to the stage model of behavioural change (see Section 4.9.2), these aspects are entry points for a process of change that might transpose people into a stage of deliberating options of change (Bamberg, 2013b).

11.7 Spillover effects

One of the underlying assumptions of environmental communication in alternative settings is that pro-environmental behaviour in one domain or context can spill over to other contexts. Thøgersen (2004) shows that people have a tendency to be consistently environmental across many different behaviours. However, the consistency is lower for behaviours that are perceived as dissimilar and for people that hold weaker norms to behave in an environmentally responsible way. A longitudinal study found signs of the spillover effect of pro-environmental behaviour from one domain to others over time (Thøgersen & Ölander, 2003). However, the effects were small, and indications for trade-off effects were also found. Another study found only signs for partial spillover effects in some domains, whereas other domains were not affected (Whitmarsh & O'Neill, 2010). It seems that spillover effects are the result of a stable overarching value orientation or self-identity if they show. However, the opposing trade-off effect, sometimes also referred to as negative spillover, has also been shown. A qualitative study found signs of a trade-off between holiday travel and everyday travel for some participants (Dickinson et al., 2010). Another study described the situation where people that purchased a fuel-efficient car were less willing to reduce their car use, probably indicating a trade-off effect (Jansson et al., 2010). Thøgersen (1999) reported that people who recycled a lot paid less attention to reduction of packaging. Another study found that a significant proportion of people that insulated their houses or invested into more efficient heating technology preferred to use the gained financial possibilities to increase comfort (Howden-Chapman et al., 2009). Another kind of potential rebound effect is discussed by De Haan et al. (2006) who analysed if a hybrid car is substituting an already fuel-efficient car or is purchased as an additional car but do find no signs of such a rebound effect.

11.8 General conclusion

Implementing environmental communication in unusual settings and using art-based expressions is a potentially effective pathway for the future, but little is known about the effects at the moment. It appears that big events such as rock festivals, sport events, or other cultural happenings have an organisational need for environmental communication, but can also act as platforms for environmental communication. Many people who attend the festival share at least some common features which might enhance the effectiveness of group psychology tools. On the other hand, these people are there to be entertained rather than educated, which challenges communication design. Depending on the context, the communication tools need to be accessible by intoxicated or distracted people. They furthermore have to be coordinated with organisations that have priorities other than environmental messages. Although there are many pitfalls of the festival format and the evaluation of the film festival installations also shows some unexpected effects that need to be attended to, the use of unconventional means of communication can be a tool which reaches out to demographics that do not usually engage with environmental messages. However, more research on the effects is certainly needed.

Review questions

- Describe the possible effects of humour on environmental communication.
- Describe some of the main challenges with environmental communication on big events.
- What are the aspects that can make environmental communication through art more effective?

Suggested readings

Doyle, J. (2011). *Mediating climate change*. Surrey, UK: Ashgate Publishing.
Jones, M. L. (2014). *Sustainable event management: A practical guide*. London: Routledge.
Sharpe, E. K. (2008). Festivals and social change: Intersections of pleasure and politics at a community music festival. *Leisure Sciences*, 30(3), 217–234.
Thøgersen, J. (1999). Spillover processes in the development of a sustainable consumption pattern. *Journal of Economic Psychology*, 20(1), 53–81.

References

Aarts, H., Verplanken, B., & Van Knippenberg, A. (1997). Habit and information use in travel mode choices. *Acta Psychologica, 96*(1), 1–14.

Abrahamse, W., & Steg, L. (2013). Social influence approaches to encourage resource conservation: A meta-analysis. *Global Environmental Change, 23*(6), 1773–1785.

Abrahamse, W., Steg, L., Vlek, C., & Rothengatter, T. (2005). A review of intervention studies aimed at household energy conservation. *Journal of Environmental Psychology, 25*(3), 273–291.

Abrahamse, W., Steg, L., Vlek, C., & Rothengatter, T. (2007). The effect of tailored information, goal setting, and tailored feedback on household energy use, energy-related behaviors, and behavioral antecedents. *Journal of Environmental Psychology, 27*(4), 265–276.

Ahn, H.-Y., Wu, L., Kelly, S., & Haley, E. (2011). A qualitative study of college student responses to conflicting messages in advertising: Anti-binge drinking public service announcements versus wine promotion health messages. *International Journal of Public Health, 56*(3), 271–279.

Ajzen, I. (1991). The theory of planned behavior. *Organizational Behavior and Human Decision Processes, 50*(2), 179–211.

Ajzen, I. (2012). Values, attitudes, and behavior. In S. Salzborn, E. Davidov & J. Reinecke (Eds.), *Methods, Theories, and Empirical Applications in the Social Sciences* (pp. 33–38). Wiesbaden: Verlag für Sozialwissenschaften.

Anable, J. (2005). "Complacent car addicts" or "aspiring environmentalists"? Identifying travel behaviour segments using attitude theory. *Transport Policy, 12*(1), 65–78.

Anable, J., & Shaw, J. (2007). Priorities, policies and (time) scales: The delivery of emissions reductions in the UK transport sector. *Area, 39*(4), 443–457.

Andresen, S. A., Lesaint Rusu, C., Thao Nguyen, T. M., Raj Pandey, B., Vilhelmsen, K., & Fjermeros, L. K. (2011). *Switch off the light*. Experts in team project reports. NTNU. Trondheim.

Anker, A. E., & Feeley, T. H. (2011). Are nonparticipants in prosocial behavior merely innocent bystanders? *Health Communication, 26*(1), 13–24.

Ardissono, L., & Goy, A. (1999). *Tailoring the interaction with users in electronic shops*. Paper presented at the 7th International Conference on User Modeling (UM-97), Banff, MA.

Armitage, C. J., & Conner, M. (2001). Efficacy of the theory of planned behaviour: A meta-analytic review. *British Journal of Social Psychology, 40*(4), 471–499.

Arnesen, M. (2013). *Saving energy through culture: A multidisciplinary model for analyzing energy culture applied to Norwegian empirical evidence*. (Master), Norwegian University of Science and Technology, Trondheim.

Aronson, E., Fried, C., & Stone, J. (1991). Overcoming denial and increasing the intention to use condoms through the induction of hypocrisy. *American Journal of Public Health, 81*(12), 1636–1638.

Artistico, D., Pinto, A. M., Douek, J., Black, J., & Pezzuti, L. (2013). The value of removing daily obstacles via everyday problem-solving theory: Developing an applied novel procedure to increase self-efficacy for exercise. *Frontiers in Psychology, 4*, 1–8.

Asch, S. E. (1951). Effects of group pressure upon the modification and distortion of judgments. In H. Guetzkow (Ed.), *Groups, Leadership, and Men* (pp. 222–236). Pittsburgh: Carnegie Press.

Ashforth, B. E., & Mael, F. (1989). Social identity theory and the organization. *Academy of Management Review, 14*(1), 20–39.

Atkinson, R. C., & Shiffrin, R. M. (1968). Human memory: A proposed system and its control processes. In K. W. Spence & J. T. Spence (Eds.), *The psychology of learning and motivation* (Vol. 2, pp. 89–195). New York: Academic Press.

Austin, J., Hatfield, D. B., Grindle, A. C., & Bailey, J. S. (1993). Increasing recycling in office environments: The effects of specific, informative cues. *Journal of Applied Behavior Analysis, 26*(2), 247–253.

Baddeley, A. D. (1997). *Human memory: Theory and practice*. Psychology Press.

Baddeley, A. D. (2000). The episodic buffer: A new component of working memory? *Trends in Cognitive Sciences, 4*(11), 417–423.

Baddeley, A. D., & Hitch, G. (1975). Working memory. *The Psychology of Learning and Motivation, 8*, 47–89.

Baddeley, A. D., Lewis, V., Eldridge, M., & Thomson, N. (1984). Attention and retrieval from long-term memory. *Journal of Experimental Psychology: General, 113*(4), 518.

Baer, M., Leenders, R. T. A., Oldham, G. R., & Vadera, A. K. (2010). Win or lose the battle for creativity: The power and perils of intergroup competition. *Academy of Management Journal, 53*(4), 827–845.

Baiocchi, G., Minx, J., & Hubacek, K. (2010). The impact of social factors and consumer behavior on carbon dioxide emissions in the United Kingdom. *Journal of Industrial Ecology, 14*(1), 50–72.

Ballantyne, R., Fien, J., & Packer, J. (2001). School environmental education programme impacts upon student and family learning: A case study analysis. *Environmental Education Research, 7*(1), 23–37.

Bamberg, S. (2002). Effects of implementation intentions on the actual performance of new environmentally friendly behaviours – results of two field experiments. *Journal of Environmental Psychology, 22*(4), 399–411.

Bamberg, S. (2006). Is a residential relocation a good opportunity to change people's travel behavior? Results from a theory-driven intervention study. *Environment and Behavior, 38*(6), 820–840.

Bamberg, S. (2007). Is a stage model a useful approach to explain car drivers' willingness to use public transportation? *Journal of Applied Social Psychology, 37*(8), 1757–1783.

Bamberg, S. (2012). Processes of change. In L. Steg, A. E. van den Berg, & J. I. M. De Groot (Eds.), *Environmental psychology: An introduction*. New York: Wiley. West Sussex, UK: Wiley & Sons.

Bamberg, S. (2013a). Applying the stage model of self-regulated behavioral change in a car use reduction intervention. *Journal of Environmental Psychology, 33*, 68–75.

Bamberg, S. (2013b). Changing environmentally harmful behaviors: A stage model of self-regulated behavioral change. *Journal of Environmental Psychology, 34*, 151–159.

Bamberg, S. (2014). Psychological contributions to the development of car use reduction interventions. In T. Gärling, D. Ettema, & M. Friman (Eds.), *Handbook of sustainable travel* (pp. 131–149). Dordrecht, NL: Springer.

Bamberg, S., Hunecke, M., & Blöbaum, A. (2007). Social context, personal norms and the use of public transportation: Two field studies. *Journal of Environmental Psychology, 27*(3), 190–203.

Bamberg, S., & Möser, G. (2007). Twenty years after Hines, Hungerford, and Tomera: A new meta-analysis of psycho-social determinants of pro-environmental behaviour. *Journal of Environmental Psychology, 27*(1), 14–25.

Banas, J. A., Dunbar, N., Rodriguez, D., & Liu, S.-J. (2011). A review of humor in educational settings: Four decades of research. *Communication Education, 60*(1), 115–144.

Bandura, A. (1982). Self-efficacy mechanism in human agency. *American Psychologist, 37*(2), 122.

Bargh, J. A., & Chartrand, T. L. (1999). The unbearable automaticity of being. *American Psychologist, 54*(7), 464–479.

Baron, R. S., Roper, G., & Baron, P. H. (1974). Group discussion and the stingy shift. *Journal of Personality and Social Psychology, 30*(4), 538.

Bell, P. A., Greene, T., Fisher, J. D., & Baum, A. (2001). *Environmental psychology* (Fifth ed.). Orlando: Harcourt College Publishers.

Berkhout, P. H., Muskens, J. C., & Velthuijsen, J. W. (2000). Defining the rebound effect. *Energy Policy, 28*(6), 425–432.

Bither, S. W., Dolich, I. J., & Nell, E. B. (1971). The application of attitude immunization techniques in marketing. *Journal of Marketing Research*, 56–61.

Bokek-Cohen, Y. a. (2011). Marital power bases as predictors of spousal influence strategies in a vacation purchase decision. *International Journal of Culture, Tourism and Hospitality Research, 5*(2), 144–157.

Bonebright, D. A. (2010). 40 years of storming: A historical review of Tuckman's model of small group development. *Human Resource Development International, 13*(1), 111–120.

Bonnes, M., & Secchiaroli, G. (1995). *Environmental psychology – a psycho-social introduction*. London: Sage.

Bordia, P. (1997). Face-to-face versus computer-mediated communication: A synthesis of the experimental literature. *Journal of Business Communication, 34*(1), 99–118.

Borgstede, C. V., Johansson, L.-O., & Nilsson, A. (2013). Social dilemmas: Motivational, individual and structural aspects influencing cooperation. In L. Steg, A. E. Van den Berg, & J. I. M. De Groot (Eds.), *Environmental psychology – an introduction* (pp. 175–184). Chichester, UK: John Wiley & Sons.

Bornstein, G., & Erev, I. (1994). The enhancing effect of intergroup competition on group performance. *International Journal of Conflict Management, 5*(3), 271–283.

Bornstein, G., Gneezy, U., & Nagel, R. (2002). The effect of intergroup competition on group coordination: An experimental study. *Games and Economic Behavior, 41*(1), 1–25.

Bostrom, A., Morgan, M. G., Fischhoff, B., & Read, D. (1994). What do people know about global climate change? 1. Mental models. *Risk Analysis, 14*(6), 959–970.

Boyes, E., & Stanisstreet, M. (2012). Environmental education for behaviour change: Which actions should be targeted? *International Journal of Science Education, 34*(10), 1591–1614.

Braun, B., & Castree, N. (2005). *Remaking reality: Nature at the millennium.* London: Routledge.

Breakwell, G. M. (2007). *The psychology of risk.* Cambridge University Press Cambridge.

Breakwell, G. M., & Barnett, J. (2001). *The impact of social amplification on risk communication.* Contract Research Report Sudbury: HSE Books.

Broadbent, D. E. (1958). *Perception and communication.* New York: Pergamon.

Buckland, D. (2012). Climate is culture. *Nature Climate Change, 2*(3), 137–140.

Burnstein, E., & Vinokur, A. (1977). Persuasive argumentation and social comparison as determinants of attitude polarization. *Journal of Experimental Social Psychology, 13*(4), 315–332.

Cammaer, G. (2009). Edward Burtynsky's Manufactured Landscapes: The ethics and aesthetics of creating moving still images and stilling moving images of ecological disasters. *Environmental Communication, 3*(1), 121–130.

Carr, T. H., McCauley, C., Sperber, R. D., & Parmelee, C. (1982). Words, pictures, and priming: On semantic activation, conscious identification, and the automaticity of information processing. *Journal of Experimental Psychology: Human Perception and Performance, 8*(6), 757.

Chapman, L. (2007). Transport and climate change: A review. *Journal of Transport Geography, 15*(5), 354–367.

Cheverst, K., Davies, N., Mitchell, K., & Smith, P. (2000). Providing tailored (context-aware) information to city visitors. In P. Brusilovski, O. Stock, & C. Strapparava (Eds.), *Adaptive hypermedia and adaptive web-based systems* (pp. 73–85). Berlin: Springer.

Child, I. L. (1968). Personality in culture. In E. F. Borgatta & W. W. Lambert (Eds.), *Handbook of personality theory and research* (pp. 82–145). Chicago: Rand McNally.

Chiu, B., & Arreglo, C. (2011). At the intersections of ecosee and just sustainability: New directions for communication theory and practice. *Environmental Communication, 5*(2), 141–145.

Chiu, Y.-T. H., Lee, W.-I., & Chen, T.-H. (2014). Environmentally responsible behavior in ecotourism: Antecedents and implications. *Tourism Management, 40*, 321–329.

Cialdini, R. B. (2003). Crafting normative messages to protect the environment. *Current Directions in Psychological Science, 12*(4), 105–109.

Cialdini, R. B. (2006). *Influence – the psychology of persuasion.* New York: Harper Business.

Clarke, A., Bell, P. A., & Peterson, G. L. (1999). The influence of attitude priming and social responsibility on the valuation of environmental public goods using paired comparisons. *Environment and Behavior, 31*(6), 838–857.

Collins, A., & Fairchild, R. (2007). Sustainable food consumption at a sub-national level: An ecological footprint, nutritional and economic analysis. *Journal of Environmental Policy & Planning, 9*(1), 5–30.

Conner, M., & Armitage, C. J. (1998). Extending the theory of planned behavior: A review and avenues for further research. *Journal of Applied Social Psychology, 28*(15), 1429–1464.

Cornelissen, G., Pandelaere, M., Warlop, L., & Dewitte, S. (2008). Positive cueing: Promoting sustainable consumer behavior by cueing common environmental behaviors as environmental. *International Journal of Research in Marketing, 25*(1), 46–55.

Costa, D. L., & Kahn, M. E. (2013). Energy conservation "nudges" and environmentalist ideology: Evidence from a randomized residential electricity field experiment. *Journal of the European Economic Association, 11*(3), 680–702.

Costa, P. T., & McCrae, R. R. (2008). The revised neo personality inventory (neo-pi-r). In G. J. Boyle, G. Matthews, & D. H. Saklofske (Eds.), *The SAGE handbook of personality theory and assessment* (Vol. 2, pp. 179–198). London: Sage.

Cox, R. (2012). *Environmental communication and the public sphere*. Thousand Oaks: Sage.

Crabtree, L., & Hes, D. (2009). Sustainability uptake in housing in metropolitan Australia: An institutional problem, not a technological one. *Housing Studies, 24*(2), 203–224.

Craig, R. T. (1999). Communication theory as a field. *Communication theory, 9*(2), 119–161.

D'Souza, C., Taghian, M., Lamb, P., & Peretiatko, R. (2007). Green decisions: Demographics and consumer understanding of environmental labels. *International Journal of Consumer Studies, 31*(4), 371–376.

Darley, J. M., & Latane, B. (1968). Bystander intervention in emergencies: Diffusion of responsibility. *Journal of Personality and Social Psychology, 8*(4), 377.

Darnton, A., Verplanken, B., White, P., & Whitmarsh, L. (2011). *Habits, routines and sustainable lifestyles: A summary report to the department for environment, food and rural affairs AD research & analysis for Defra*. London: Defra.

De Haan, P., Mueller, M. G., & Peters, A. (2006). Does the hybrid Toyota Prius lead to rebound effects? Analysis of size and number of cars previously owned by Swiss Prius buyers. *Ecological Economics, 58*(3), 592–605.

Deetz, S. (1973). Words without things: Toward a social phenomenology of language. *Quarterly Journal of Speech, 59*(1), 40–51.

Delmas, M. A., Fischlein, M., & Asensio, O. I. (2013). Information strategies and energy conservation behavior: A meta-analysis of experimental studies from 1975 to 2012. *Energy Policy, 61*, 729–739.

Deutsch, J. A., & Deutsch, D. (1963). Attention: Some theoretical considerations. *Psychological Review, 70*(1), 80.

DeVries, R. (2000). Vygotsky, Piaget, and education: A reciprocal assimilation of theories and educational practices. *New Ideas in Psychology, 18*(2), 187–213.

Diamantopoulos, A., Schlegelmilch, B. B., Sinkovics, R. R., & Bohlen, G. M. (2003). Can socio-demographics still play a role in profiling green consumers? A review of the evidence and an empirical investigation. *Journal of Business Research, 56*(6), 465–480.

Dickerson, C. A., Thibodeau, R., Aronson, E., & Miller, D. (1992). Using cognitive dissonance to encourage water conservation. *Journal of Applied Social Psychology, 22*(11), 841–854.

Dickinson, J. E., Robbins, D., & Lumsdon, L. (2010). Holiday travel discourses and climate change. *Journal of Transport Geography, 18*(3), 482–489.

Diekmann, A., & Preisendörfer, P. (2003). Green and greenback the behavioral effects of environmental attitudes in low-cost and high-cost situations. *Rationality and Society, 15*(4), 441–472.

Dietz, T., Gardner, G. T., Gilligan, J., Stern, P. C., & Vandenbergh, M. P. (2009). Household actions can provide a behavioral wedge to rapidly reduce US carbon emissions. *Proceedings of the National Academy of Sciences, 106*(44), 18452–18456.

Dogan, E., Bolderdijk, J. W., & Steg, L. (2014). Making small numbers count: Environmental and financial feedback in promoting eco-driving behaviours. *Journal of Consumer Policy, 37*(3), 1–10.

Dono, J., Webb, J., & Richardson, B. (2010). The relationship between environmental activism, pro-environmental behaviour and social identity. *Journal of Environmental Psychology, 30*(2), 178–186.

Douglas, M. (1986). *Risk acceptability according to the social sciences.* Russell Sage Foundation.

Douglas, M., & Wildavsky, A. (1982). How can we know the risks we face? Why risk selection is a social process. *Risk Analysis, 2*(2), 49–58.

Doyle, J. (2011). *Mediating climate change.* Surrey, UK: Ashgate Publishing.

Dunaway, F. (2009). Seeing global warming: Contemporary art and the fate of the planet. *Environmental History, 14*(1), 9–31.

Duncan, O. D. (1961). From social system to ecosystem. *Sociological Inquiry, 31*(2), 140–149.

Dunlap, R. E., Van Liere, K. D., Mertig, A. G., & Jones, R. E. (2000). New trends in measuring environmental attitudes: Measuring endorsement of the new ecological paradigm: A revised NEP scale. *Journal of Social Issues, 56*(3), 425–442.

Duryea, E. J. (1983). Utilizing tenets of inoculation theory to develop and evaluate a preventive alcohol education intervention. *Journal of School Health, 53*(4), 250–256.

Eisenack, K. (2013). A climate change board game for interdisciplinary communication and education. *Simulation & Gaming, 44*(2–3), 328–348.

Eisend, M. (2009). A meta-analysis of humor in advertising. *Journal of the Academy of Marketing Science, 37*(2), 191–203.

Elias, E. W., Dekoninck, E., & Culley, S. J. (2009). Designing for "use phase" energy losses of domestic products. Proceedings of the Institution of Mechanical Engineers, Part B. *Journal of Engineering Manufacture, 223*(1), 115–120.

Ellen, P. S., Wiener, J. L., & Cobb-Walgren, C. (1991). The role of perceived consumer effectiveness in motivating environmentally conscious behaviors. *Journal of Public Policy & Marketing*, 102–117.

Elliot, A. J., & Fryer, J. W. (2008). The goal construct in psychology. *Handbook of Motivation Science, 18*, 235–250.

Eltantawy, N., & Wiest, J. B. (2011). The Arab Spring. Social media in the Egyptian revolution: Reconsidering resource mobilization theory. *International Journal of Communication, 5*, 18.

Engel, J. F., Kollat, D. T., & Blackwell, R. D. (1969). Personality measures and market segmentation: Evidence favors interaction view. *Business Horizons, 12*(3), 61–70.

Erev, I., Bornstein, G., & Galili, R. (1993). Constructive intergroup competition as a solution to the free rider problem: A field experiment. *Journal of Experimental Social Psychology, 29*(6), 463–478.

Ernst, A., Schulz, C., Schwarz, N., & Janisch, S. (2008). Modelling of water use decisions in a large, spatially explicit, coupled simulation system. In B. Edmonds, K. G. Troitzsch, & C. Hernandez Iglesias (Eds.), *Social simulation: Technologies, advances and new discoveries*. (pp. 138–149). New York: Hershey.

Evans, D. (2011). Blaming the consumer–once again: The social and material contexts of everyday food waste practices in some English households. *Critical Public Health, 21*(4), 429–440.

Fairchild, R. J. (2008). The manufacturing sector's environmental motives: A game-theoretic analysis. *Journal of Business Ethics, 79*(3), 333–344.

Fardzadeh, H. E., Baginski, M., Wasike, S. N., Wilkund, T. A., & Marealle Njama, W. (2010). *Assessing and communicating the environmental impact of a rock festival*. Experts in team project reports. NTNU. Trondheim.

Feldman, D. C. (1984). The development and enforcement of group norms. *Academy of Management Review, 9*(1), 47–53.

Festinger, L. (1962). *A theory of cognitive dissonance* (Vol. 2). Stanford: Stanford University Press.

Fielding, K. S., Terry, D. J., Masser, B. M., & Hogg, M. A. (2008). Integrating social identity theory and the theory of planned behaviour to explain decisions to engage in sustainable agricultural practices. *British Journal of Social Psychology, 47*(1), 23–48.

Fischer, P., Krueger, J. I., Greitemeyer, T., Vogrincic, C., Kastenmüller, A., Frey, D., ... Kainbacher, M. (2011). The bystander-effect: A meta-analytic review on bystander intervention in dangerous and non-dangerous emergencies. *Psychological Bulletin, 137*(4), 517.

Fischhoff, B., Slovic, P., Lichtenstein, S., Read, S., & Combs, B. (1978). How safe is safe enough? A psychometric study of attitudes towards technological risks and benefits. *Policy Sciences, 9*(2), 127–152.

Fishbein, M., & Ajzen, I. (1975). *Belief, attitude, intention, and behavior: An introduction to theory and research*. Reading, MA: Addison-Wesley.

Fisman, L. (2005). The effects of local learning on environmental awareness in children: An empirical investigation. *The Journal of Environmental Education, 36*(3), 39–50.

Flora, J. A., Schooler, C., Mays, V. M., & Cochran, S. D. (1996). Exploring a model of symbolic social communication. The case of "Magic" Johnson. *Journal of Health Psychology, 1*(3), 353–366.

Floyd, D. L., Prentice-Dunn, S., & Rogers, R. W. (2000). A meta-analysis of research on protection motivation theory. *Journal of Applied Social Psychology, 30*(2), 407–429.

Folk, C. L., & Remington, R. W. (2008). Bottom-up priming of top-down attentional control settings. *Visual Cognition, 16*(2–3), 215–231.

Frank, R. H. (1997). *Microeconomics and behavior*. New York: McGraw-Hill

Frewer, L. (2004). The public and effective risk communication. *Toxicology Letters, 149*(1), 391–397.

Friman, M., Larhult, L., & Gärling, T. (2013). An analysis of soft transport policy measures implemented in Sweden to reduce private car use. *Transportation, 40*(1), 109–129.

Fujii, S., & Gaerling, T. (2004). *Temporary structural change: A strategy to break car-use habit and promote public transport*. Paper presented at the International Conference of Traffic and Transport Psychology, Nottingham, UK.

Fujii, S., & Kitamura, R. (2003). What does a one-month free bus ticket do to habitual drivers? An experimental analysis of habit and attitude change. *Transportation, 30*(1), 81–95.

Gajic, N., Nii-Boye Quarshie, E., Tsegaye, M. A., Hazar, O., & Storsveen, S. (2010). *Smoothy bike*. Experts in team project reports. NTNU. Trondheim.

Gardner, B., & Abraham, C. (2008). Psychological correlates of car use: A meta-analysis. *Transportation Research Part F: Traffic Psychology and Behaviour, 11*(4), 300–311.

Gavelin, S., & Sjöström, A. (2014). Värderingar och villighet att betala extra: En kvantitativ studie gällande miljömärkning och social produktmärkning av mobiltelefoner [Personal values and willingness to pay more: A quantitative study regarding eco-labelled and fairtrade mobile phones]. Trollhättan: Högskolan Vest.

Geller, E. S. (2002). The challenge of increasing proenvironment behavior. In R. B. Bechtel & A. Churchman (Eds.), *Handbook of environmental psychology* (pp. 525–540). New York: John Wiley & Sons.

Gergen, K. J. (2011). The self as social construction. *Psychological Studies, 56*(1), 108–116.

Goffman, E. (1959). *The presentation of self in everyday life*. Garden City, NY: Doubleday.

Goldstein, N. J., Cialdini, R. B., & Griskevicius, V. (2008). A room with a viewpoint: Using social norms to motivate environmental conservation in hotels. *Journal of Consumer Research, 35*(3), 472–482.

Graham, C. R. (2003). A model of norm development for computer-mediated teamwork. *Small Group Research, 34*(3), 322–352.

Gram-Hanssen, K., Christensen, T. H., & Petersen, P. E. (2012). Air-to-air heat pumps in real-life use: Are potential savings achieved or are they transformed into increased comfort? *Energy and Buildings, 53*, 64–73.

Gronau, W., & Kagermeier, A. (2004). Mobility management outside metropolitan areas: Case study evidence from North Rhine-Westphalia. *Journal of Transport Geography, 12*(4), 315–322.

Gröger, M., & Bruckner, T. (2011, 16.–18.2.2011). *Lebensstile und Investitionsverhalten im Wärmemarkt*. Paper presented at the Internationale Energiewirtschaftstagung (IEWT 2011), Wien.

Guagnano, G. A., Stern, P. C., & Dietz, T. (1995). Influences on attitude-behavior relationships a natural experiment with curbside recycling. *Environment and Behavior, 27*(5), 699–718.

Gustafsson, A., Katzeff, C., & Bang, M. (2009). Evaluation of a pervasive game for domestic energy engagement among teenagers. *Computers in Entertainment (CIE), 7*(4), 54.

Haas, P. M. (2004). Addressing the global governance deficit. *Global Environmental Politics, 4*(4), 1–15.

Handgraaf, M. J., Van Lidth de Jeude, M. A., & Appelt, K. C. (2013). Public praise vs. private pay: Effects of rewards on energy conservation in the workplace. *Ecological Economics, 86*, 86–92.

Hanley, N., Shogren, J. F., & White, B. (2007). *Environmental economics in theory and practice* (2nd ed.). New York: Palgrave Macmillan.

Hannigan, J. (2006). *Environmental sociology* (2nd ed.). New York: Routledge.

Hardeman, W., Johnston, M., Johnston, D., Bonetti, D., Wareham, N., & Kinmonth, A. L. (2002). Application of the theory of planned behaviour in behaviour change interventions: A systematic review. *Psychology and Health, 17*(2), 123–158.

Hardin, G. (1968). The tragedy of the commons. *Science, 162*(3859), 1243–1248.

Hargreaves, T. (2011). Practice-ing behaviour change: Applying social practice theory to pro-environmental behaviour change. *Journal of Consumer Culture, 11*(1), 79–99.

Harland, P., Staats, H., & Wilke, H. A. (2007). Situational and personality factors as direct or personal norm mediated predictors of pro-environmental behavior: Questions derived from norm-activation theory. *Basic and Applied Social Psychology, 29*(4), 323–334.

Heath, Y., & Gifford, R. (2006). Extending the theory of planned behavior: Predicting the use of public transportation. *Journal of Applied Social Psychology, 32*(10), 2154–2189.

Hergesell, A., & Dickinger, A. (2013). Environmentally friendly holiday transport mode choices among students: The role of price, time and convenience. *Journal of Sustainable Tourism, 21*(4), 596–613.

Hertwich, E. G., & Peters, G. P. (2009). Carbon footprint of nations: A global, trade-linked analysis. *Environmental Science & Technology, 43*(16), 6414–6420.

Hicks, J. J. (2001). The strategy behind Florida's "truth" campaign. *Tobacco Control, 10*(1), 3–5.

Higgins, E. T. (1987). Self-discrepancy: A theory relating self and affect. *Psychological Review, 94*(3), 319.

Hines, J. M., Hungerford, H. R., & Tomera, A. N. (1987). Analysis and synthesis of research on responsible environmental behavior: A meta-analysis. *The Journal of Environmental Education, 18*(2), 1–8.

Hirsh, J. B. (2010). Personality and environmental concern. *Journal of Environmental Psychology, 30*(2), 245–248.

Hirsh, J. B., & Dolderman, D. (2007). Personality predictors of consumerism and environmentalism: A preliminary study. *Personality and Individual Differences, 43*(6), 1583–1593.

Hjelmar, U. (2011). Consumers' purchase of organic food products: A matter of convenience and reflexive practices. *Appetite, 56*(2), 336–344.

Hogan, K., & Stubbs, R. (2003). *Can't Get Through: Eight Barriers to Communication.* Gretna: Pelican Publishing.

Hogg, M. A., Turner, J. C., & Davidson, B. (1990). Polarized norms and social frames of reference: A test of the self-categorization theory of group polarization. *Basic and Applied Social Psychology, 11*(1), 77–100.

Holm, L. (2003). Blaming the consumer: On the free choice of consumers and the decline in food quality in Denmark. *Critical Public Health, 13*(2), 139–154.

Homburg, A., & Stolberg, A. (2006). Explaining pro-environmental behavior with a cognitive theory of stress. *Journal of Environmental Psychology, 26*(1), 1–14.

Hoogendoorn-Lanser, S., & Van Nes, R. (2004). Multimodal choice set composition: Analysis of reported and generated choice sets. *Transportation Research Record: Journal of the Transportation Research Board, 1898*(1), 79–86.

Hopper, J. R., & Nielsen, J. M. (1991). Recycling as altruistic behavior normative and behavioral strategies to expand participation in a community recycling program. *Environment and Behavior, 23*(2), 195–220.

Howden-Chapman, P., Viggers, H., Chapman, R., O'Dea, D., Free, S., & O'Sullivan, K. (2009). Warm homes: Drivers of the demand for heating in the residential sector in New Zealand. *Energy Policy, 37*(9), 3387–3399.

Hunecke, M., Blöbaum, A., Matthies, E., & Höger, R. (2001). Responsibility and environment ecological norm orientation and external factors in the domain of travel mode choice behavior. *Environment and Behavior, 33*(6), 830–852.

Hutchcroft, P. D. (2001). Centralization and decentralization in administration and politics: Assessing territorial dimensions of authority and power. *Governance, 14*(1), 23–53.

Hutton, R. B., Mauser, G. A., Filiatrault, P., & Ahtola, O. T. (1986). Effects of cost-related feedback on consumer knowledge and consumption behavior: A field experimental approach. *Journal of Consumer Research*, 327–336.

Inglehart, R., & Welzel, C. (2005). *Modernization, cultural change, and democracy: The human development sequence*: Cambridge University Press.

Inglehart, R., & Welzel, C. (2010). Changing mass priorities: The link between modernization and democracy. *Perspectives on Politics, 8*(02), 551–567.

Jager, W., & Gotts, N. (2013). Simulating social environmental systems. In L. Steg, A. E. van den Berg, & J. I. M. De Groot (Eds.), *Environmental Psychology – An Introduction* (pp. 281–291). Oxford: Blackwell.

Jager, W., Janssen, M., De Vries, H., De Greef, J., & Vlek, C. (2000). Behaviour in commons dilemmas: Homo economicus and Homo psychologicus in an ecological-economic model. *Ecological Economics, 35*(3), 357–379.

Janssen, M., & Hamm, U. (2012). Product labelling in the market for organic food: Consumer preferences and willingness-to-pay for different organic certification logos. *Food Quality and Preference, 25*(1), 9–22.

Jansson, J., Marell, A., & Nordlund, A. (2009). Elucidating green consumers: A cluster analytic approach on proenvironmental purchase and curtailment behaviors. *Journal of Euromarketing, 18*(4), 245–267.

Jansson, J., Marell, A., & Nordlund, A. (2010). Green consumer behavior: Determinants of curtailment and eco-innovation adoption. *Journal of Consumer Marketing, 27*(4), 358–370.

Jansson, J., Marell, A., & Nordlund, A. (2011). Exploring consumer adoption of a high involvement eco-innovation using value-belief-norm theory. *Journal of Consumer Behaviour, 10*(1), 51–60.

Jellison, J., & Arkin, R. (1977). Social comparison of abilities: A self-presentation approach to decision making in groups. In J. M. Suls & R. L. Miller (Eds.), *Social comparison processes: Theoretical and empirical perspectives* (pp. 235–258). Washington: Hemisphere.

Jiménez-Parra, B., Rubio, S., & Vicente-Molina, M.-A. (2014). Key Drivers in the Behavior of Potential Consumers of Remanufactured Products: A study on laptops in Spain. *Journal of Cleaner Production*.

Johannessen, B., Bangs, C., Randmæl, T., & Xie, Q. (2010). *Assessing and communicating the environmental impact of a rock festival*. Experts in team project reports. NTNU. Trondheim.

Johnson-Laird, P. N. (1980). Mental models in cognitive science. *Cognitive Science, 4*(1), 71–115.

Johnson, B. B., & Slovic, P. (1995). Presenting uncertainty in health risk assessment: Initial studies of its effects on risk perception and trust. *Risk Analysis, 15*(4), 485–494.

Johnson, B. B., & Slovic, P. (1998). Lay views on uncertainty in environmental health risk assessment. *Journal of Risk Research, 1*(4), 261–279.
Johnson, D., & Johnson, F. (2013). *Joining together: Group theory and group skills*. Boston: Pearson.
Jones, M. L. (2014). *Sustainable event management: A practical guide*. London: Routledge.
Jurin, R. R., Roush, D., & Danter, J. (2010). Communicating without words. In R. R. Jurin, D. Roush, & J. Danter (Eds.), *Environmental communication. Second edition* (pp. 221–230). Dordrecht: Springer.
Kahneman, D., Knetsch, J. L., & Thaler, R. H. (1986). Fairness and the assumptions of economics. *Journal of Business*, S285–S300.
Kahneman, D., & Tversky, A. (1984). Choices, values, and frames. *American Psychologist, 39*(4), 341.
Kaiser, F. G., Hübner, G., & Bogner, F. X. (2005). Contrasting the theory of planned behavior with the value-belief-norm model in explaining conservation behavior. *Journal of Applied Social Psychology, 35*(10), 2150–2170.
Kaklamanou, D., Jones, C. R., Webb, T. L., & Walker, S. R. (2013). Using public transport can make up for flying abroad on holiday: Compensatory green beliefs and environmentally significant behavior. *Environment and Behavior, 47*(2), 184–204.
Kaplan, A. M., & Haenlein, M. (2010). Users of the world, unite! The challenges and opportunities of social media. *Business Horizons, 53*(1), 59–68.
Kasperson, J. X., Kasperson, R. E., Pidgeon, N., & Slovic, P. (2003). The social amplification of risk: Assessing fifteen years of research and theory. In N. Pigeon, R. E. Kasperson, & P. Slovic (Eds.), *The social amplification of risk* (pp. 13–46). Cambridge: Cambridge University Press.
Kasperson, R. E., Renn, O., Slovic, P., Brown, H. S., Emel, J., Goble, R., ... Ratick, S. (1988). The social amplification of risk: A conceptual framework. *Risk Analysis, 8*(2), 177–187.
Katzev, R. D., & Johnson, T. R. (1984). Comparing the effects of monetary incentives and foot-in-the-door strategies in promoting residential electricity conservation. *Journal of Applied Social Psychology, 14*(1), 12–27.
Keizer, K., Lindenberg, S., & Steg, L. (2011). The reversal effect of prohibition signs. *Group Processes & Intergroup Relations, 14*(5), 681–688.
Keizer, K., Lindenberg, S., & Steg, L. (2013). The importance of demonstratively restoring order. *PloS One, 8*(6), e65137.
Kelley, H. H. (1973). The processes of causal attribution. *American psychologist, 28*(2), 107.
Kemp, B., Randle, M., Hurlimann, A., & Dolnicar, S. (2012). Community acceptance of recycled water: Can we inoculate the public against scare campaigns? *Journal of Public Affairs, 12*(4), 337–346.
Kim, H., Lee, E.-J., & Hur, W.-M. (2012). The normative social influence on eco-friendly consumer behavior: The moderating effect of environmental marketing claims. *Clothing and Textiles Research Journal, 30*(1), 4–18.
Klöckner, C. A. (2004). *How single events change travel mode choice–a life span perspective*. Paper presented at the 3rd International Conference on Traffic and Transport Psychology Nottingham, UK.
Klöckner, C. A. (2012). Nye måter å fremme miljøvennlig atferd på – kan miljøvernbudskap tilpasses en rockefestival? In A. Fyhri, Å. L. Hauge, &

H. Nordh (Eds.), *Norsk Miljøpsykologi – Mennesker og Omgivelser*. Oslo: Sintef akademisk forlag.

Klöckner, C. A. (2013a). A comprehensive model of the psychology of environmental behaviour – A meta-analysis. *Global Environmental Change, 23*(5), 1028–1038.

Klöckner, C. A. (2013b). *The effects of environmental art presented at a film festival on the audience*. Unpublished study. NTNU. Trondheim.

Klöckner, C. A. (2013c). How powerful are moral motivations in environmental protection? In K. Heinrichs, F. Oser, & T. Lovat (Eds.), *Handbook of moral motivation* (pp. 447–472). Rotterdam: Sense Publishers.

Klöckner, C. A. (2014). The dynamics of purchasing an electric vehicle – A prospective longitudinal study of the decision-making process. *Transportation Research Part F: Traffic Psychology and Behaviour, 24*, 103–116.

Klöckner, C. A., Beisenkamp, A., & Hallmann, S. (2010a). Klimawandel aus der Sicht 9-14jähriger Kinder – Emotionen, Bewältigungsressourcen und allgemeines Wohlbefinden. *Umweltpsychologie, 14*(2), 121–142.

Klöckner, C. A., Beisenkamp, A., & Hallmann, S. (2010b). Wie motivieren klimawandelbezogene Emotionen Kinder zum Klimaschutz? Ein Arbeitsmodell. *Umweltpsychologie, 14*(2), 143–159.

Klöckner, C. A., & Blöbaum, A. (2010). A comprehensive action determination model: Toward a broader understanding of ecological behaviour using the example of travel mode choice. *Journal of Environmental Psychology, 30*(4), 574–586.

Klöckner, C. A., & Matthies, E. (2004). How habits interfere with norm-directed behaviour: A normative decision-making model for travel mode choice. *Journal of Environmental Psychology, 24*(3), 319–327.

Klöckner, C. A., & Matthies, E. (2012). Two pieces of the same puzzle? Script based car choice habits between the influence of socialization and past behavior. *Journal of Applied Social Psychology, 42*(4), 793–821.

Klöckner, C. A., Matthies, E., & Hunecke, M. (2006). Problems of operationalizing habits and integrating habits in normative decision making models. *Journal of Applied Social Psychology, 33*(2), 396–417.

Klöckner, C. A., Nayum, A., & Mehmetoglu, M. (2013). Positive and negative spillover effects from electric car purchase to car use. *Transportation Research Part D: Transport and Environment, 21*, 32–38.

Klöckner, C. A., & Ohms, S. (2009). The importance of personal norms for purchasing organic milk. *British Food Journal, 111*(11), 1173–1187.

Klöckner, C. A., & Oppedal, I. O. (2011). General vs. domain specific recycling behaviour – Applying a multilevel comprehensive action determination model to recycling in Norwegian student homes. *Resources, Conservation and Recycling, 55*(4), 463–471.

Klöckner, C. A., Sopha, B. M., Matthies, E., & Bjørnstad, E. (2013). Energy efficiency in Norwegian households – identifying motivators and barriers with a focus group approach. *International Journal of Environment and Sustainable Development, 12*(4), 396–415.

Klöckner, C. A., & Verplanken, B. (2012). Yesterday's habits preventing change for tomorrow? About the influence of automaticity on environmental behaviour In L. Steg, A. E. van den Berg, & J. I. M. De Groot (Eds.), *Environmental psychology: An introduction* (pp. 197–209): Wiley-Blackwell.

Kollmuss, A., & Agyeman, J. (2002). Mind the gap: Why do people act environmentally and what are the barriers to pro-environmental behavior? *Environmental Education Research, 8*(3), 239–260.

Krotoski, A. (2010). Serious fun with computer games. *Nature, 466*(7307), 695.

Kuhn, K. M. (2000). Message format and audience values: Interactive effects of uncertainty information and environmental attitudes on perceived risk. *Journal of Environmental Psychology, 20*(1), 41–51.

Kuhn, M. H. (1964). Major trends in symbolic interaction theory in the past twenty-five years. *The Sociological Quarterly, 5*(1), 61–68.

Lachter, J., Forster, K. I., & Ruthruff, E. (2004). Forty-five years after Broadbent (1958): Still no identification without attention. *Psychological Review, 111*(4), 880.

Laing, J., & Frost, W. (2010). How green was my festival: Exploring challenges and opportunities associated with staging green events. *International Journal of Hospitality Management, 29*(2), 261–267.

Lantz-Andersson, A., Vigmo, S., & Bowen, R. (2013). Crossing boundaries in Facebook: Students' framing of language learning activities as extended spaces. *International Journal of Computer-Supported Collaborative Learning, 8*(3), 293–312.

Lanzendorf, M. (2002). Mobility styles and travel behavior: Application of a lifestyle approach to leisure travel. *Transportation Research Record: Journal of the Transportation Research Board, 1807*(1), 163–173.

Lazer, W. (1963). Life style concepts and marketing. In S. Greyser (Ed.), *Toward scientific marketing* (pp. 140–151). Chicago: American Marketing Association.

Leiserowitz, A. A. (2004). Day After Tomorrow: Study of climate change risk perception. *Environment: Science and Policy for Sustainable Development, 46*(9), 22–39.

Lemos, M. C., & Agrawal, A. (2006). Environmental governance. *Annual Review of Environmental Resources, 31*, 297–325.

Lightfoot, J. M. (2006). A comparative analysis of e-mail and face-to-face communication in an educational environment. *The Internet and Higher Education, 9*(3), 217–227.

Lindenberg, S., & Steg, L. (2007). Normative, gain and hedonic goal frames guiding environmental behavior. *Journal of Social Issues, 63*(1), 117–137.

Littlejohn, S. W., & Foss, K. A. (2009). *Encyclopedia of communication theory*. New York: Sage.

Littlejohn, S. W., & Foss, K. A. (2011). *Theories of human communication*. Long Grove, IL: Waveland Press.

Lokhorst, A. M., Werner, C., Staats, H., van Dijk, E., & Gale, J. L. (2013). Commitment and behavior change. A meta-analysis and critical review of commitment-making strategies in environmental research. *Environment and Behavior, 45*(1), 3–34.

Luchs, M. G., & Mooradian, T. A. (2012). Sex, personality, and sustainable consumer behaviour: Elucidating the gender effect. *Journal of Consumer Policy, 35*(1), 127–144.

Maass, A., & Clark, R. D. (1984). Hidden impact of minorities: Fifteen years of minority influence research. *Psychological Bulletin, 95*(3), 428.

Mallett, R. K., Melchiori, K. J., & Strickroth, T. (2013). Self-confrontation via a carbon footprint calculator increases guilt and support for a proenvironmental group. *Ecopsychology, 5*(1), 9–16.

Markowitz, E. M., Goldberg, L. R., Ashton, M. C., & Lee, K. (2012). Profiling the "pro-environmental individual": A personality perspective. *Journal of Personality, 80*(1), 81–111.

Marx, J. D. (2000). Online fundraising in the human services. *Journal of Technology in Human Services, 17*(2–3), 137–152.

Matthies, E., Klöckner, C. A., & Preißner, C. L. (2006). Applying a modified moral decision making model to change habitual car use: How can commitment be effective? *Applied Psychology, 55*(1), 91–106.

Matthies, E., & Krömker, D. (2000). Participatory planning – A heuristic for adjusting interventions to the context. *Journal of Environmental Psychology, 20*(1), 65–74.

Matthies, E., Selge, S., & Klöckner, C. A. (2012). The role of parental behaviour for the development of behaviour specific environmental norms-The example of recycling and re-use behaviour. *Journal of Environmental Psychology, 32*(3), 277–284.

McCalley, L. T., Kaiser, F., Midden, C., Keser, M., & Teunissen, M. (2006). Persuasive appliances: Goal priming and behavioral response to product-integrated energy feedback. In W. A. Ijsselsteijn, Y. A. W. de Kort, C. Midden, B. Eggen, & E. van den Hoven (Eds.), *Persuasive technology* (pp. 45–49). Berlin: Springer.

McCalley, L. T., & Midden, C. J. (2002). Energy conservation through product-integrated feedback: The roles of goal-setting and social orientation. *Journal of Economic Psychology, 23*(5), 589–603.

McDaniels, T., Axelrod, L. J., & Slovic, P. (1996). Perceived ecological risks of global change: A psychometric comparison of causes and consequences. *Global Environmental Change, 6*(2), 159–171.

McGonigal, J. (2011). *Reality is broken: Why games make us better and how they can change the world*. New York: Penguin Press.

McGuire, W. J. (1964). Inducing resistance to persuasion – some contemporary approaches. In L. Berkowitz (Ed.), *Advances in experimental social psychology* (Vol. 1, pp. 191–229). New York: Academic Press.

McNally, A. M., Palfai, T. P., & Kahler, C. W. (2005). Motivational interventions for heavy drinking college students: Examining the role of discrepancy-related psychological processes. *Psychology of Addictive Behaviors, 19*(1), 79.

Messerlian, C., & Derevensky, J. (2006). Social marketing campaigns for youth gambling prevention: Lessons learned from youth. *International Journal of Mental Health and Addiction, 4*(4), 294–306.

Miao, L., & Wei, W. (2013). Consumers' pro-environmental behavior and the underlying motivations: A comparison between household and hotel settings. *International Journal of Hospitality Management, 32*, 102–112.

Miller, G. A. (1956). The magical number seven, plus or minus two: Some limits on our capacity for processing information. *Psychological Review, 63*(2), 81.

Mills, T. M. (1967). *The sociology of small groups*. Englewood Cliffs, NJ: Prentice-Hall.

Mitchell, R. B. (2012). Technology is not enough. Climate change, population, affluence, and consumption. *The Journal of Environment & Development, 21*(1), 24–27.

Moscardo, G., Pearce, P., & Morrison, A. (2001). Evaluating different bases for market segmentation: A comparison of geographic origin versus activity participation for generating tourist market segments. *Journal of Travel & Tourism Marketing, 10*(1), 29–49.

Moscovici, S., Lage, E., & Naffrechoux, M. (1969). Influence of a consistent minority on the responses of a majority in a color perception task. *Sociometry, 32*(4), 365–380.

Mowen, J. C., & Minor, M. (1997). *Consumer behavior* (5th ed.). New Jersey: Prentice-Hall.

Nawijn, J., & Peeters, P. (2014). Rose tinted memories as a cause of unsustainable leisure travel. In T. Gärling, D. Ettema, & M. Friman (Eds.), *Handbook of sustainable travel* (pp. 185–197). New York: Springer.

Nayum, A., & Klöckner, C. A. (2014). A comprehensive socio-psychological approach to car type choice. *Journal of Environmental Psychology, 40*, 401–411.

Nayum, A., Klöckner, C. A., & Prugsamatz, S. (2013). Influences of car type class and carbon dioxide emission levels on purchases of new cars: A retrospective analysis of car purchases in Norway. *Transportation Research Part A: Policy and Practice, 48*, 96–108.

Neal, D. T., Wood, W., & Quinn, J. M. (2006). Habits – A repeat performance. *Current Directions in Psychological Science, 15*(4), 198–202.

Nie, C., & Zepeda, L. (2011). Lifestyle segmentation of US food shoppers to examine organic and local food consumption. *Appetite, 57*(1), 28–37.

Nolan, J. M. (2010). "An Inconvenient Truth" increases knowledge, concern, and willingness to reduce greenhouse gases. *Environment and Behavior, 42*(5), 643–658.

Nomura, H., John, P. C., & Cotterill, S. (2011). The use of feedback to enhance environmental outcomes: A randomised controlled trial of a food waste scheme. *Local Environment, 16*(7), 637–653.

Nordhøy, F. (1962). *Group interaction in decision-making under risk.* Cambridge: School of Industrial Management, MIT.

Nordlund, A. M., & Garvill, J. (2002). Value structures behind proenvironmental behavior. *Environment and Behavior, 34*(6), 740–756.

Oosterbeek, H., Sloof, R., & Van De Kuilen, G. (2004). Cultural differences in ultimatum game experiments: Evidence from a meta-analysis. *Experimental Economics, 7*(2), 171–188.

Oreg, S., & Katz-Gerro, T. (2006). Predicting proenvironmental behavior cross-nationally values, the theory of planned behavior, and value-belief-norm theory. *Environment and Behavior, 38*(4), 462–483.

Ostrom, E. (1990). *Governing the commons: The evolution of institutions for collective action.* Cambridge, US: Cambridge University Press.

Ouellette, J. A., & Wood, W. (1998). Habit and intention in everyday life: The multiple processes by which past behavior predicts future behavior. *Psychological Bulletin, 124*(1), 54–74.

Oyserman, D., Terry, K., & Bybee, D. (2002). A possible selves intervention to enhance school involvement. *Journal of Adolescence, 25*(3), 313–326.

Ozaki, R. (2011). Adopting sustainable innovation: What makes consumers sign up to green electricity? *Business Strategy and the Environment, 20*(1), 1–17.

Ozaki, R., & Dodgson, M. (2010). Adopting and consuming innovations. *Prometheus, 28*(4), 311–326.

Patt, A. G., & Schrag, D. P. (2003). Using specific language to describe risk and probability. *Climatic Change, 61*(1–2), 17–30.

Pearson, J. C., Nelson, P. E., Titsworth, S., & Harter, L. (2011). *Human communication*. New York: McGraw-Hill.

Peirce, C. S. (1974). *Collected papers of Charles Sanders Peirce* (Vol. 3). Cambridge: Harvard University Press.

Peters, A., Gutscher, H., & Scholz, R. W. (2011). Psychological determinants of fuel consumption of purchased new cars. *Transportation Research Part F: Traffic Psychology and Behaviour, 14*(3), 229–239.

Peterson, L., & Peterson, M. J. (1959). Short-term retention of individual verbal items. *Journal of Experimental Psychology, 58*(3), 193.

Pettersson, A., Olsson, U., & Fjellström, C. (2004). Family life in grocery stores – a study of interaction between adults and children. *International Journal of Consumer Studies, 28*(4), 317–328.

Petty, R. E., & Cacioppo, J. T. (1986). The elaboration likelihood model of persuasion. In L. Berkowitz (Ed.), *Advances in experimental social psychology* (Vol. 19, pp. 123–203). New York: Academic Press.

Plummer, J. T. (1974). The concept and application of life style segmentation. *Journal of Marketing, 38*(1), 33–37.

Poumadere, M., Mays, C., Le Mer, S., & Blong, R. (2005). The 2003 heat wave in France: Dangerous climate change here and now. *Risk Analysis, 25*(6), 1483–1494.

Power, M. R. (1998). *Working through communication*. Queensland: Bond University.

Prestin, A., & Pearce, K. E. (2010). We care a lot: Formative research for a social marketing campaign to promote school-based recycling. *Resources, Conservation and Recycling, 54*(11), 1017–1026.

Prochaska, J. O., & DiClemente, C. C. (1994). *The transtheoretical approach: Crossing traditional boundaries of therapy*. Malaba, FL: Krieger Pub.

Procter-Scherdtel, A., & Collins, D. (2013). Social norms and smoking bans on campus: Interactions in the Canadian university context. *Health Education Research, 28*(1), 101–112.

Prugsamatz, S., Klöckner, C. A., Matthies, E., Bamberg, S., & Stern, P. C. (2014a). Stage of change and information self-tailoring. *Manuscript in preparation*.

Prugsamatz, S., Klöckner, C. A., Matthies, E., Bamberg, S., Stern, P. C., & Steg, L. (2014b). Tailored interventions and stage progression. *Manuscript in preparation*.

Pruneau, D., Gravel, H., Bourque, W., & Langis, J. (2003). Experimentation with a socio-constructivist process for climate change education. *Environmental Education Research, 9*(4), 429–446.

Pöttker, H. (2003). News and its communicative quality: The inverted pyramid – when and why did it appear? *Journalism Studies, 4*(4), 501–511.

Rapoport, A. (1965). *Prisoner's dilemma: A study in conflict and cooperation* (Vol. 165). Ann Arbor: University of Michigan Press.

Ratcliff, R. (1978). A theory of memory retrieval. *Psychological Review, 85*(2), 59–108.

Rebich, S., & Gautier, C. (2005). Concept mapping to reveal prior knowledge and conceptual change in a mock summit course on global climate change. *Journal of Geoscience Education, 53*(4), 355–365.

Reckien, D., & Eisenack, K. (2013). Climate change gaming on board and screen: A review. *Simulation & Gaming, 44*(2–3), 253–271.

Reckwitz, A. (2002). Toward a Theory of Social Practices A development in culturalist theorizing. *European Journal of Social Theory, 5*(2), 243–263.
Rippl, S. (2002). Cultural theory and risk perception: A proposal for a better measurement. *Journal of Risk Research, 5*(2), 147–165.
Rivis, A., & Sheeran, P. (2003). Descriptive norms as an additional predictor in the theory of planned behaviour: A meta-analysis. *Current Psychology, 22*(3), 218–233.
Roebers, C. M., Moga, N., & Schneider, W. (2001). The role of accuracy motivation on children's and adults' event recall. *Journal of Experimental Child Psychology, 78*(4), 313–329.
Rogers, E. M. (2003). *Diffusion of innovations*. New York: Free Press.
Rogers, R. W. (1975). A protection motivation theory of fear appeals and attitude change. *The Journal of Psychology, 91*(1), 93–114.
Roig, M. A., Ortiz, S. B., & i Palmer, P. F. (2011). Greening events: Waste reduction through the integration of life cycle management into event organisation at ESCi. In M. Finkbeiner (Ed.), *Towards life cycle sustainability management* (pp. 239–245). New York: Springer.
Ross, L. (1977). The intuitive psychologist and his shortcomings: Distortions in the attribution process. In L. Berkowitz (Ed.), *Advances in experimental social psychology* (Vol. 10, pp. 173–220).
Rothgerber, H. (2013). Real men don't eat (vegetable) quiche: Masculinity and the justification of meat consumption. *Psychology of Men & Masculinity, 14*(4), 363.
Rubens, L., Gosling, P., Bonaiuto, M., Brisbois, X., & Moch, A. (2013). Being a hypocrite or committed while I am shopping? A comparison of the impact of two interventions on environmentally friendly behavior. *Environment and Behavior, 47*(1), 3–16.
Sadler, T. D., Chambers, F. W., & Zeidler, D. L. (2004). Student conceptualizations of the nature of science in response to a socioscientific issue. *International Journal of Science Education, 26*(4), 387–409.
Sahin, D. Y., & Atik, D. (2013). Celebrity influences on young consumers: Guiding the way to the ideal self. *Izmir Review of Social Sciences, 1*(1), 65–82.
Salvucci, D. D., & Taatgen, N. A. (2008). Threaded cognition: An integrated theory of concurrent multitasking. *Psychological Review, 115*(1), 101.
Sams, M., Hari, R., Rif, J., & Knuutila, J. (1993). The human auditory sensory memory trace persists about 10 sec: Neuromagnetic evidence. *Journal of Cognitive Neuroscience, 5*(3), 363–370.
Sanfey, A. G., Rilling, J. K., Aronson, J. A., Nystrom, L. E., & Cohen, J. D. (2003). The neural basis of economic decision-making in the ultimatum game. *Science, 300*(5626), 1755–1758.
Schelling, T. C. (1971). Dynamic models of segregation. *Journal of mathematical sociology, 1*(2), 143–186.
Schlegelmilch, B. B., Bohlen, G. M., & Diamantopoulos, A. (1996). The link between green purchasing decisions and measures of environmental consciousness. *European Journal of Marketing, 30*(5), 35–55.
Schnaiberg, A. (1980). *The environment: From surplus to scarcity*. New York: Oxford University Press.
Schwartz, S. H. (1994). Are there universal aspects in the structure and contents of human values? *Journal of Social Issues, 50*(4), 19–45.

Schwartz, S. H. (2006). A theory of cultural value orientations: Explication and applications. *Comparative Sociology, 5*(2–3), 137–182.

Schwartz, S. H., & Howard, J. A. (1981). A normative decision-making model of altruism. In J. P. Rushton, Sorrentino, R. M. (Ed.), *Altruism and helping behavior* (pp. 189–211). Hillsdale: Lawrence Erlbaum.

Schwarz, N., & Ernst, A. (2009). Agent-based modeling of the diffusion of environmental innovations – an empirical approach. *Technological Forecasting and Social Change, 76*(4), 497–511.

Schweizer, S., Davis, S., & Thompson, J. L. (2013). Changing the conversation about climate change: A theoretical framework for place-based climate change engagement. *Environmental Communication: A Journal of Nature and Culture, 7*(1), 42–62.

Schösler, H., De Boer, J., & Boersema, J. J. (2012). A theoretical framework to analyse sustainability relevant food choices from a cultural perspective: Caring for food and sustainability in a pluralistic society. In T. Potthast & S. Meisch (Eds.), *Climate change and sustainable development: Ethical perspectives on land use and food production* (pp. 335–341). Wageningen: Springer/ Wageningen Academic Publishers.

Sharpe, E. K. (2008). Festivals and social change: Intersections of pleasure and politics at a community music festival. *Leisure Sciences, 30*(3), 217–234.

Shove, E. (2010). Beyond the ABC: Climate change policy and theories of social change. *Environment and Planning. A, 42*(6), 1273.

Shove, E. (2011). On the difference between chalk and cheese – a response to Whitmarsh et al.'s comments on "Beyond the ABC: Climate change policy and theories of social change". *Environment and Planning A, 43*(2), 262–264.

Shove, E., & Pantzar, M. (2005). Consumers, producers and practices understanding the invention and reinvention of Nordic walking. *Journal of Consumer Culture, 5*(1), 43–64.

Shove, E., Pantzar, M., & Watson, M. (2012). *The dynamics of social practice: Everyday life and how it changes*. London: Sage.

Siero, F. W., Bakker, A. B., Dekker, G. B., & Van Den Burg, M. T. (1996). Changing organizational energy consumption behaviour through comparative feedback. *Journal of Environmental Psychology, 16*(3), 235–246.

Simon, H. A. (1972). Theories of bounded rationality. In C. B. McGuire & R. Radner (Eds.), *Decision and organization* (pp. 161–176). Amsterdam: North Holland Publishing Company.

Sinha, P. K., & Uniyal, D. P. (2005). Using observational research for behavioural segmentation of shoppers. *Journal of Retailing and Consumer Services, 12*(1), 35–48.

Sinus-Sociovision. (2002). *Strategische Zielgruppenanalyse für den Öko-Ernährungs-Markt. Untersuchung für die CMA*. Sinus-Sociovision. Heidelberg.

Sinus-Sociovision. (2009). *Die Sinus-Milieus*. Heidelberg, Deutschland: Sinus Sociovision.

Sjöberg, L. (1996). A discussion of the limitations of the psychometric and cultural theory approaches to risk perception. *Radiation Protection Dosimetry, 68*(3–4), 219–225.

Sjöberg, L. (2000). Factors in risk perception. *Risk Analysis, 20*(1), 1–12.

Sjöberg, L. (2003). *Risk perception is not what it seems: The psychometric paradigm revisited*. Paper presented at the Valdor conference.

Skinner, B. F. (1938). *The behavior of organisms: An experimental analysis.* Oxford: Appleton-Century.

Slovic, P. (1987). Perception of risk. *Science, 236*(4799), 280–285.

Slovic, P., Fischhoff, B., & Lichtenstein, S. (1986). The psychometric study of risk perception risk evaluation and management (pp. 3–24). New York: Springer.

Smith, J. (2005). Dangerous news: Media decision making about climate change risk. *Risk Analysis, 25*(6), 1471–1482.

Sopha, B. M., & Klöckner, C. A. (2011). Psychological factors in the diffusion of sustainable technology: A study of Norwegian households' adoption of wood pellet heating. *Renewable and Sustainable Energy Reviews, 15*(6), 2756–2765.

Sopha, B. M., Klöckner, C. A., & Hertwich, E. G. (2010a, 6–9 September 2010). The influence of the social network structure on the diffusion of heating system in Norway. Paper presented at the World Congress on Social Simulation, Kassel, Germany.

Sopha, B. M., Klöckner, C. A., & Hertwich, E. G. (2011a). Adopters and non-adopters of wood pellet heating in Norwegian households. *Biomass and Bioenergy, 35*(1), 652–662.

Sopha, B. M., Klöckner, C. A., & Hertwich, E. G. (2011b). Exploring policy options for a transition to sustainable heating system diffusion using an agent-based simulation. *Energy Policy, 39*(5), 2722–2729.

Sopha, B. M., Klöckner, C. A., & Hertwich, E. G. (2013). Adoption and diffusion of heating systems in Norway: Coupling agent-based modeling with empirical research. *Environmental Innovation and Societal Transitions, 8*(0), 42–61.

Sopha, B. M., Klöckner, C. A., Skjevrak, G., & Hertwich, E. G. (2010b). Norwegian households' perception of wood pellet stove compared to air-to-air heat pump and electric heating. *Energy Policy, 38*(7), 3744–3754.

Souchet, L., & Girandola, F. (2013). Double foot-in-the-door, social representations, and environment: Application for energy savings. *Journal of Applied Social Psychology, 43*(2), 306–315.

Sparks, P., & Shepherd, R. (1992). Self-identity and the theory of planned behavior: Assessing the role of identification with "green consumerism". *Social Psychology Quarterly, 55*(4), 388–399.

Srivastava, R. K., & Anderson, B. B. (2010). Gender roles and family decision making: A study of Indian automobile purchases. *International Journal of Services, Economics and Management, 2*(2), 109–120.

Staats, H., Harland, P., & Wilke, H. A. (2004). Effecting durable change a team approach to improve environmental behavior in the household. *Environment and Behavior, 36*(3), 341–367.

Staats, H., Wit, A., & Midden, C. (1996). Communicating the greenhouse effect to the public: Evaluation of a mass media campaign from a social dilemma perspective. *Journal of Environmental Management, 46*(2), 189–203.

Stefan, V., Van Herpen, E., Tudoran, A. A., & Lähteenmäki, L. (2013). Avoiding food waste by Romanian consumers: The importance of planning and shopping routines. *Food Quality and Preference, 28*(1), 375–381.

Steg, L., Dreijerink, L., & Abrahamse, W. (2005). Factors influencing the acceptability of energy policies: A test of VBN theory. *Journal of Environmental Psychology, 25*(4), 415–425.

Steg, L., van den Berg, A. E., & de Groot, J. I. M. (2012). *Environmental psychology: An introduction.* Oxford, UK: Wiley-Blackwell.

Steg, L., & Vlek, C. (2009). Encouraging pro-environmental behaviour: An integrative review and research agenda. *Journal of Environmental Psychology, 29*(3), 309–317.
Stern, P. C. (1999). Information, incentives, and proenvironmental consumer behavior. *Journal of Consumer Policy, 22*(4), 461–478.
Stern, P. C. (2000). New environmental theories: Toward a coherent theory of environmentally significant behavior. *Journal of Social Issues, 56*(3), 407–424.
Stetsenko, A., & Arievitch, I. (1997). Constructing and deconstructing the self: Comparing post-Vygotskian and discourse-based versions of social constructivism. *Mind, Culture, and Activity, 4*(3), 159–172.
Stolzenbach, S., Bredie, W. L., Christensen, R. H., & Byrne, D. V. (2013). Impact of product information and repeated exposure on consumer liking, sensory perception and concept associations of local apple juice. *Food Research International, 52*(1), 91–98.
Stoner, J. A. (1968). Risky and cautious shifts in group decisions: The influence of widely held values. *Journal of Experimental Social Psychology, 4*(4), 442–459.
Straughan, R. D., & Roberts, J. A. (1999). Environmental segmentation alternatives: A look at green consumer behavior in the new millennium. *Journal of Consumer Marketing, 16*(6), 558–575.
Strengers, Y. (2012). Peak electricity demand and social practice theories: Reframing the role of change agents in the energy sector. *Energy Policy, 44*, 226–234.
Su, C., Fern, E. F., & Ye, K. (2003). A temporal dynamic model of spousal family purchase-decision behavior. *Journal of Marketing Research, 40*(3), 268–281.
Suppipat, S., Thomlison, J., Osei, E. A., & Syltern, A. J. (2009). *Communicating environmental aspects on the PSTEREO rock festival in Trondheim*. Experts in team project reports. NTNU. Trondheim.
Susi, T., Johannesson, M., & Backlund, P. (2007). *Serious games: An overview*. Skövde, Sweden: School of Humanities and Informatics, University of Skövde.
Sussman, R., Greeno, M., Gifford, R., & Scannell, L. (2013). The effectiveness of models and prompts on waste diversion: A field experiment on composting by cafeteria patrons. *Journal of Applied Social Psychology, 43*(1), 24–34.
Tajfel, H. (2010). *Social identity and intergroup relations* (Vol. 7). Cambridge: Cambridge University Press.
Taniguchi, A., Fujii, S., Azami, T., & Ishida, H. (2014). Persuasive communication aimed at public transportation-oriented residential choice and the promotion of public transport. *Transportation, 41*(1), 75–89.
Taniguchi, A., Hara, F., Takano, S. e., Kagaya, S. i., & Fujii, S. (2003). Psychological and behavioral effects of Travel Feedback Program for travel behavior modification. *Transportation Research Record: Journal of the Transportation Research Board, 1839*(1), 182–190.
Tanner, C. (1999). Constraints on environmental behaviour. *Journal of Environmental Psychology, 19*(2), 145–157.
Thaler, R. H. (1988). Anomalies: The ultimatum game. *The Journal of Economic Perspectives*, 195–206.
Thompson, M., Ellis, R., & Wildavsky, A. (1990). *Cultural theory*. Boulder, CO: Westview Press.
Thøgersen, J. (1999). Spillover processes in the development of a sustainable consumption pattern. *Journal of Economic Psychology, 20*(1), 53–81.

Thøgersen, J. (2004). A cognitive dissonance interpretation of consistencies and inconsistencies in environmentally responsible behavior. *Journal of Environmental Psychology, 24*(1), 93–103.

Thøgersen, J. (2005). Main effects and side effects of environmental regulation. In K. G. Grunert & J. Thøgersen (Eds.), *Consumers, policy and the environment* (pp. 311–324). New York: Springer.

Thøgersen, J. (2006). Norms for environmentally responsible behaviour: An extended taxonomy. *Journal of Environmental Psychology, 26*(4), 247–261.

Thøgersen, J. (2009). Promoting public transport as a subscription service: Effects of a free month travel card. *Transport Policy, 16*(6), 335–343.

Thøgersen, J., & Ölander, F. (2003). Spillover of environment-friendly consumer behaviour. *Journal of Environmental Psychology, 23*(3), 225–236.

Tilyard, B. A. (2011). *Seeing Green and Becoming Green: Applying Normative Social Influence to Promote Pro-Environmental Behaviour Across Two New Zealand Contexts.* (Master), Victoria University of Wellington, Wellington, New Zealand. Retrieved from http://researcharchive.vuw.ac.nz/xmlui/bitstream/handle/10063/1829/thesis.pdf?sequence=1.

Timmermans, H., Borgers, A., Van Dijk, J., & Oppewal, H. (1992). Residential choice behaviour of dual earner households: A decompositional joint choice model. *Environment and Planning A, 24*, 517–533.

Tonglet, M., Phillips, P. S., & Read, A. D. (2004). Using the theory of planned behaviour to investigate the determinants of recycling behaviour: A case study from Brixworth, UK. *Resources, Conservation and Recycling, 41*(3), 191–214.

Treisman, A. M. (1960). Contextual cues in selective listening. *Quarterly Journal of Experimental Psychology, 12*(4), 242–248.

Tuckman, B. W., & Jensen, M. A. C. (1977). Stages of small-group development revisited. *Group & Organization Management, 2*(4), 419–427.

Tulving, E. (1972). Episodic and semantic memory. In E. Tulving & W. Donaldson (Eds.), *Organization of memory* (pp. 381–405). New York: Academic Press.

Tulving, E., & Schacter, D. L. (1990). Priming and human memory systems. *Science, 247*(4940), 301–306.

Tulving, E., & Thomson, D. M. (1973). Encoding specificity and retrieval processes in episodic memory. *Psychological Review, 80*(5), 352.

Tversky, A., & Kahneman, D. (1973). Availability: A heuristic for judging frequency and probability. *Cognitive Psychology, 5*(2), 207–232.

Tversky, A., & Kahneman, D. (1974). Judgment under uncertainty: Heuristics and biases. *Science, 185*(4157), 1124–1131.

Tversky, A., & Kahneman, D. (1981). The framing of decisions and the psychology of choice. *Science, 211*(4481), 453–458.

Tversky, A., & Kahneman, D. (1986). Rational choice and the framing of decisions. *Journal of Business, 59*(4), 251–278.

Ukenna, S., Nkamnebe, A. D., Nwaizugbo, I. C., Moguluwa, S. C., & Olise, M. C. (2012). Profiling the environmental sustainability-conscious (ESC) consumer: Proposing the SPP model. *Journal of Management & Sustainability, 2*(2), 197–210.

Ullman, M. T. (2004). Contributions of memory circuits to language: The declarative/procedural model. *Cognition, 92*(1), 231–270.

Ungar, S. (2000). Knowledge, ignorance and the popular culture: Climate change versus the ozone hole. *Public Understanding of Science, 9*(3), 297–312.
Uzunboylu, H., Cavus, N., & Ercag, E. (2009). Using mobile learning to increase environmental awareness. *Computers & Education, 52*(2), 381–389.
Van Houwelingen, J. H., & Van Raaij, W. F. (1989). The effect of goal-setting and daily electronic feedback on in-home energy use. *Journal of Consumer Research, 16*(1), 98–105.
Van Vugt, M., Van Lange, P. A., & Meertens, R. M. (1996). Commuting by car or public transportation? A social dilemma analysis of travel mode judgements. *European Journal of Social Psychology, 26*(3), 373–395.
Venhoeven, L. A., Bolderdijk, J. W., & Steg, L. (2013). Explaining the paradox: How pro-environmental behaviour can both thwart and foster well-being. *Sustainability, 5*(4), 1372–1386.
Vermeir, I., & Verbeke, W. (2008). Sustainable food consumption among young adults in Belgium: Theory of planned behaviour and the role of confidence and values. *Ecological Economics, 64*(3), 542–553.
Verplanken, B., Aarts, H., & Van Knippenberg, A. (1997). Habit, information acquisition, and the process of making travel mode choices. *European Journal of Social Psychology, 27*(5), 539–560.
Verplanken, B., & Wood, W. (2006). Interventions to break and create consumer habits. *Journal of Public Policy & Marketing, 25*(1), 90–103.
Voelpel, S. C., Eckhoff, R. A., & Förster, J. (2008). David against Goliath? Group size and bystander effects in virtual knowledge sharing. *Human Relations, 61*(2), 271–295.
Von Neumann, J., & Morgenstern, O. (2007). *Theory of games and economic behavior (60th anniversary commemorative edition)*. Princeton: Princeton university press.
Wallach, M. A., Kogan, N., & Bem, D. J. (1962). Group influence on individual risk taking. *Journal of Abnormal and Social Psychology, 65*(2), 75–86.
Wallach, M. A., Kogan, N., & Bem, D. J. (1964). Diffusion of responsibility and level of risk taking in groups. *The Journal of Abnormal and Social Psychology, 68*(3), 263.
Walther, J. B., & Bunz, U. (2005). The rules of virtual groups: Trust, liking, and performance in computer-mediated communication. *Journal of Communication, 55*(4), 828–846.
Walther, J. B., & D'Addario, K. P. (2001). The impacts of emoticons on message interpretation in computer-mediated communication. *Social Science Computer Review, 19*(3), 324–347.
Wauters, E., Bielders, C., Poesen, J., Govers, G., & Mathijs, E. (2010). Adoption of soil conservation practices in Belgium: An examination of the theory of planned behaviour in the agri-environmental domain. *Land Use Policy, 27*(1), 86–94.
Weber, E. U. (2006). Experience-based and description-based perceptions of long-term risk: Why global warming does not scare us (yet). *Climatic Change, 77*(1–2), 103–120.
Wedel, M., & Kamakura, W. A. (2000). *Market segmentation: Conceptual and methodological foundations*. New York: Springer.
Weiner, B. (1972). *Theories of motivation: From mechanism to cognition*. Oxford: Markham.

Weiner, B. (2001). Intrapersonal and interpersonal theories of motivation from an attribution perspective. In F. Salili, C.-Y. Chiu, & Y.-Y. Hong (Eds.), *Student motivation* (pp. 17–30). New York: Springer.
Wells, N. M., & Lekies, K. S. (2006). Nature and the life course: Pathways from childhood nature experiences to adult environmentalism. *Children Youth and Environments, 16*(1), 1–24.
Welp, M., Anne, C., Stoll-Kleemann, S., & Fürstenau, C. (2006). Science-based stakeholder dialogues in climate change research. In R. Allan, U. Förstner, W. Salomons, S. Stoll-Kleemann, & M. Welp (Eds.), *Stakeholder dialogues in natural resources management* (pp. 213–240). Berlin: Springer.
Whitmarsh, L., & O'Neill, S. (2010). Green identity, green living? The role of pro-environmental self-identity in determining consistency across diverse pro-environmental behaviours. *Journal of Environmental Psychology, 30*(3), 305–314.
Whitmarsh, L., O'Neill, S., & Lorenzoni, I. (2011). Climate change or social change? Debate within, amongst, and beyond disciplines. *Environment and Planning A, 43*(2), 258–261.
Wiedmann, K. P., Reeh, M.-O., & Schumacher, H. (2009). Near field communication in mobile marketing. In H. H. Bauer, T. Dirks, & M. Bryant (Eds.), *Erfolgsfaktoren des mobile marketing* (pp. 305–325). Berlin: Springer.
Wildavsky, A. (1993). The comparative study of risk perception: A beginning. In B. Rnck (Ed.), *Risk is a construct* (pp. 89–94). München: Knesebeck.
Wildavsky, A., & Dake, K. (1990). Theories of risk perception: Who fears what and why? *Daedalus, 119*(4), 41–60.
Wilke, H. A. (1991). Greed, efficiency and fairness in resource management situations. *European Review of Social Psychology, 2*(1), 165–187.
Wood, R., Baxter, P., & Belpaeme, T. (2012). A review of long-term memory in natural and synthetic systems. *Adaptive Behavior, 20*(2), 81–103.
Wood, W., Quinn, J. M., & Kashy, D. A. (2002). Habits in everyday life: Thought, emotion, and action. *Journal of Personality and Social Psychology, 83*(6), 1281.
Zachrisson, J., & Boks, C. (2012). Exploring behavioural psychology to support design for sustainable behaviour research. *Journal of Design Research, 10*(1), 50–66.
Zeelenberg, M., Nelissen, R. M., Breugelmans, S. M., & Pieters, R. (2008). On emotion specificity in decision making: Why feeling is for doing. *Judgment and Decision making, 3*(1), 18–27.
Zepeda, L., & Deal, D. (2008). Think before you eat: Photographic food diaries as intervention tools to change dietary decision making and attitudes. *International Journal of Consumer Studies, 32*(6), 692–698.
Zur, I., & Klöckner, C. A. (2014). Individual motivations for limiting meat consumption. *British Food Journal, 116*(4), 629–642.

Index

Aarts, H., 91
ABM, see agent-based modelling (ABM)
Abraham, C., 39
Abrahamse, W., 24, 33, 81, 167, 169, 176, 192
agent-based modelling (ABM)
 advantage of, 114
 applications of, 115–16
 basic assumptions of, 114–15
 computer simulations with core elements, 114–15
 decision rules, 115
 description of, 113–14
 diffusion of wood pellet, 116
 strengths and weaknesses of, 116–17
 water-use model, 116
agents, computer simulations, 114
Agrawal, A., 10
agreeableness, 153–4
Agyeman, J., 58
Ahn, H.-Y., 135
Ajzen, I., 70, 72, 111
Anable, J., 4, 153
anchoring heuristics, 63
Anderson, B. B., 181
Andresen, S. A., 223
Anker, A. E., 188
Appelt, K. C., 85
Ardissono, L., 158
Arievitch, I., 65
Arkin, R., 187
Armitage, C. J., 72, 74
Arnesen, M., 12
Aronson, E., 172
arrangement, aspects of speech, 46
Arreglo, C., 225
art-based communication, 126
Artistico, D., 173
Asch, S. E., 188, 189
Asch study, 188–9
ascription of responsibility, 76
Asensio, O. I., 33

Ashforth, B. E., 190
Ashton, M. C., 154
Atik, D., 170
Atkinson, R. C., 54
attention, sociopsychological communication theory, 51–3
attitude, behaviours, 71
attribution, sociopsychological communication theory, 56–7
Austin, J., 165, 166
automatic processes, in communication
 heuristics, 62–4
 mental models, 64
availability heuristic, 63
awareness of consequences, 76, 80
awareness of need, 76, 168

Baddeley, A. D., 54, 55
Baer, M., 191
Baiocchi, G., 149
Ballantyne, R., 175, 176
Bamberg, S., 24, 39, 78, 94–7, 105, 147, 151, 155, 156, 172, 174, 233
Banas, J. A., 218
Bandura, A., 204
Bargh, J. A., 86
Barnett, J., 138, 140, 141, 142
Baron, P. H., 187
Baron, R. S., 187
Baum, A., 6
BBC, see British Broadcasting Company (BBC)
behavioural decision-making, 207–8
behavioural segmentation approaches, 149–50
behaviours
 attitudes towards, 71
 communication, see communication behaviour
 in consumption of goods domain, 36, 37

258

environmental psychology focus on, 31
in food domain, 33, 34
vs. human, 16
individual, household and group, 181–5
ipsative theory of, 88–9
in leisure activities domain, 40–1
meat-eating, 35
in mobility domain, 38, 39
models to prevalent goal frame, 84
PBC, 71–2
performance of, 176
plasticity of, 30
pro-social, 188
risk-related, 138
in shelter domain, 31, 32
subjective norms, 71
see also specific types
Bell, P. A., 6, 11, 87, 166, 167, 169, 176
Berkhout, P. H., 5
Bither, S. W., 61
Blackwell, R. D., 153
Blöbaum, A., 77, 92, 173
"block-leader" approach, 171
board games
benefits of, 205
CO_2, 202–3
description of, 201
effective, 203–4
in environmental communication, 205
Green Deal, 203
Settlers of Catan Oil Springs Scenario, 201–2
Boersema, J. J., 36
Bogner, F. X., 81
Bohlen, G. M., 148, 149
Bokek-Cohen, Y. a., 181, 182
Boks, C., 23
Bolderdijk, J. W., 85
Bonebright, D. A., 186
Bonetti, D., 101
Bonnes, M., 11
Bordia, P., 14, 15
Borgstede, C. V., 207, 208
Bornstein, G., 191
Bostrom, A., 64
Boyes, E., 175

Braun, B., 29
Breakwell, G. M., 127, 130, 138, 140, 141, 142, 186
British Broadcasting Company (BBC), 122
Broadbent, D. E., 52
Bruckner, T., 152
Buckland, D., 224
Bunz, U., 185
Burnstein, E., 187
bystander effect, 188

Cacioppo, J. T., 58, 59, 189
Cammaer, G., 225, 231
carbon emission reduction, 26–7
Carr, T. H., 86
Castree, N., 29
Chapman, L., 4, 233
Chartrand, T. L., 86
"the chasm", 109
Cheverst, K., 158
Child, I. L., 153
Chiu, B., 225
Chiu, Y.-T. H., 41
Christensen, T. H., 5
Cialdini, R. B., 57, 61, 170
Clarke, A., 87
Clark, R. D., 189
classical behavioural psychology, 166
classification system of intervention techniques, 176
climate change, household actions to mitigate, 26–7
Climate Diplomat, 205–6
Cobb-Walgren, C., 150
cognitive dissonance theory, 57–8
Collins, A., 149
Collins, D., 171
commitment, 169
communication
automatic processes in, 51, 62
direct person-to-person, 13–14
dyadic, 13, 19
e-mail, 15
environmental governance, part of, 11
and environmental interventions, 21–9
exchanging meaning process, 18

communication – *continued*
   face-to-face, 125
   forms of, 4, 13–16
   human-to-human, 13
   identity creation, role of, 66–7
   mediated person-to-person, 14–15
   and other strategies, interactions, 28–9
   vs. policy change, 27–8
   role of, 29
   vs. structural change, 24–5
   structures, defined, 185
   vs. technological developments, 25–7
   via media, 15–16
communication-based intervention techniques
   awareness, increasing, 168
   "block-leader" approach, 171
   classification system of, 176
   commitment, 169
   competition, 168–9
   description of, 163–4
   environmental education, 174–6
   experience, 172–3
   feedback, 167
   foot-in-the-door, 171
   goal setting, 168
   hypocrisy paradigm, 172
   information, providing, 164–5
   problem-solving abilities, 173
   product bans, 174
   prompts, 165–6
   rewards and punishments, 166–7
   self-discrepancy theory, 171–2
   social models, 169–71
   structural changes, 173–4
   structured overview of, 177
communication behaviour, 4
   defined, 16
   dimensions of, 4
   vs. human behaviour, 16
communication in social systems
   ABM, 113–17
   diffusion of innovation theory, 104–13
communication theory
   critical, 48–9
   cybernetic, 49–50
   overview, 45–6
   phenomenological, *see* phenomenological communication theory
   rhetorical, 46–7
   semiotic, 47–8
   sociocultural, 50–1
   sociopsychological, *see* sociopsychological communication theory
compatibility, characteristics of innovation, 107
competition, 168–9
   element of, 168–9
   group, 191–2
complexity, characteristics of innovation, 107
comprehensive action determination model, 92–3
computer-based learning, 200
computer games, 197
   advantage of, 200
   Energy Saving Game, 199
   in environmental communication, 200
   Fate of the World, 198–9
   potential mechanisms, 199–200
computer-mediated communication, 15
computer simulations with core elements, 114–15
concept-mapping study, 207
confirmation for innovation adoption, 106
Conner, M., 72, 74
conscientiousness, 153–4
conservational psychology, 11
conservation behaviour, 86
consumer behaviour, 26, 73
   observation of, 149
context, role of, *see* role of context
contradictory messages, effect of, 134–5
control beliefs, 71
coping appraisal, 132
Cornelissen, G., 63
Costa, D. L., 170
Costa, P. T., 153
coverage, length and timing of, 141–2

Cox, R., 17, 18
Crabtree, L., 111
Craig, R. T., 46, 47, 49–51, 205
critical communication theory, 48–9
cultural theory, 129–30
  bias types, 130
  "grid" dimension, 130
  "group" dimension, 130
cybernetic communication theory, 45, 49–50

D'Addario, K. P., 14
Dake, K., 128
Darley, J. M., 188
Darnton, A., 9
Davies, N., 158
Deal, D., 168
decentralised level, environmental governance, 10
decision-making
  children roles and abilities in, 181
  group, 184
  household, 181–3
  individual, 180–1
  marital, 182–3
  routine, 90
decision vs. change models
  implications for environmental communication, 98–9
  self-regulated behavioural change, 95–8
  trans-theoretical model, 94–5
Deetz, S., 48
de Groot, J. I. M., 11
De Haan, P., 233
delivery, aspects of speech, 46
Delmas, M. A., 33
democratisation, 125
demographic segmentation approaches, 147–8
Derevensky, J., 219
descriptive norms, 169–70
Deutsch, D., 52, 53
Deutsch, J. A., 52, 53
DeVries, R., 65
Diamantopoulos, A., 148, 149
Dickerson, C. A., 172
Dickinger, A., 40
Dickinson, J. E., 233

DiClemente, C. C., 94, 105
Diekmann, A., 87
Dietz, T., 26, 30
diffusion network characteristics, 109–10
diffusion of innovation theory, 104–13
  applications of, 110–12
  characteristics of, 107–8
  decision process of, 105–6
  innovator characteristics, 108–9
  network characteristics, 109–10
  S-shaped diffusion curve, 104–5
  strengths and weaknesses of, 112
diffusion of responsibility in groups, 187–8
direct person-to-person communication, 13–14, 15
documentary-style movies, 126
Dodgson, M., 112
Dogan, E., 39
Dolderman, D., 154
domains of life, environmental communication
  consumption of goods, 36–8
  food, 33–6
  leisure activity, 40–1
  mobility, 38–40
  shelter, 31–3
Douglas, M., 128, 129
Doyle, J., 225
Dreijerink, L., 81
D'Souza, C., 148
Dunaway, F., 225
Duncan, O. D., 7, 8
Dunlap, R. E., 80
Duryea, E. J., 61
dyadic communication, 13, 19
dynamic webpages, 158

early adopters, 108
early majority, 108
echoic memory, information storage, 54
eco kettle, 23
ecological risk perception, 129
ecosystem metaphor, 8
ecovators, 111
editors, importance of, 140–1

efficiency, 207–8
  technology, 5
egalitarians, 130
Eisenack, K., 198, 205
Eisend, M., 218
elaboration likelihood model, 58–60, 59
Elias, E.W., 23
Ellen, P. S., 150
Elliot, A. J., 83
Eltantawy, N., 125
e-mail communication, 15
emotional instability, 153
encoding, information storage, 53–4
Energy Saving Game, 199
Engel, J. F., 153
environmental behaviour, 92, 193
  causes of, 57
  comprehensive model, framework for, 100
  determinants of, 73, 87
  German research on, 152
  implication of, 21
  individual feedback on, 192
  MOA model, 22
  performance of, 22
  psychology of, 11
  research on, 152
  Stern's ABC model, 21
environmental communication, 186
  attribution theory, implication for, 57
  board games, 201–5
  computer games, 198–200
  defined, 17–18
  dilemmas of, 217–18
  in domains of life, 30–41
  economics, 6–7
  forms of, 13–16
  games and simulations, 197–211
  governance, 10–11
  humour in, 218–19
  impacts groups, 180
  implications for, 91, 93, 112–13, 137–8
  importance of, 29
  integrated perspectives, 11–13
  media in, role, 120–7
  model for, 60
  overview, 3–4
  potential and limitations of, 20–41
  potential impact of, 24, 30–41
  psychology, 11
  as risk communication, 127–38
  rock festival (case study), 219–24
  role plays as, 205–7
  social dilemmas, 207–10
  sociology, 7–9
  spillover effects, 233
  technology-centred approach, 4–5
  through visual art at film festival, 224–33
environmental design, 23
environmental domain, ABM in, 115–16
environmental economics, 6–7
environmental education programs, 174–6
environmental games, 198
environmental governance, 10–11
  communication, part of, 11
  defined, 10
  levels of, 10
environmental impact
  contributions of reducing, 215–17
  improving, 214
environmental interventions, group competition in, 191
environmentalism, 194, 202
environmental psychology, 11–13, 21, 30, 31, 72, 76, 88, 91, 94
environmental sociology, 7–9, 11
  description of, 7, 9
  focus of, 9
  POET model of, 7–8
equality principle, 208
equity principle, 208
Erev, I., 191
Ernst, A., 116
Evans, D., 25
everyday behaviour, specifics of, 90
"everyday problem solving", 173
exclusion, 125
experience, 172–3
external reward/punishment scheme, 167
extraversion, 153

face-to-face communication, 125
Fairchild, R. J., 149, 209
fairness, 207–8
Fardzadeh, H. E., 223
fatalists, 130
Fate of the World game, 198–9
feedback-based techniques, 167
Feeley, T. H., 188
Feldman, D. C., 185
feminist communication theory, 49
Festinger, L., 57, 172
fictional books, 126
fictional films, 126
Fielding, K. S., 190
Fischer, P., 188
Fischhoff, B., 128
Fischlein, M., 33
Fishbein, M., 70
Fisher, J. D., 6, 166
Fisman, L., 175
five-dimensional system of basic personality factors, 153
Flora, J. A., 170
Floyd, D. L., 130, 131
Folk, C. L., 86
food-related lifestyle segmentation, 154–5
foot-in-the-door technique, 171
Foss, K. A., 16, 17, 46–51, 66
Frank, R. H., 6
Frewer, L., 133
Friman, M., 39
Frost, W., 217, 218
Fryer, J. W., 83
fundamental attribution error, 57

Gaerling, T., 174
Gajic, N., 223
Galili, R., 191
game-based learning, 200
games
  based on role playing, 197
  board, 201–5
  computer, 198–200
  environmental, 198
game theory, 208–9
Gardner, B., 39
Garvill, J., 81
Gautier, C., 206, 207

Gavelin, S., 37
GEF hypothesis, 207–8
Geller, E. S., 25
geodemographic analysis, 149
geographic segmentation approaches, 148–9
Gergen, K. J., 29, 41
Gifford, R., 72
Girandola, F., 171
globalised level, environmental governance, 10
goal, defined, 83
goal feasibility, 97
goal-framing theory
  applications of, 85
  implications for environmental communication, 86–7
  strengths and weaknesses, 85–6
  variables and structure of, 83–5
goal priming, 86
goal setting intervention technique, 168
Goffman, E., 66
Goldberg, L. R., 154
Goldstein, N. J., 170
Gotts, N., 113
Goy, A., 158
Graham, C. R., 185
Gram-Hanssen, K., 5
greed, 207–8
green consumer behaviour, 73
green consumers, 150
Greene, T., 6
Gröger, M., 152
Gronau, W., 89
group-centred intervention techniques, 190–1
  competition, 191–2
  feedback, 192
  participatory, 192–3
  social practice approach, 193–4
group competition, 191–2
group creativity, positive influence on, 191
group decision-making, 184
group feedback, 192
group polarisation, 186–7

group psychology
  diffusion of responsibility, 187–8
  establishing norms in, 185–6
  group polarisation and risky shift, 186–7
  majority and minority influence in, 188–90
  social identity, 190
groups
  on decision-making, 185
  defined, 184
  development of, 186
  negative effects of, 185
  norms, 184
  process of, 195
  virtual, 184–5
group theory, 184
Guagnano, G. A., 21
Gustafsson, A., 200

Haas, P. M., 10
habit-deactivating techniques, 169
habits, routines and, 91
habitual behaviour, in everyday life, 90
Haenlein, M., 125
Hamm, U., 35
Handgraaf, M. J., 85
Hanley, N., 6
Hannigan, J., 7, 8
haptic memory, information storage, 54
Hardeman, W., 74
Hardin, G., 6, 207
Hargreaves, T., 193, 194
Harland, P., 77, 78
Heath, Y., 72
Hergesell, A., 40
hermeneutic circle, 48
Hertwich, E. G., 30, 116
Hes, D., 111
heuristics
  anchoring, 63
  availability, 63
  description of, 62–3
  representativeness, 63
Hicks, J. J., 219
hierarchists, 130
Higgins, E. T., 98, 171

Hines, J. M., 164
Hirsh, J. B., 154
Hitch, G., 54
Hjelmar, U., 34
Hogan, K., 17
Höger, R., 77
Hogg, M. A., 187
Holm, L., 25
Homburg, A., 132
Hoogendoorn-Lanser, S., 88
Hopper, J. R., 171
household decision-making, 181–3
Howard, J. A., 76, 77
Howden-Chapman, P., 233
Hubacek, K., 149
Hübner, G., 81
human communication, theory of, 46
human-to-human communication, 13
humour messages in environmental communication, 218–19
Hunecke, M., 77, 91
Hutchcroft, P. D., 10
Hutton, R. B., 167
hypocrisy paradigm, 172

iconic memory, information storage, 54
identity creation, 66–7
implementation of innovation adoption, 106
implications, environmental communication
  in ABM, 117
  decision vs. change models, 98–9
  in diffusion of innovation theory, 112–13
  goal-framing theory, 86–7
  integrated approaches, 93
  norm-activation theory, 79
  risk communication, 137–8
  role of context, 89–90
  theory of planned behaviour, 74–5
  value-belief-norm theory, 82–3
individual behavioural change, 167
individual behaviour in social contexts, 12
individual communication, 123–4
individual competition, 191–2
individual decision-making, 180–1

individual feedback
  on environmental behaviour, 192
  and goal setting, 192
individualists, 130
individual journalists, importance of, 140–1
influence in groups, 188–9
influential psychological theory of attention, 52
informational strategies, 24
information, providing, 164–5
information storage/retrieval, 54–6
  human memory, model of, 55
  memory process, 53–4
  sensory buffer/register, 54
infotainment, significance of, 139
Inglehart, R., 82, 152
injunctive norms, 170–1
innovation adoption process, 105–6
innovation theory
  diffusion of, *see* diffusion of innovation theory
  principles, 193
innovator characteristics of diffusion, 108–9
integrated approaches, 91–2
  comprehensive action determination model, 92–3
  implications for environmental communication, 93
Intergovernmental Panel on Climate Change (IPCC), 134
Internet-based communication, 123–4
interpersonal comparison theory, 187
interventions, 156
intrapersonal communication, 13
invention, aspects of speech, 46
investigative journalism, 141
IPCC, *see* Intergovernmental Panel on Climate Change (IPCC)
ipsative theory of behaviour, 88–9

Jager, W., 113, 115
Janssen, M., 35
Jansson, J., 81, 111, 233
Jensen, M. A. C., 186
Jiménez-Parra, B., 36
Johannessen, B., 222
Johnson, B. B., 133
Johnson, D., 184
Johnson, F., 184
Johnson-Laird, P. N., 64
Johnson, T. R., 171
Jones, C. R., 41
Jones, M. L., 215
Jones, R. E., 80
Jurin, R. R., 17, 18

Kagermeier, A., 89
Kahneman, D., 7, 62, 63, 209
Kahn, M. E., 170
Kaiser, F. G., 81, 86
Kaklamanou, D., 41
Kamakura, W. A., 147
Kaplan, A. M., 125
Kashy, D. A., 90
Kasperson, J. X., 135
Kasperson, R. E., 135–6
Katzev, R. D., 171
Katz-Gerro, T., 81
Keizer, K., 86
Kelley, H. H., 56
Kemp, B., 61
Keser, M., 86
Kim, H., 37
Kitamura, R., 174
Klöckner, C. A., 5, 33, 35, 38, 78, 91–3, 110, 116, 156, 168, 173–5, 181, 220, 227
knowledge, innovation adoption, 105–6
Kollat, D. T., 153
Kollmuss, A., 58
Krömker, D., 192
Krotoski, A., 200
Kuhn, K. M., 133
Kuhn, M. H., 66

Lachter, J., 52
laggards, 108
Laing, J., 217, 218
"lakeland study", 115
Lamb, P., 148
Lantz-Andersson, A., 125
Lanzendorf, M., 155
Latane, B., 188
Lazer, W., 154
leader personalities, 187

learning, computer- and game-based, 200
Lee, K., 154
Lee, W.-I., 41
Leiserowitz, A. A., 225
Lekies, K. S., 173
Lemos, M. C., 10
Lichtenstein, S., 128
lifestyles
  concept of, 154
  food-related, 154–5
Lightfoot, J. M., 15
Lindenberg, S., 83, 84, 86
Littlejohn, S. W., 16, 17, 46, 47, 48, 49, 50, 51, 66
Lokhorst, A. M., 169
Lorenzoni, I., 12
low cost hypothesis, 87
Luchs, M. G., 154

Maass, A., 189
Mael, F., 190
magazines, 120–1
Mallett, R. K., 167
Marell, A., 81, 111
marital decision-making, 182–3
market- and agent-focused, environmental governance, 10
market failure, 6
Markowitz, E. M., 154
Marx, J. D., 14
mass communication, 13, 15, 19, 113
Matthies, E., 77, 91, 93, 169, 174, 175, 192
McCalley, L. T., 86, 168
McCauley, C., 86
McCrae, R. R., 153
McDaniels, T., 129
McGonigal, J., 198, 200
McGuire, W. J., 61, 135
McNally, A. M., 172
measurement instrument, 156–7
meat-eating behaviour, model of, 35
media
  channels, 119
  communication via, 15–16
  effective environmental communication through, 138–43
  elements of, 142
  environmental risk communication via, 134
  individual journalists and editors, importance of, 140–1
  investigative journalism, 141
  length and timing of coverage, 141–2
  limitations of, 120
  pressure groups in, role of, 142
  "real science", 140
  role of, 120–7
  scare stories, 138–9
  significance of infotainment, 139
  significance of interactions between, 141
  uncertainty and controversy, 142–3
mediated person-to-person communication, 14–15
Mehmetoglu, M., 5
Melchiori, K. J., 167
memory, aspects of speech, 46
mental models, automatic processes in communication, 64
Mertig, A. G., 80
Messerlian, C., 219
Miao, L., 85
Midden, C. J., 86, 168
Miller, G. A., 54
Mills, T. M., 184
Minor, M., 147, 148, 149
Minx, J., 149
Mitchell, K., 158
Mitchell, R. B., 5
MOA, see motivation-opportunity-ability (MOA)
mobility behaviour, 155
Mock Environmental Summit, 206
model groups, 155–6
Moguluwa, S. C., 147
Mooradian, T. A., 154
Morgenstern, O., 208
Morrison, A., 147
Moscardo, G., 147
Moscovici, S., 189
Möser, G., 78
motivation-opportunity-ability (MOA), 22

movies, 126
Mowen, J. C., 147, 148, 149
multi-store model, memory, 54
music, 126–7
Muskens, J. C., 5

Nawijn, J., 40
Nayum, A., 5, 38
Neal, D. T., 91
near-field communication, 158
need principle, 208
negative spillover, 233
NEP, *see* new ecological paradigm (NEP)
neuroticism, 153
new ecological paradigm (NEP), 80
new media for environmental communication
  democratisation and exclusion, 125
  Internet, 123–4
  smartphones and tablets, 124
  social media, 124–5
  newspapers, 120–1
new technology approaches, 157–9
Nie, C., 154
Nielsen, J. M., 171
Nkamnebe, A. D., 147
Nolan, J. M., 225
Nomura, H., 36
non-verbal communication, 3, 4, 14, 16–17, 18, 46
Nordhøy, F., 187
Nordlund, A. M., 81, 111
norm-activation theory, 92, 97
  applications of, 77–8
  communication techniques and, 79
  implications for environmental communication, 79
  strengths and weaknesses of, 78–9
  variables and structure of, 76–7, 78
norms
  group, 184, 185–6
  personal, 76, 77
  taxonomy of, 77
Norwegian system, 167
Nwaizugbo, I. C., 147

object, defined, 83
objective constraints, 89, 92

observability, characteristics of innovation, 108
Ohms, S., 168
Ölander, F., 233
Olise, M. C., 147
O'Neill, S., 12, 66, 233
"one-size-fits-all" communication, 146
Oosterbeek, H., 209
openness, 153, 154
Oppedal, I. O., 92
Oreg, S., 81
organisation, structuring framework and construction, 194
orientational others, 66
Ostrom, E., 6
Ouellette, J. A., 91
Oyserman, D., 172
Ozaki, R., 110, 112

Pantzar, M., 9
paper recycling, 166
Parmelee, C., 86
participatory intervention, 190, 193
Patt, A. G., 134
PBC, *see* perceived behavioural control (PBC)
Pearce, K. E., 219
Pearce, P., 147
Pearson, J. C., 13, 16, 18
Peeters, P., 40
Peirce, C. S., 47
perceived availability, 73
perceived behavioural control (PBC), 70, 71–2, 156
perceived consumer effectiveness, 73
perceived control, 36
  on behaviour, 72
  components of, 73
  goal feasibility, 97
  sub-dimensions of, 77
Peretiatko, R., 148
periphery route of persuasion, 53
personal commitment, 169
personal experience, 172–3
personality
  and pro-environmentalism, 154
  variables, 153–4
personal norms, 76, 77
  activating, 175

persuasion, environmental communication
  cognitive dissonance theory, 57–8
  elaboration likelihood model, 58–60, 59
  psychological research on, 57
  theory of inoculation, 61
  weapons of influence, 61–2
persuasive argument theory, 187
Peters, A., 38, 233
Petersen, P. E., 5
Peters, G. P., 30
Peterson, G. L., 87
Peterson, L., 54
Peterson, M. J., 54
Pettersson, A., 181
Petty, R. E., 58, 59, 189
phenomenological communication theory, 48
  hermeneutic circle, 48
  principles of, 48
planned behaviour theory, 92
  applications of, 72–3
  communication techniques and, 75
  to green consumer behaviour, 73
  implications for environmental communication, 74–5
  strengths and weaknesses of, 73–4
  variables and structure of, 70–2
Plummer, J. T., 154
POET, see Population-Organization-Environment-Technology (POET)
point-of-decision prompts, 165–6
polarisation, group, 186–7
policy-making instrument, 117
Population-Organization-Environment-Technology (POET), 7, 8
post-colonialist theory, 49
Pöttker, H., 140
Poumadere, M., 137
"Power Agent" game, 200
power failure project, 223
Power, M. R., 17
Preisendörfer, P., 87
pressure groups in media, 142
Prestin, A., 219
printed publications, 120–1

print media, non-periodical forms of, 125
problem-solving abilities, 173
problem-solving procedure, 98
Prochaska, J. O., 94, 105
Procter-Scherdtel, A., 171
product bans, 174
pro-environmental behaviours, 24, 28, 166, 173, 233
pro-environmental beliefs, 165
pro-environmentalism, personality and, 154
prompts, point-of-decision, 165–6
pro-social behaviour, 188
protection motivation theory, 130–3
Prugsamatz, S., 156
Pruneau, D., 65
psychometrical segmentation approaches, 150–7
  lifestyles, 154–5
  personality, 153–4
  stage models of behaviour change, 155–7
  values, 151–3
psychometric paradigm, 128–9
public commitment, 169
public communication, 13, 146
punishing behaviour, 166–7

quick response codes (QR codes), 158
Quinn, J. M., 90, 91

radio, 121–2
Rapoport, A., 209
Ratcliff, R., 54
Rebich, S., 206, 207
Reckien, D., 198, 205
Reckwitz, A., 8
Reeh, M.-O., 158
relative advantage, characteristics of innovation, 107
Remington, R. W., 86
representativeness heuristic, 63
rewarding behaviour, 166–7
rhetorical communication theory, 46–7
ripple effect, 137
Rippl, S., 130

risk
  characteristics of, 129
  defining elements, 127
  described, 127
  perception theories, 127–30
  social definition of, 137
  theory, social amplification of, 135–7
risk communication
  effect of contradictory messages, 134–5
  implications for environmental communication, 137–8
  protection motivation theory, 130–3
  risk perception theories, 127–30
  role of uncertainty, 133–4
  social amplification of risk theory, 135–7
risk-related behaviours, 138
risky shift
  mechanism in, 187
  reasons for, 186–7
Rivis, A., 71
Roberts, J. A., 153
rock festival (case study)
  pilot study, 220–2
  project ideas, 223–4
  start-up workshop, 219–20
Roebers, C. M., 55
Rogers, E. M., 103, 104–5, 108–9, 111–12, 123, 137, 189, 193, 218
Rogers, R. W., 130
Roig, M. A., 215
role of context
  generation of choice sets, 88
  impact of, 87–8
  implications for environmental communication, 89–90
  ipsative theory of behaviour, 88–9
  objective vs. subjective constraints, 88
role of uncertainty, 133–4
role play, environmental communication
  Climate Diplomat, 205–6
  effective, 206–7
  in environmental communication, 207
  Mock Environmental Summit, 206

Ross, L., 57
Rothgerber, H., 35
routines
  decision-making, potential advantages of, 90
  and habits, 91
Rubens, L., 172

Sadler, T. D., 134
Sahin, D. Y., 170
Salvucci, D. D., 53
Sams, M., 52
Sanfey, A. G., 209
SARF, see social amplification of risk framework (SARF)
satisficing, concept of, 62
scare stories strategy, 138–9
Schacter, D. L., 86
Schelling, T. C., 114
Schlegelmilch, B. B., 148, 149
Schnaiberg, A., 8
school environmental programs, 175
Schösler, H., 36
Schrag, D. P., 134
Schumacher, H., 158
Schwartz, S. H., 73, 76, 77, 82, 227
  basic value orientations, 151
Schwarz, N., 116
Schweizer, S., 175
Secchiaroli, G., 11
sectarians, 130
self-discrepancy theory, 98, 171–2
self-efficacy, 98, 173
self-regulated behavioural change, 95–8
semiotic communication theory, 47–8
sensory buffer, information, 54
sensory memory/register, 52, 54
"serious games", 197
Sharpe, E. K., 214, 218
Shaw, J., 4
Sheeran, P., 71
Shepherd, R., 74
Shiffrin, R. M., 54
Shogren, J. F., 6
Shove, E., 9, 11, 193
Siero, F. W., 192
signs, communication, 47
Simon, H. A., 62

Sinha, P. K., 149, 150
Sinkovics, R. R., 148
Sinus milieus, *see* value-based segmentation approach
Sjöberg, L., 128–9
Sjöström, A., 37
Skinner, B. F., 166
Slovic, P., 128, 133
small-group communication, 13
smartphones, 124
Smith, J., 122, 124
Smith, P., 158
smoothie bike project, 223
social amplification of risk framework (SARF), 119, 135–8, 145
social constructivism, description of, 65
social definition process, 138
social dilemmas, environmental communication
   characterization, 207
   game theory, 208–10
   research, 207–8
social identity theory, 190
socialisation, 9, 181
social media, 124–5
social models, 169–71
social networks, 109, 110, 115, 124, 125, 210
social practices, 8
   approach, 193–4
   elements of, 9
sociocultural communication theory, 50–1, 64
   identity creation, 66–7
   social constructivism, 65
sociopsychological communication theory, 50, 51–64
   attention, *see* attention, sociopsychological communication theory
   attribution, 56–7
   human memory, model of, 55
   information storage/retrieval, 53–6
   persuasion, 57
Sopha, B. M., 33, 92, 114, 116
Souchet, L., 171
Sparks, P., 74
Sperber, R. D., 86

spillover effects, 233
Srivastava, R. K., 181
Staats, H., 77, 165, 169, 210
stage models of behaviour change, 155–7
Stanisstreet, M., 175
Stefan, V., 36
Steg, L., 11, 24, 28, 30, 33, 39, 81, 83–6
Stern, P. C., 21, 26, 79–80, 87
Stetsenko, A., 65
Stolberg, A., 132
Stolzenbach, S., 35
Stoner, J. A., 186
Straughan, R. D., 153
Strengers, Y., 8
Strickroth, T., 167
structural changes, intervention techniques, 173–4, 177
Stubbs, R., 17
style, aspects of speech, 46
subjective constraints, 89
subjective norms, behaviours, 71
Su, C., 182
Suppipat, S., 223
Susi, T., 197
Sussman, R., 169
switch off the light project, 223

Taatgen, N. A., 53
tablets, 124
Taghian, M., 148
Tajfel, H., 190–2
Taniguchi, A., 33, 167
Tanner, C., 88–9
targeted approaches, 157–9
target group segmentation, 146
   behavioural, 149–50
   demographic, 147–8
   geographic, 148–9
   new technology, 157–9
   psychometrical, 150–7
technology-centred approach, 4–5
technophilic optimism, technology, 5
television, 122–3
Teunissen, M., 86
Thaler, R. H., 209
theatre, 126–7
theoretical framework model, 12
theory of inoculation, 61

theory of planned behaviour, *see* planned behaviour theory
Thøgersen, J., 22, 28–9, 58, 77, 233
Thompson, M., 128, 130
Thomson, D. M., 55
threat appraisal, 132
Tilyard, B. A., 191
time, agent-based model, 115
Timmermans, H., 31
Tonglet, M., 72
trans-theoretical model, 94–5
Treisman, A. M., 52
trialability, characteristics of innovation, 107–8
Tuckman, B. W., 186
Tulving, E., 54–5, 86
Tversky, A., 7, 62, 63

Ukenna, S., 147–50, 154
Ullman, M. T., 54
unattended stimuli, information processing for, 52
Ungar, S., 203
Uniyal, D. P., 149–50
urbanisation, 8
Uzunboylu, H., 168

value-based segmentation approach, 151–3
value-belief-norm theory
    applications of, 81
    implications for environmental communication, 82–3
    strengths and weaknesses, 81–2
    variables and structure of, 80–1
van den Berg, A. E., 11
Vandenbergh, M. P., 26
Van Den Burg, M. T., 192
Van Houwelingen, J. H., 167
Van Knippenberg, A., 91
Van Lidth de Jeude, M. A., 85
Van Liere, K. D., 80
Van Nes, R., 88
Van Raaij, W. F., 167
Van Vugt, M., 208
Velthuijsen, J.W., 5
Venhoeven, L. A., 85
verbal communication, 3, 14
    vs. non-verbal, 16–17

Verbeke, W., 73
Vermeir, I., 73
Verplanken, B., 9, 91, 173
Vilhelmsen, K., 223
Vinokur, A., 187
virtual groups, 184–5
visual art, 126–7
visual art at film festival (case study), 224–33
Vlek, C., 24, 28, 30, 173, 224
Voelpel, S. C., 188
Von Neumann, J., 208

Walker, S. R., 41
Wallach, M. A., 187–8
Walther, J. B., 14, 185
waste voting project, 223
water-saving technology, 116
Watson, M., 9, 193
Wauters, E., 72
weapons of influence, persuasion
    authority, 62
    commitment and consistency, 61
    linking, 62
    reciprocity, 61
    scarcity, 62
    social proof, 62
Webb, T. L., 41
Weber, E. U., 48, 126, 204
Wedel, M., 147
Weiner, B., 56
Wei, W., 85
Wells, N. M., 173
Welp, M., 205
Welzel, C., 82, 152
White, B., 6
White, P., 9
Whitmarsh, L., 9, 12, 66, 233
Wiedmann, K. P., 158
Wiener, J. L., 150
Wiest, J. B., 125
Wildavsky, A., 128, 129–30
Wilke, H. A., 77, 207
Wood, R., 54
Wood, W., 90, 91, 173

Zachrisson, J., 23
Zepeda, L., 154, 168
Zur, I., 35

GPSR Compliance
The European Union's (EU) General Product Safety Regulation (GPSR) is a set of rules that requires consumer products to be safe and our obligations to ensure this.

If you have any concerns about our products, you can contact us on

ProductSafety@springernature.com

In case Publisher is established outside the EU, the EU authorized representative is:

Springer Nature Customer Service Center GmbH
Europaplatz 3
69115 Heidelberg, Germany

www.ingramcontent.com/pod-product-compliance
Ingram Content Group UK Ltd.
Pitfield, Milton Keynes, MK11 3LW, UK
UKHW021325180426
11947UKWH00017B/1434